PAPA
HEMINGWAY

PAPA
HEMINGWAY

a personal memoir

A. E. HOTCHNER

CARROLL & GRAF PUBLISHERS, INC.
NEW YORK

For Sally Hotchner

First Carroll & Graf edition 1999
Carroll & Graf Publishers, Inc.
19 West 21st Street
New York, NY 10010-6805

Quotations from "A Clean, Well-lighted Place," *A Moveable Feast* and *The Old Man and the Sea,* by Ernest Hemingway, used by permission of Charles Scribner's Sons.

Portrait of Hemingway, p. ii: Photo by Paul Radka. Photograph on p. 12 of insert by Larry Burrows. All other photographs by A.E. Hotchner

Captions
PART-TITLE ONE: Ernest wrote literature standing up, checks sitting down. Either way it bored Black Dog, who preferred hunting lizards at the pool *(photo by George Leavens, Photographic Researchers).*
PART-TITLE TWO: On our way to Nice, high in the Italian Alps, Ernest momentarily forgot his crash injuries as he was warmed and cheered by the spring sun reflected off the snow, 1954. This was his favorite photograph.
PART-TITLE THREE: Ernest, after nearly drowning on the beach at Valencia, with the author, 1959.
PART-TITLE FOUR: The ground floor of the white tower was a preserve for the twenty-five resident cats.

Library of Congress Cataloging-in Publication Data is available.
ISBN: 0-7867-0592-2

Manufactured in the United States of America

Also by A. E. Hotchner

There are some things which cannot
be learned quickly, and time, which is all we have,
must be paid heavily for their acquiring.
They are the very simplest things,
and because it takes a man's life to know them
the little new that each man gets from life
is very costly and the only heritage
he has to leave.

ERNEST HEMINGWAY

Contents

Preface ◆ 1999

Hemingway: The name conjures up a man of courage and daring both in his writing and his way of life. On this, the one hundredth anniversary of his birth, his books sell as well as they did when he was alive, and young people universally know about him.

I think that a large part of Ernest's enduring appeal is rooted in the fact that he was a romantic until the day he died, about women, about his writing, about the life he lived. I was privileged to be a part of that life for fourteen years, to participate in it, to share many of his poignant, intimate moments. Thinking back on our first meeting in Havana in 1948, when I was sent down there by *Cosmopolitan* magazine to invite the renowned Hemingway to write an article on the future of literature, I wonder why he was so kind to me. He had a reputation for being pugnaciously inaccessible, and yet he virtually overwhelmed me with his hospitality, taking me out on his boat to catch marlin, inviting me to a jai alai game and a cockfight, having me to dinner with his friends.

Perhaps the explanation lies in the fact that I was young and struggling and vulnerable. During the years of our friendship, I saw this incredible generosity toward young people demonstrated time and again, both with money and with the commodity that Ernest regarded as infinitely more valuable than money—his time.

I wrote *Papa Hemingway* a few years after his death when the events of those years I spent with him were still fresh but when I hadn't yet the perspective to assess what his friendship meant to me and the impact that his philosophy exerted on my life.

Now, thirty-eight years later, with ample time for reflection, I can identify what I learned from him: that true friendship requires forgiveness but that no friendship can withstand the abuse of duplicity; that anger and compassion are not too far apart and that, whenever possible, spent anger should give way to compassion; that pride is a desirable trait that rescues one from a fall and not vice versa—e.g. after the brutal critical assault that followed the publication of *Across the River and Into the Trees*, it was Ernest's pride that defied the naysayers and goaded him into writing *The Old Man and the Sea*; that deviousness is permissible if it is innocuous; that good times should be orchestrated and not left to the uncertainties of chance; that discipline is more desirable than inspiration; that courage is a matter of one's conscience, not beholden to the evaluation of others; that love is more durable than hate.

Part of the mystique about Ernest stems from the manner in which he blurred the demarcation between fiction and fact. Fiction is a magnification of reality, he once observed, and when he told a story (and a splendid storyteller he was), it was hard to know whether it was fantasy laced with fact, fact seasoned with fiction, or pure fantasy. Did he really have sex with the beautiful girlfriend of the vicious gangster Legs Diamond on the stair landing at 21 in New York City? Did he actually toss a lion out of Harry's New York Bar in Paris? When he was on African safari with his wife, Mary, did he really marry an eighteen-year-old Wakamba beauty named Debba and in the process acquire ownership of her seventeen-year-old widowed sister? And did the threesome sleep on a goatskin bed fourteen feet wide? This Wakamba troika figures prominently in the latest posthumous Hemingway "discovery," *True at First Light*, but Ernest's son Patrick, who was a white hunter and present during much of that safari, says he has no knowledge of any such matrimonial liaison; certainly Ernest never mentioned writing this book to me, though he did confide to me, "September I will have an African son. Before I left I gave a herd of goats to my bride's family. Most over-goated family in Africa. Feels good to have African son. Never regretted anything I ever did." I can honestly say I believed him, although how he received word about the pregnancy and how in deepest Africa, without benefit of sonogram, they could foretell the sex of his offspring, went unexplained.

We know full well that contrary to his colorful account of his sexual escapade with the celebrated World War I spy Mata Hari ("One night I fucked her very well," he once told me, "although I found her to be very heavy throughout the hips and to have more desire for what was done for her than what she was giving the man"), such an encounter could not possibly have taken place since Mata Hari had been executed by the French in 1917 and Ernest had first gone abroad in 1918 as a Red Cross ambulance driver in Italy. Still, when writing *Papa Hemingway*, I was simply trying to re-create the man as I knew him, and what he told me is unjudgmentally presented.

On page 199, I recount a time when I accompanied Ernest on a visit to an English class in a high school located in Hailey, a town a few miles south of where he lived in Ketchum. In response to one student's question, he enunciated his philosophy about fiction writing: "Fiction is inventing out of what knowledge you have. If you invent successfully, it is more true than if you try to remember it. A big lie is more plausible than truth. People who write fiction, if they had not taken it up, might have become very successful liars."

On another occasion, he said, "All good books have one thing in common—they are truer than if they had really happened, and after you've read one of them you will feel that all that happened, happened to you and then it belongs to you forever: the happiness and unhappiness, good and evil, ecstasy and sorrow, the food, wine, beds, people and the weather. If you can give that to readers, then you're a writer."

Since Ernest's death in 1961, scores of books have been written about him. His fourth wife, his first wife, his brother, sister, youngest son, assorted college professors who never met him, various cronies and phonies and even a self-proclaimed mistress have all written books about him, and, predictably, he emerges as a different man in each one of them. And in one way or another, Mary Hemingway published most of Ernest's letters written to family, friends, editors, business associates and others during his lifetime.

When I wrote *Papa Hemingway*, Mary unsuccessfully tried to enjoin its publication in an attempt to suppress the revelation that Ernest had in reality committed suicide and had not shot himself accidentally while cleaning a loaded shotgun in July, as she had insisted. Needless to say, she was not cooperative in allowing me the use of passages from letters I had received from Ernest.

But in writing about the years I knew Ernest, to portray

him accurately, I felt it was essential to convey what he was thinking and doing between those times I was with him; these periods were fully covered in the many letters that he wrote to me. At first, I attempted to paraphrase vital passages from some of these letters (an artificial but permitted circumambulatory device), but no matter how I tried paraphrasing, what resulted had an ersatz ring to it that seemed to vitiate the uniqueness and energy of what he said in his letters, which were conversational in tone, quite like when he was talking to me in person. I felt strongly that some parts of these letters were needed to portray the true essence of how he was those last fourteen years of his life. I decided, therefore, to disguise certain excerpts from his letters, so that I could preserve his actual voice and emotions and meld them into the conversation we had when we were together.

◆   ◆   ◆

At the time I wrote *Papa Hemingway*, five years after Ernest's death, Mary was still "wounded" by his violent suicide; out of deference to her, I did not fully discuss their relationship during the last few years of his life. I realized that she was struggling against her deep feelings of guilt, a guilt so strong that for years Mary could not accept the fact that shortly after having returned with her from the Mayo Clinic to their Ketchum home, Ernest committed suicide while she slept in her upstairs bedroom.

From a wife's point of view, it is hard to imagine a more painful rejection than that, and I think it partly explains Mary's postmortem behavior, not only toward me but toward anyone who dared to write about her departed husband. Soon after the original publication of *Papa Hemingway*, the late Leonard

Lyons, who wrote a syndicated gossip column and who was an old friend of the Hemingways, confided to me some details about Ernest's suicide that I had not known at the time I wrote the book, details about what actually transpired on that tragic morning in Ketchum when Ernest put the muzzle of his Boss shotgun in his mouth and pulled the trigger.

"When Mary heard the blast and came running down the stairs," Lyons said Mary told him, "she found Ernest sprawled near the front door, most of his head blown away, blood splattered everywhere. The first thing she did was to go to the phone and put in a call to my New York apartment. She was told I was in Los Angeles, whereupon she put in a follow-up call to my Beverly Hills hotel and woke me up.

"'Lennie,' she said, very calmly, 'I'm calling you because Papa has killed himself.'

"After I recovered from the shock of her announcement, I asked her how it had happened.

"'With a shotgun. Now what I'd like you to do is this—arrange for a press conference at your hotel—make sure all the wire services are there—and tell them I have informed you that while Ernest was cleaning his shotgun this morning, in preparation for going on a shoot, it accidentally discharged and shot him in the head. Got that?'

"Only after she arranged all this with me did she phone Ernest's doctor and tell him what had happened."

Despite her animosity after the publication of *Papa Hemingway*, I continued to feel sorry for Mary, who had been a close friend of mine for so many years. It must be remembered that the book Ernest was struggling to finish when he killed himself (*A Moveable Feast*) was, in effect, a tribute of love to his first wife, Hadley; that he shot himself in Mary's presence while affirming his love for his first wife—this was obviously a rejection that inflicted deep pain and humiliation.

I think another part of Mary's guilt stemmed from the altercations she and Ernest had in steadily increasing frequency and hostility during the period preceding his death. For example, her truculence over the diamond pin Ernest brought her from Cartier's instead of the much more expensive diamond earrings, which she coveted; a truculence that spilled over into Mary's petulant refusal to "play the cook and hostess" for Antonio Ordoñez and his wife, Carmen, when they came to visit the Hemingways in Ketchum. Ernest cared very much about making Antonio's visit enjoyable, and Mary's hostility caused a running battle with Ernest. Once, after a particularly violent exchange with Mary, Ernest said to me, "I wish I could leave her, I really do, but I'm too old now to afford a fourth divorce and the hell Mary would put me through."

One of the most painful fights I witnessed occurred when Gary Cooper and his friend Pat di Cicco, once married to Gloria Vanderbilt, came to Ketchum to hunt with us. Di Cicco was attended by a manservant who carried a movie camera in one hand to record his master's every move and in the other hand held the leash of a Labrador retriever who was poised to fetch his master's birds; unfortunately the poor Labrador failed to find the one bird di Cicco succeeded in shooting. That evening, Coop and di Cicco came to dinner, and Ernest ragged di Cicco about the Labrador, saying, "Pat, the Labrador you've got is sure a shitty example of the dog-maker's art." Mary was at the stove overseeing the cooking of some ducks, but she angrily turned on Ernest for his use of the word *shitty*.

"You overuse that word! Seems to me you could find some other word, for Christ's sake, but no, it's shitty this and shitty that—you're supposed to be a writer and to have some vocabulary at your command!"

"What you don't seem to know," Ernest shot back, "is that when you fight, *shit* or *merde* has a particular meaning."

"I haven't fought, huh? That's what you're telling me? I guess I wasn't in the blitz."

"You've been bombed on—that's different from fighting."

"And what about you? You've never been anything but a combat voyeur—a war watcher."

"I didn't fight in Hertgen...?"

"You've never been in the uniform of any army or air force..."

"And I also haven't fucked generals in order to get a story for *Time* magazine."

"Name one—name one general I fucked. You know the men I fucked and you're just jealous, that's all, and it wasn't for a story."

"Jealous? Of what—that creep journalist? Fucking him must be as exciting as having your ticket punched on the Metro."

And on and on, swirling in intensity, out of control, the dinner ruined; and I recall thinking then, sitting uncomfortably in their living room cringing at the violent exchange, that it was possible that what underlay this hostility was that they no longer had a sex life, at least with each other.

That would also account for another nasty quarrel they had, this time in Spain. We were all living at Bill Davis' villa in Churriana at the time. Ernest and Bill had gone into nearby Malaga for the mail, and they had run into Ernest's old friends Slim Hayward (Lady Keith) and Lauren Bacall. Ernest invited them for lunch, and they were very amusing and witty and, of course, quite decorative around the pool in their fashionable bikinis.

In the late afternoon, Ernest suggested that since we were all having such a fine time the ladies should stay for dinner, but they said that although they'd like to, they had no change of clothes, whereupon Ernest offered to drive them back to their hotel in Malaga to change. While Ernest was in his room getting out of his wet bathing suit, Mary, who had withdrawn to her room soon after lunch, marched up to Slim and Betty, who were sitting poolside, and confronted them.

"You two show up here tonight," she said, "and I'll show you I know how to use these." She plunked down two bullets on the table in front of them and marched off.

Needless to say, the women did not return for dinner, but when Ernest got wind of what had happened, he really lit into Mary, and she returned his fire. They didn't speak to each other for days.

There were many other such confrontations, growing in frequency and intensity during the final year of Ernest's life, and looking back on them, they seem to blend into Ernest's final turbulent aberrations. In fact, Mary herself has described many of her fights with Ernest in her book *How It Was.* "The man has his house," she writes, "his children, his cats, Nothing is mine...I can't fight for areas of personal domination...that Ernest was to blame for my troubles I never questioned."

Mary bombards the reader with one complaint after another, to the point where the reader wonders why she is in a relationship with Ernest. "I had a good life until I met you," she tells him. "I am a practical nurse for you in your old age and your kids." She says she even urged him to seek reconciliation with his second wife. "I loved Ernest in spite of himself," she says repeatedly. On one occasion, she reports, Ernest railed at her:

"You goddamn, smirking, useless female war correspondent, all evening and without cease, you insulted my friends. You could not have behaved more horribly." On still another occasion, Mary says, Ernest threw her typewriter to the floor and called her a camp follower and scavenger with the face of a Torquemada.

Mary says that her response was, "Your failure is that you have been careless and increasingly unthinking of my feeling...undisciplined in your daily living. Both privately and in public you have insulted me and my dignity as a human being."

◆   ◆   ◆

For years it was believed that Ernest's obsession that he was being stalked by Federal Bureau of Investigation agents was evidence of his crack-up. Only recently, thanks to the surrender of certain FBI documents under the Freedom of Information Act, has it been revealed that J. Edgar Hoover had indeed had Ernest under surveillance, even going so far as to bug his phone at the Mayo Clinic hospital. The FBI harassment was not primarily responsible for his attempts at suicide, but certainly it was a contributing factor.

The FBI file on Ernest commenced when he became involved with the Lincoln Brigade during the Spanish Civil War and worked tirelessly to produce a documentary about the war, *The Spanish Earth*. Ernest was also active in recruiting members and money for the Brigade (Hollywood pledged twenty ambulances), which intensified the FBI's surveillance of him.

In 1949, when William Faulkner won the Nobel Prize for Literature, Ernest said, "No son of a bitch who ever won the Nobel Prize ever wrote anything worth reading afterwards." At the time, Ernest's observation was discounted as sour grapes, but applied to his own life, it was certainly an apt prophecy. In my view, winning the Prize was more contributory to Ernest's decline than the air crashes in Africa, what might have been the onset of impotence, the altercations with his wife, and having to leave Cuba and the *finca*, the Pilar and his good workplace. How often Ernest spoke with envy of Jean-Paul Sartre who had had the prescience to refuse the Nobel Prize when it had been offered to him.

"I guess Sartre knew," Ernest once said rather ruefully, "that the Prize is a whore who can seduce you and give you an incurable disease. I knew that once but now I've got her and she's got me, and you know who she is, this whore called 'Fame'? Death's little sister."

On this centennial of his birth, I am pleased that *Papa Hemingway* is again being published in honor of this man who contributed so significantly to American literature and, on a personal basis, so much to me in my formative years. Random memories: His trenchant observations as we traveled by car through Italy, France and Spain. I particularly recall one afternoon when we stopped on the road to observe a chimney nest that housed a stork and her young—Ernest was very fond of the storks, which are indigenous to Spain, and for twenty minutes or so he regaled us with splendid stork lore.

Ernest kept no diaries or notebooks but at any given moment he could conjure up vivid details of events that had transpired long ago, as quickly and surely as a computer screen reveals its storage. One day as we drove across the Riviera, he pointed out the exact itinerary he had followed with F. Scott Fitzgerald when they had bicycled through there in the 1920s; when we walked the streets of Paris, his recall of places and people was prodigious—for instance, when we climbed the steep ascent to the Place du Tertre in Montmartre, he gave a running commentary on the houses, stores, cafés and restaurants that we passed, recalling who lived in them in the twenties and with whom he had dined— even incredibly recalling special wines and food. It was certainly a learning process for me, being introduced to the subtleties of the wines we drank, the nuances of oysters ranging from the lowly Portuguese to the imperial Belons, the poetry of waterbirds, the classic faenas of a great matador who literally dances with the bull, the difference between Titian and Tintoretto, Monet and Renoir, Gaugin and Seurat, Picasso and Braque and why he felt Cezanne could not be compared to anyone else. He told me how to use one's built-in shit detector, how to enjoy idle time, when to be aggressive, when to give ground, how to set your hook on a hit from a sailfish, how to swing your shotgun to transect the flight of a pheasant, how to evaluate a racehorse during the paddock parade, how to trim the fat from the sinews and bones of writing.

Ernest has never been very far out of my life. How I have lived, the principles I live by, my attitude toward survival, toward love, toward friendship, toward trust, toward believing in myself and in the simple truths he impressed upon me—I owe that to him and more. He was my father, my brother, my ancestor who passed his secrets along to me. Looking back on the thirty-eight years since his death, all those years that have passed without him, I'd say that the most vital thing I learned from him was this: Don't fear failure, and don't over-estimate success. It was a tenet he lived by, and a legacy I treasure.

A. E. HOTCHNER

Foreword

On July 2, 1961, a writer whom many critics call the greatest writer of this century, a man who had a zest for life and adventure as big as his genius, a winner of the Nobel Prize and the Pulitzer Prize, a soldier of fortune with a home in Idaho's Sawtooth Mountains, where he hunted in the winter, an apartment in New York, a specially rigged yacht to fish the Gulf Stream, an available apartment at the Ritz in Paris and the Gritti in Venice, a solid marriage, no serious physical ills, good friends everywhere—on that July day, that man, the envy of other men, put a shotgun to his head and killed himself.

How did this come to pass?

Why?

I was his close friend for fourteen years, right up to the day he died. I knew about his life: the adventures, the conversations, the dreams and disillusions, the triumphs and defeats of this complicated, unique, humorous, intense, fun-loving man who was Ernest Hemingway but I cannot tell you why. No one can.

But to tell about his life, I must inevitably tell of his death and the events which preceded it. I gave long and hard thought to that—whether it should be gone into at all, or parts of it suppressed, or generalized and disguised. But in the end I was guided by what Ernest had told me when I wondered whether I should be as frank and open as he was about Scott Fitzgerald. "Every man's life ends the same way," Ernest had said, "and it is only the details of how he lived and how he died that distinguishes one man from another."

He said that for him there was only one way to account for things—to tell the whole truth about them, holding back nothing; tell the reader the way it truly happened, the ecstasy and sorrow, remorse and how the weather was, and, with any luck, the reader will find his way to the heart of the thing itself.

That is what I have tried to do, holding back nothing, and it is as close as I can get to the Why.

A. E. HOTCHNER

Rome, 1965

PAPA
HEMINGWAY

Part One

I am glad we do not have to try to kill
the stars. Imagine if each day a man must
try to kill the moon. The moon runs away.
But imagine if a man each day should
have to try to kill the sun? We are born lucky.
Yes, we are born lucky.

THE OLD MAN AND THE SEA

Chapter One

Havana ◆ 1948

In the spring of 1948 I was dispatched to Cuba to make a horse's ass out of myself by asking Ernest Hemingway to write an article on "The Future of Literature." I was on the staff of the magazine *Cosmopolitan*, and the editor was planning an issue on The Future of Everything: Frank Lloyd Wright on Architecture, Henry Ford II on Automobiles, Picasso on Art, and, as I said, Hemingway on Literature.

Of course, no writer knows the future of literature beyond what he'll write the next morning, and many can't see even that far ahead, but here was I checking into the Nacional Hotel for the express purpose of cornering Mr. Hemingway, introducing myself, and asking him to gaze into a literary crystal ball for good old *Cosmo*.

Horse's ass isn't strong enough. From the time I read my first Hemingway work, *The Sun Also Rises*, as a student at Soldan High School in St. Louis, I was struck with an affliction common to my generation: Hemingway Awe. In my schoolboy fantasies I had identified with Nick Adams (he was approximately my age and was the protagonist of many Hemingway short stories) as he made his way through a murky world of punch-drunk fighters, killers, suiciding Indians, dope addicts and whores, and the rigors of war on the Italian front. During the Second World War, as an Air Force officer in France, I had been further awed by War Correspondent Hemingway's mili-

tary exploits. He had entered the hostilities and affiliated himself in a nonjournalistic manner with Colonel Buck Lanham's
Twenty-second Infantry Regiment, as it moved through Nor-
mandy, the grim action in Luxembourg, and the terror of Hürtgen Forest, where the Twenty-second suffered 2060 casualties
out of 3200 men.

I had tried to evade this *Cosmopolitan* assignment, but had
been summarily ordered to try to get this asinine article *or else.*
The *or else* had quite a bite to it, as I was in my mid-twenties,
only six months on the job, which was the first I had been able
to find after dissipating my Air Force severance pay with a year
in Paris. I had Hemingway's address in the little town of San
Francisco de Paula, which is about twenty minutes outside Havana, but the more I considered going out there and knocking at
his door and disturbing him face to face, which is what the editor had instructed me to do, the more my blood congealed. After
two days of sitting by the Nacional pool in a semicomatose state
induced by pure cowardice, I finally decided, the hell with it,
there were other editorial jobs, I would not go banging on his
door; and even had I had his unlisted telephone number, which
I hadn't, I couldn't have managed to phone him.

So I took the coward's way out and wrote him a note saying
that I had been sent down on this ridiculous mission but did
not want to disturb him, and if he could simply send me a few
words of refusal it would be enormously helpful to The Future
of Hotchner.

Early the next morning the phone rang. "This Hotchner?"
"Yes."

"Dr. Hemingway here. Got your note. Can't let you abort
your mission or you'll lose face with the Hearst organization,
which is about like getting bounced from a leper colony. You
want to have a drink around five? There's a bar called La
Florida. Just tell the taxi."

At that time the Florida (that was its proper name but everyone called it Floridita) was a well-lighted old-fashioned bar-
restaurant with ceiling fans, informal waiters and three musicians who wandered around or sat at a table near the bar. The
bar was of massive, burnished mahogany; the bar stools were

high and comfortable, and the bartenders cheerful, skilled veterans who produced a variety of frozen daiquiris of rare quality. On the wall there were several framed photographs of the Hemingways drinking La Florida's most publicized product— the Hemingway daiquiri, or Papa Doble. Requested by most tourists, a Papa Doble was compounded of two and a half jiggers of Bacardi White Label Rum, the juice of two limes and half a grapefruit, and six drops of maraschino, all placed in an electric mixer over shaved ice, whirled vigorously and served foaming in large goblets. I sat on a stool at the Obispo Street end of the bar, in the corner under the framed photos, and ordered a Papa Doble.

Before leaving for Havana, I had searched for a Hemingway biography but could find none. All I knew about his life was that he was born in Oak Park, Illinois, outside Chicago, on July 21, 1899, the second of six children; he was devoted to his father, a doctor, who passed along his keen interest and skill in fishing and hunting to young Ernest. However, Ernest's inability to get along with his mother made his home life chaotic, and soon after graduation from Oak Park High School, he left home.

Not yet eighteen, he wangled a reporting job on the Kansas City *Star*, and the following year, having been rejected by the U.S. Army because of his defective eyesight, he managed to get accredited by the Red Cross as an ambulance driver on the Italian front. In July, 1918, at Fossalta di Piave, he was hit by an Austrian trench mortar and severely wounded.

After the war, with his mutilated leg patched up, he returned to the States and then got a job on the Toronto *Star*. In 1920 he married a St. Louis girl, Hadley Richardson, with whom he had a son. That marriage was dissolved in 1927, when he married Pauline Pfeiffer, a Paris writer for *Vogue*, who became the mother of his two other sons. In 1940 Pauline divorced him. The writer Martha Gellhorn became his third wife, and she was supplanted in 1946 by Mary Welsh, also a writer.

Early in the Twenties, married to Hadley, he lived in Paris, where he wrote *The Sun Also Rises*, a novel about his generation which brought him quick and enduring fame. He then enhanced his literary position with *A Farewell to Arms*, which he

completed after returning to the United States to live in Key
West. *To Have and Have Not* was a reflection of those Key
West years.

Between books he traveled far and wide, fished for marlin
and tuna, hunted big game on safari, and followed the bulls in
Spain. When civil war broke out in that country, he fought on
the side of the Loyalists and later wrote about it in *For Whom
the Bell Tolls*, the most widely read of all of his books. That's
about all the data I had.

Hemingway arrived a little late. He was wearing khaki pants
held up by a wide old leather belt with a huge buckle inscribed
GOTT MIT UNS, a white linen sport shirt that hung loose, and
brown leather loafers without socks. His hair was dark with
gray highlights, flecked white at the temples, and he had a
heavy mustache that ran past the corners of his mouth, but no
beard. He was massive. Not in height, for he was only an inch
over six feet, nor in weight, but in impact. Most of his two
hundred pounds was concentrated above his waist: he had
square heavy shoulders, long hugely muscled arms (the left one
jaggedly scarred and a bit misshapen at the elbow), a deep
chest, a belly-rise but no hips or thighs. Something played off
him—he was intense, electrokinetic, but in control, a race horse
reined in. He stopped to talk to one of the musicians in fluent
Spanish and something about him hit me—*enjoyment:* God, I
thought, how he's *enjoying* himself! I had never seen anyone
with such an aura of fun and well-being. He radiated it and
everyone in the place responded. He had so much more in his
face than I had expected to find from seeing his photographs.

As he came toward the bar, greeting the barmen, I noticed
that on his forehead, well above his left eye, there was a large
oblong welt that looked as if a patch of flesh-colored clay had
been stuck there haphazardly.

"Hotchner," he said, shaking hands, "welcome to the Cub
Room." His hands were thick and square, the fingers rather
short, the nails squared off. The bartender placed two frozen
daiquiris in front of us; they were in conical glasses twice the
size of my previous drink. "Here we have the ultimate achieve-

ment of the daiquiri-maker's art," Hemingway said. "Made a
run of sixteen here one night."

"This size?"

"House record," the barman, who had been listening, said.

Hemingway sampled his drink by taking a large mouthful,
holding it a long moment, then swallowing it in several installments. He nodded approval. "Hotchner . . . that's a very suspi-
cious name. Where you from?"

"St. Louis."

"What part, Chouteau Avenue? Did your grandfather fight
Nut Sigel?"

"Do you know St. Louis?"

"First three wives from St. Louis." He shook his head sadly.
"I know St. Louis. Only good person I know who didn't leave
there was Martha Gellhorn's ma." The bartender placed on the
bar in front of us a platter heaped with unshelled shrimp.
"Couple of years ago," Hemingway said, picking up one of the
shrimp, "I founded the Royal Order of Shrimp Eaters. Want to
join?"

"Sure. What do I do?"

"Members of the order eat the heads and tails." He bit off
a shrimp's head and crunched it happily.

I bit off a head and crunched it, but not happily.

"It grows on you," he said, picking up another. Two more
vases of daiquiris arrived. The bartender handed Hemingway
a letter; he looked at the return address, folded it and put it
into his pocket. "Basque friend of mine is a prolific letter writer
and each letter ends the same way: Send money." The trio,
which consisted of a big, happy guitarist, a serious, unsmiling
guitarist, and a thin, dark-skinned vocalist who also played the
maracas, began to play and sing a spirited number.

"Pals of mine," Hemingway said. "They're singing a song I
wrote for them. Wish Mary was here. She sings it best. One
night we were in here, bar crowded, everyone having a good
time, when in came three eager young gents to have a drink at
the bar, and they have FBI written all over them. So I send
word to these boys and at the stroke of midnight they break

into 'Happy Birthday' in English, everyone joining in, and when we get to 'Happy birthday, dear FBI,' those three J. Edgars nearly caved in. They cleared out fast."

We chain-drank daiquiris and discussed Havana as a place to live and work. "Character like me," Hemingway said, "the whole world to choose from, they naturally want to know why here. Usually don't try to explain. Too complicated. The clear, cool mornings when you can work good with just Black Dog awake and the fighting cocks sending out their first bulletins. Where else can you train cocks and fight them and bet those you believe in and be legal? Some people put the arm on fighting cocks as cruel? But what the hell else does a fighting cock like to do?

"Then there's the bird population—wonder birds, truly—resident and migratory, quail that drink at the swimming pool before the sun comes up. And lizards that hunt out of the arbors at the pool and the vines on the house. Am very fond of lizards.

"You want to go to town, you just slip on a pair of loafers; always a good town to get away from yourself; these Cuban girls, you look into their black eyes, they have hot sunlight in them. If you don't want to get away from yourself, you can shut out everything by not going to town and jamming the phone.

"A half hour away from the *finca* you've got your boat set up so you're in the dark-blue water of the Gulf Stream with four lines out fifteen minutes after you board her. Or maybe you feel like shooting live pigeons at the shooting club just down the way from the *finca*. Matches for big money if that's the way you want it. That's the way we had it when Tommy Shevlin, Pichon Aguilera, Winston Guest and Thorwald Sanchez were around to make teams, and you can't ask for better shoots than when the Dodgers are training and we have match-ups with Hugh Casey, Billy Herman, Augie Galan, Curt Davis and some of the others who are all crack shots. The same people who crusade against fighting cocks also blast you for the pigeon shoot. Although it's barred in a lot of places it's legal here and it's the most exciting betting-sport I know—for the shooters. To watch it is a deadly bore."

"But doesn't it get monotonous to go through an entire year without changes of seasons?" I asked. "Don't you miss the spring and fall the way it is in New England?"

"We have changes in the seasons here too," he said. "They are subtle, not abrupt as in New England, where our parents took off from because it was cropped out and the soil no damn good. But let me have Red Lodge, Montana, or even Cody, Wyoming, or West Yellowstone, with Big Jim Savage dealing off the bottom of the deck so wonderful that only the boys can see it, or Billings on a Saturday night, or even, hell, Casper, which is an oil town where Miss Mary was hospitalized."

The daiquiris kept coming as we discussed Robert Flaherty's documentary films, which Hemingway greatly admired, Ted Williams, the Book-of-the-Month-Club, Lena Horne, Proust, television, swordfish recipes, aphrodisiacs, and Indians, until eight o'clock, not threatening the Hemingway daiquiri-record but setting an all-time Hotchner high of seven. Hemingway took a drink with him for the road, sitting in the front seat of the station wagon next to his chauffeur, Juan; and I somehow managed to retain in the rum-mist of my head that he was going to pick me up the following morning to go out on his boat. I also managed—don't ask me how—to make some notes on our conversation for the benefit of the *Cosmopolitan* editor. This was the beginning of a practice I followed during the entire time I knew him. Later on I augmented these journals with conversations recorded on pocket tape transistors that we carried when we traveled.

There were two Pilars in Hemingway's life: one, the lusty partisan of *For Whom the Bell Tolls;* the other, a forty-foot black and green cabin cruiser—both named after the Spanish shrine. The seagoing *Pilar* was docked in the Havana harbor, ready to roll when we got there. It had a flying bridge with topside controls, outsized riggers that could handle ten-pound skipping bait, and the capacity to fish four rods. Ernest introduced me to her with old affection.

First, though, he introduced me to a lean Indian-skinned man who was Gregorio Fuentes, mate on the *Pilar* since 1938. Went

to sea when he was four," Ernest said, "out of Lanzarote in the
Canaries. Met him at Dry Tortugas when we were stormbound
there. Before Gregorio, had another wonderful mate, Carlos
Gutierrez, but somebody lured him away with more dough
while I was away in the Spanish Civil War. But Gregorio is a
marvel: got *Pilar* through three hurricanes with his absolute
seamanship, is a peerless fisherman, and cooks the best pom-
pano you ever tasted."

The big engines turned over; Ernest climbed topside and
steered her out of port, past Morro Castle, and up the coast
about seven miles, toward the fishing village of Cojimar, which
was destined to be the village of *The Old Man and the Sea*.
Gregorio set out four lines, two with feathers, two with meat
bait. I was topside with Ernest.

He took out some tequila and we both had a sip to see if it
was cold enough. "It's getting there," he said. "Wish you had
been along on the last trip. The kids were down on ten days'
vacation and I took them to Cay Sal and Double-Headed Shot
Keys in the Bahamas. We caught around eighteen hundred
pounds of game fish, turned three big turtles, got lots of crayfish
and had wonderful swimming. That water is almost virgin fishing and the kids had a wonderful time."

He then began talking about the *Pilar* with extraordinary
pride. "She sleeps seven but in the war she slept nine."

"She was in the war?"

"From 1942 to 1944 we turned her into a Q-boat and pa-
trolled the waters off the north shore of Cuba. Antisub. Worked
under Naval Intelligence. We posed as a commercial fishing
boat but changed *Pilar's* disguise several times so it didn't look
like any one boat was fishing too much. Had thirty-five hundred
dollars' worth of radio equipment in the head; the actual head
was however you could manage over the side. We had machine
guns, bazookas and high explosives, all disguised as something
else, and the plan was to maneuver ourselves into a position
where we were hailed and ordered alongside by a surfacing
U-boat. A U-boat not on alert could have been taken by our
plan of attack. Crew was Spanish, Cuban and American, very

good at their jobs, all brave, and I think our capture attack
would have worked."

"But you never got a chance to try it out?"

"No, but we were able to send in good information on U-boat
locations and were credited by Naval Intelligence with locating
several Nazi subs which were later bombed out by Navy depth
charges and presumed sunk. Got decorated for that."

"Was Gregorio along?"

"Sure. I explained to the crew the dangers involved, since
Pilar was no match for any U-boat that wanted to blast it, but
Gregorio was very happy to go out because we were insured
ten thousand dollars a man and Gregorio had never figured he
was worth that much. Quarters very cramped but crew got
along fine. No fights. One tour we stayed out fifty-seven days."

"Feesh! Feesh, Papa, Feesh!" Gregorio was calling from the
stern. We looked quickly starboard; I saw brown flashing that
turned to dark purple, pectoral fins that showed lavender, the
symmetry of a submarine. "Marlin," Ernest said, "let's go." He
took hold of the topside rail and swung himself down. Gregorio
handed him the rod with the meat bait. "Ever boat one of
these?" Ernest asked.

"Never been deep-sea fishing."

"Then cut your teeth on this," he said, handing me the rod.
I felt a touch of panic. Here was one of the world's great
fishermen, a lightning-fast marlin whose size I couldn't believe,
a big, complicated rod and reel—and here was I, who had never
caught anything larger than a ten-pound bass out of my friend
Sam Epstein's rowboat off Southold, Long Island.

But I had not reckoned with a quality of Ernest's I was to
observe and enjoy many times over the ensuing years: his
superb skill at instruction and his infinite patience with his
pupil. In a quiet, even voice Ernest guided me every step of
the way, from when to pull up to set the big hook in his mouth
to when to bring him in close to be taken. A half hour later
we were looking down at the beauty of that boated marlin;
"We just might have a new *syndicat des pêcheurs*—Hotchner
and Hemingway, Marlin Purveyors," Ernest said. I realized that

he had tentatively knighted me as a potential co-adventurer; for thirteen years it was to be an invigorating, entertaining, educational, exasperating, uplifting, exhausting, surprising partnership.

As we returned from the boat to the Nacional, Ernest made his first and only reference to the note I had sent him on The Future of Literature. I was going back to New York the following morning, and we were shaking hands on the sidewalk in front of the hotel. "The fact is I do not know a damn about the future of anything," he said.

I was startled by the abrupt reference. "Oh, sure, just forget . . ."

"What are they paying?"

"Fifteen thousand."

"Well, that's enough to perk up The Future of Literature in itself. Tell you what—send me tear sheets or manuscripts of what any of your other master minds have written so I get the pitch. Also a contract. If it still legally checks out that pieces contracted for by a bona-fide nonresident and written outside the States are tax-free so long as the nonresident stays out of country twelve consecutive months, then will write a good straight piece about what I think and will try to straighten up and think as good as I can."

Over the years, with the exception of 1956 and 1957, when I was living in Rome, I visited Ernest in Cuba at least once a year, often more, and daiquiris at the Floridita, pigeon shoots, excursions on the *Pilar*, and days at the *finca* became familiar. There was often a "business" reason behind these Havana trips and other trips to meet Ernest elsewhere in the world, but his approach to dealing with business matters was widely circuitous. He invariably allotted a minimum of two days to "cooling out"—I from the trip, he from working or if not working, then from some mysterious pressure he never clearly identified. We would cool out by indulging in the local distractions—if in Cuba, fishing, shooting pigeons, attending jai-alai matches and betting on them, matching Ernest's stable of fighting cocks and so on; if in Ketchum, Idaho, the cool-out was hunting the wild

duck, goose, pheasant, elk, deer, dove, chukker, Hungarian partridge, and cooking and eating same; the Spanish cool-out was
all aspects of bullfighting, the Prado, touring, eating, drinking
and joining the *ambiance*. I said the minimum was two days.

The maximum? I went to Spain in June, 1959, to discuss a
series of Hemingway-based special dramas that I was destined
to write and produce for the Columbia Broadcasting System.
I met Ernest in Alicante on June 28th, and on August 17th, as
we were riding back from the bull ring, he said, "Been thinking
about those television plays. Let's talk about them."

Six months after my first visit I returned to Havana. The
fifteen thousand dollars had been advanced but the article on
The Future of Literature had not been written. Instead, Ernest
had an alternate idea that he wanted me to come down to
discuss. The little town of San Francisco de Paula, where
Ernest's Finca Vigía (Lookout Farm) was located, was itself
a poverty-stricken shambles. But the Hemingway property was
fence-enclosed and consisted of thirteen acres of flower and
vegetable gardens, a cow pasture with a half-dozen cows, fruit
trees, a defunct tennis court, a large swimming pool, and a
low, once-white limestone villa which was a bit crumbled but
dignified. Eighteen kinds of mangoes grew on the long slope
from the main gate up to the house that Ernest called his
"charming ruin." Immediately in front of the house was a giant
ceiba tree, sacred in voodoo rites, orchids growing from its
grizzled trunk, its massive roots upheaving the tiled terrace and
splitting the interior of the house itself. But Ernest's fondness
for the tree was such that despite its havoc, he would not
permit the roots to be touched. A short distance from the main
house was a white frame guest house. Behind the main house,
to one side, was a new white gleaming three-storied square
tower with an outside winding staircase.

The walls of the dining room and the nearly fifty-foot living
room of the main house were populated with splendidly horned
animal heads, and there were several well-trod animal skins on
the tiled floors. The furniture was old, comfortable and undistinguished. Inside the front door was an enormous magazine rack
that held an unceasing deluge of American and foreign-lan-

guage periodicals. A large library off the living room was crammed with books that lined the walls from the floor to the high ceiling. Ernest's bedroom, where he worked, was also walled with books; there were over five thousand volumes on the premises. On the wall over his bed was one of his favorite paintings, Juan Gris' "Guitar Player." Another Gris, Miró's "Farm," several Massons, a Klee, a Braque, and Waldo Peirce's portrait of Ernest as a young man were among the paintings in the living room and Mary's room.

In Ernest's room there was a large desk covered with stacks of letters, newspapers and magazine clippings, a small sack of carnivores' teeth, two unwound clocks, shoehorns, an unfilled pen in an onyx holder, a wood-carved zebra, wart hog, rhino and lion in single file, and a wide assortment of souvenirs, mementos and good-luck charms. He never worked at the desk. Instead, he used a stand-up work place he had fashioned out of the top of a bookcase near his bed. His portable typewriter was snugged in there and papers were spread along the top of the bookcase on either side of it. He used a reading board for longhand writing. There were some animal heads on the bedroom walls, too, and a worn, cracked skin of a lesser kudu decorated the tiled floor.

His bathroom was large and cluttered with medicines and medical paraphernalia which bulged out of the cabinet and onto all surfaces; the room was badly in need of paint but painting was impossible because the walls were covered with inked records, written in Ernest's careful hand, of dated blood-pressure counts, and weights, prescription numbers and other medical and pharmaceutical intelligence.

The staff for the *finca* normally consisted of the houseboy René, the chauffeur Juan, a Chinese cook, three gardeners, a carpenter, two maids and the keeper of the fighting cocks. The white tower had been built by Mary in an effort to get the complement of thirty cats out of the house, and to provide Ernest with a place more becoming to work in than his makeshift quarters in his bedroom. It worked with the cats but not with Ernest. The ground floor of the tower was the cats' quarters, with special sleeping, eating and maternity accommodations, and they all lived there with the exception of a few favorites like Crazy Christian, Friendless' Brother and Ecstasy, who were allowed house privileges. The top floor of the tower, which had a sweeping view of palm tops and green hillocks clear to the sea, had been furnished with an imposing desk befitting an Author of High Status, bookcases, and comfortable reading chairs, but Ernest rarely wrote a line there—except when he occasionally corrected a set of galleys.

On this first visit to the *finca* my wife and I were to be quartered in the guest house, but Mary Hemingway, a golden vivacious woman, greeted us with apologies that it was not quite ready. "Jean-Paul Sartre showed up unexpectedly yesterday with a lady friend," she said, "and the sheets haven't been changed yet."

On our way up to the main house Ernest confided: "You know what Sartre told me at dinner last night? That a newspaperman made up the word 'existentialism' and that he, Sartre, had nothing to do with it."

We went into the living room and Ernest looked up at the ceiling a moment. "The Duke and Duchess of Windsor were here last week but they only seemed fascinated by the falling plaster."

I noticed that Ernest had three long, deep scratches on his forearm and I asked about them. "Cotsies," he said. "They had a circus pitched near here with two good five-year-old cats. Brothers. It was wonderful to hear them roar in the morning. Made friends with the trainer. He let me work them and I worked them good with a rolled-up newspaper, but you have to be careful not to turn your back.

"Have a wonderful number to do in public figured out. The trainer is going to announce me as an illustrious *domador del norte*, now retired from the profession, but who, through his *afición*, dedicates this rather special number to the Cuban public. The climax is when I lie down and both cotsies put their front feet on my chest. I started to practice this but got raked on the arm a couple of times gentling them."

I said I thought lion-baiting was a rather dangerous pursuit for a writer who wanted to continue practicing his trade.

"Miss Mary agrees with you," Ernest said. "Promised her I wouldn't work cotsies any more until the big book is finished. She left when I started gentling them and got raked. I am her security and it is wicked, I guess, to lay it on the line just for fun. But know no other place as good to lay it as on the line."

That evening after dinner, Ernest showed me around the house. From a shelf in the library he took down first editions inscribed to him by James Joyce, Scott Fitzgerald, Gertrude Stein, Sherwood Anderson, John Dos Passos, Robert Benchley, Ford Maddox Ford, Ezra Pound and many others. He went through a trunk of old photos and scrapbooks. In one vintage photograph album there was a picture of Ernest, age five or six. Written on the back, in his mother's hand, was the notation: "Ernest was taught to shoot by Pa when 2½ and when 4 could handle a pistol."

We also came across a photograph of a very young-looking Marlene Dietrich, inscribed To Ernest With Love. "You know how we met, the Kraut and me?" Ernest asked. "Back in my broke days I was crossing cabin on the *Ile*, but a pal of mine who was traveling first loaned me his reserve tux and smuggled me in for meals. One night we're having dinner in the salon, my pal and I, when there appears at the top of the staircase this unbelievable spectacle in white. The Kraut, of course. A long, tight white-beaded gown over *that* body; in the area of what is known as the Dramatic Pause, she can give lessons to anybody. So she gives it that Dramatic Pause on the staircase, then slowly slithers down the stairs and across the floor to where Jock Whitney, I think it was, was having a fawncy dinner party. Of course, nobody in that dining room has touched food to lips since her entrance. The Kraut gets to the table and all the men hop up and her chair is held at the ready, but she's counting. Twelve. Of course, she apologizes and backs off and says she's sorry but she is very superstitious about being thirteen at anything and with that she turns to go, but I have naturally risen to the occasion and grandly offer to save the party by being the fourteenth. That was how we met. Pretty romantic, eh? Maybe I ought to sell it to Darryl F. Panic."

On our way back to the living room, we passed a large in-

scribed photograph of Ingrid Bergman. I stopped to look at it.
"Can post photo of any lady Miss Mary's not jealous of," Ernest
said. "So far she's batting a thousand in the no-cause-for-jeal-
ousy league."

We settled down in the living room, Ernest sitting in Papa's
Chair, a big overstuffed lopsided easy chair with a faded, well-
worn slip cover; Black Dog curled up at his feet. Black
Dog, who was mostly a springer spaniel, had wandered into
Ernest's Sun Valley ski cabin one afternoon, cold, starved,
fear-ridden and sub-dog in complex—a hunting dog who was
scared stiff of gunfire. Ernest had brought him back to Cuba
and patiently and lovingly built up his weight, confidence and
affection to the point, Ernest said, that Black Dog believed he
was an accomplished author himself. "He needs ten hours' sleep
but is always exhausted because he faithfully follows my schedule. When I'm between books he is happy, but when I'm working he takes it very hard. Although he's a boy who loves his
sleep, he thinks he has to get up and stick with me from first
light on. He keeps his eyes open loyally. But he doesn't like it."

The talk went from Black Dog, to the animal heads on the
walls, to Africa. "Had an English friend," Ernest related, "who
wanted to shoot a lion with bow and arrow. One White Hunter
after another turned him down until finally a Swede White
Hunter agreed to take him. Englishman was the kind of Englishman who took a portable bar on safari. Swede, who was a very
good hunter, warned against the bow and arrow as effectives,
but his Lordship insisted so Swede briefed him on the lion—
can run one hundred yards in four seconds, see only in silhou-
ette, should be hit at fifty yards, all that. They finally stalk the
lion, set it up, lion charges, Englishman pulls back bow, hits
lion in the chest at fifty yards, lion bites off the arrow, keeps
coming, eats the ass right off one of the native guides in one
gulping tear before Swede can drop him. Englishman is shook
up. Comes over to look at the bloody mess of native guide and
lion lying side by side. Swede says, 'Well, your Lordship, you
may now put the bow and arrow away.' Englishman says, 'I
think we might.'

"This was the same Englishman I had met in Nairobi with

his wife. She was a young Irish beauty who had come un-
announced to my room. The following evening the Englishman
asked me to have a drink with him at the hotel bar. 'Ernest,'
he said, 'you are a gentleman so you did nothing wrong, but
my wife should not make a fool out of me.' "

Mary steered the conversation back to animals. Ernest told
about a very big, cocky black bear out West, who had made
life miserable for everyone by standing in the middle of the
road and refusing to budge when cars came along. It got so
that no one could use the road. But Ernest heard about him and
drove along the road to seek him out; suddenly, sure enough—
there was the bear. A really *big* bear. He was on his hind legs
and his upper lip was pulled back in a sneer. Ernest got out of
the car and went over to him. "Do you realize that you're nothing
but a miserable, common black bear?" Ernest said to him in a
loud, firm voice. "Why, you sad son-of-a-bitch, how can you be
so cocky and stand there and block cars when you're nothing
but a *miserable* bear and a black bear at that—not even a polar
or a grizzly or anything worth-while."

Ernest said he really laid it on him and the poor black bear began to hang his head, then he lowered himself to all fours and
pretty soon he walked off the road. Ernest had destroyed him.
From that time on he used to run behind a tree and hide
whenever he saw a car coming and shake with fear that Ernest
might be inside, ready to dress him down.

René soon appeared with the movie projector and we settled
down to a twin bill that was Ernest's favorite: a Tony Zale
versus Rocky Graziano slugfest, plus *The Killers* with Burt
Lancaster and Ava Gardner. The curtain raiser was the fight,
which Ernest followed avidly and commented upon, but five
minutes into *The Killers* he was sound asleep. "Never saw him
last past the first reel," Mary said.

We had been at the *finca* for three days when Ernest got
around to his substitute idea for The Future of Literature
article: he would write two short stories instead. Some of his
stories, "The Short Happy Life of Francis Macomber," for one,
had been published in *Cosmo*, he said, and it would be better

for him and the magazine if he did fiction, which was his forte, instead of a think piece, which was not. He pointed out, however, that one article did not equal two short stories in value; subsequently the editor increased the payment to twenty-five thousand dollars.

The dinner regulars during those days at the *finca* were Roberto Herrera, a bald, deaf, powerful, unprepossessing, gentle, devoted Spaniard, in his late thirties, who, according to Ernest, had had five years of medicine in Spain and who had come to Cuba after having been imprisoned for fighting on the republican side in the Civil War; Sinsky Dunabeitia, a salty, roaring, boozing, fun-loving Basque sea captain who manned a freighter run from the States to Cuba and was a constant at the *finca* whenever his ship was in port; Father Don Andres, called Black Priest, a Basque who had been in the Bilbao Cathedral when the Civil War broke out. Don Andres had climbed into the pulpit and exhorted all the parishioners to go get their guns and fill the streets and shoot what they could and the hell with spending their time in church. After that, he enrolled as a machine-gunner in the republican army. Of course, when the war ended he was kicked out of Spain. He sought refuge in Cuba, but the Church there took a dim view of his past behavior and assigned him the poorest parish in the worst section. Thus, the name Black Priest. Ernest had befriended him, as he befriended scores of Franco refugees, and Black Priest, wearing a brightly colored sport shirt, would come to the Hemingway *finca* on his days away from his parish and devote himself to eating, drinking, swimming in the pool, and exchanging reminiscences with Ernest and Roberto. There were other guests, too: a Spanish grandee Ernest had known in the Civil War, a gambler from the old days in Key West, an anti-Batista (sub-rosa) Cuban politician and his wife, and a semiretired pelota player, once of great prominence. "Mondays to Thursdays I try to maintain quiet," Mary said. "But the week ends are always on the verge of uproar, and sometimes over the verge. Papa doesn't like to go to other people's houses because he says he can't trust the food and drink. The last time he accepted a dinner invitation was about a year ago. They served sweet champagne which he had to drink to be polite, and it took ten days for him to get it out of his system."

In early 1949, before he left for a trip to Venice, Ernest telephoned me in New York from the *finca*. He began by discussing the triumph of Mr. Truman over Mr. Dewey, but finally got to the point: "About the two stories, agreement is—deadline end of December and I deliver two stories or give back the dough, right? Wrote one story after you left but think it is too rough for *Cosmopolitan* so I better save it for the book."

"What book?"

"New book of short stories. Or book of new short stories— take your pick. Don't think I'll have time in Venice, but plan to get back to Cuba in early May, take the kids on a trip, then write two good stories for you. I may have to let them lay awhile and then go over them, but think if I have no bad luck, I should surely have two before the deadline. The story I just finished is about forty-five hundred words and much better than that Waugh crap they just ran. But I can beat it for you."

All through the spring of 1949 I received letters from Ernest from the Gritti Palace hotel in Venice and from the Villa Aprile in Cortina d'Ampezzo, which is magnificent ski country to the north. He wrote about Mary breaking her leg in a ski accident and about a serious eye infection for which he was hospitalized, but did not mention the stories. It was during this period that Ernest instigated my first meeting with Charles Scribner, Sr.; and afterward he said, "Hope you liked Charlie. He liked you very much and he likes almost nobody. Hates authors." Scribner was a silver-haired, gentle-featured man of charm, wit and good humor, and he loved Ernest as a proud father loves a gloried son. Ernest once said of Scribner: "Now that Max Perkins is gone, Charlie is all I've got left to help keep the franchise."

The first time Mr. Scribner and I met, it was to discuss Ernest's medical statement which he had sent to Scribner from Italy for release to the press. Ernest suggested that this statement might take the pressure off. "Especially off me, here in the hospital, making my fight and under siege of news hawks like Hector was be-Greeked at Troy."

The statement was: "It certainly is odd, though not particularly I suppose, for people to think you are a phony. I would not let the photographers nor any reporters in because I was too tired and was making my fight and because face was incrusted like after a flash burn. Had streptococcus infection, straphilococcus (probably misspelled) infection plus erysipelas, thirteen and one half million units of Penicillium, plus three and one half million when it started to relapse. The doctors in Cortina thought it might go into the brain and make a menengitis since the left eye was completely involved and closed completely tight so that every time I opened it with boric solution a big part of the eye-lashes would pull out.

"It could have been from the dust on the secondary roads as well as from fragments from the wad.*

"Still can't shave. Have tried it twice and up come the welts and patches and then the skin peels like postage stamps. So run a clippers over face every week. That way it looks unshaven but not as though you were sporting a beard. All above is true and accurate and you can release it to anybody, including the press."

Ernest was back in Cuba by the summer of 1949, and in late July he telephoned to report that the *Cosmopolitan* two-story project had taken another turn and suggested I visit him in September. I said that this time I would take a cottage at the Kawama Club at Varadero Beach and not inconvenience them.

"No inconvenience," Ernest said, "but Varadero beauty place. When you come down I will knock off work for two or three days and bring the boat to Varadero and we can have some fun. Will work hard for balance of July and August so that will rate the vacation."

"Arthur wants to know," I said, referring to *Cosmo*'s editor, Arthur Gordon, "if you want the additional ten thousand."

---

* Ernest is referring here to wadding fragments that fall from shotgun shells on overhead duck shots. During his hospitalization the erysipelas infected both his eyes and then spread to other parts of his face. When his eyes swelled and shut tight his doctors thought it might be fatal.

"No. Tell Arthur thanks very much, but am okay on dough. Our fighting chickens won thirty-eight out of forty-two fights. The joint is producing what we need to eat. The Deep-Freeze is full. I'm shooting hot on pigeons and should be able to pick up three to four G's. The kids are all suited, Italian moneyed, and leave on Tuesday. My oldest boy, Jack, is back as a captain of infantry in Berlin and self-supporting—so far. If Kid Gavilan wins over Robinson, am okay through Christmas. He'll probably lose, though, and am covering."

I asked if I could bring him anything. "Well, yes." he said. "If you can manage it, bring a tin of béluga caviar from Maison Glass and a Smith-Corona portable, pica type. About the stories, believe I have a pretty nice surprise for you. Have been hotter—working—than the grill they roasted San Lorenzo on."

The surprise was that Ernest had started one of the *Cosmopolitan*-promised stories, originally titled "A Short Story," when he was hospitalized in Italy; he said he had started it to pay for his imminent funeral expenses. As he improved, however, the story grew until now it gave every indication of becoming a novel. Ernest was calling it *Across the River and into the Trees*. "All of my books started as short stories," he said. "I never sat down to write a novel."

We were on the *Pilar* when he gave me the first chapters to read, sitting beside me, reading over my shoulder. (It was impossible with him breathing in my ear, and I was only vaguely aware of what I was reading. In years ahead I was to learn that all works-in-progress would be shown to me in this manner; although it wasn't easy, I eventually learned to detach myself from the author at my shoulder.) Now, however, Ernest completely distracted me with his reactions to the manuscript—laughing at places, commenting at others, as if it were someone else's book. He started to put it away (Ernest always treated the pages of a manuscript-in-progress as Crown Jewels), but I asked whether I could go through it a second time; and so later I succeeded in really reading it.

"Did Papa tell you," Mary asked, "that he's back at the cotsies again?"

"I thought you swore off," I said, surprised.

"Momentary relapse. This was a big cat, five years old. Worked him when the trainer quit on account of the cat was getting bad and I think I did okay. Takes your mind off things."

"Papa, I really think it's foolish to go in with cats when you're not training them and yourself every day," I said.

"You're right. For me to work cotsies is foolish, of course. I only do it to show off in front of some woman or for straight fun. The fun is to see how they react to discipline without provocation. But you can't work more than two at once because it is dangerous to let them get behind you. Same thing applies to some people I know."

Great black cumulus puffs were forming in the sky to the west, and the sea was getting choppy. The four lines trolled efficiently but there were no takers. The black sky began to infect the north and the water took on a luminous sheen.

"What month Gerry in?" Ernest asked.

"Fourth."

"Then not a good idea to risk hurricane or even all-out storm. If it weren't for being pregnant, we would head up into this and ride it out. Can be wonderful fun." He told Gregorio to turn the *Pilar* around, and I suggested that we all have lunch at the Kawama Club. During the two hours it took us to get there we did not have a single strike.

Gregorio anchored the boat several hundred yards from the beach. The water was very turbulent now, but the Kawama Club had no launch facilities, so we had to swim ashore. Mary could borrow clothes from Geraldine, but Ernest looked me up and down with narrowed eyes and shook his head. "Hotchner, an exchange of pawnts is hopeless. I'll carry mine." I thought he meant he would put a pair in a watertight bag and tow it in—but that was the easy way.

The women dived off and started to swim. Ernest had taken a pair of shorts and a shirt, rolled them up tightly, with a bottle of good claret inside because he didn't trust the Kawama wine, and secured the roll with his GOTT MIT UNS leather belt. He descended the boat's ladder and lowered himself carefully into the water. He had the roll in his left hand, which he held straight up over his head to keep it dry, and began to swim powerfully against the tossing sea, keeping the upper part of his torso out of the water, using only his right arm and kick for locomotion. It was a remarkable exhibition of balance and strength; I swam alongside him and even with two arms found it arduous going.

I arrived on the beach a few moments in advance of Ernest, and as I stood and watched him negotiating the last few yards, his left arm relentlessly aloft, holding the dry pants-roll like a tubular pennant on the top of a muscled mast, he was an immortal sea god, not from Oak Park, Illinois, at all, but Poseidon, emerging from his aquatic kingdom. He came out of the sea dripping, smiling happily at his dry pants, not even short of breath.

Ernest phoned frequently about *Across the River*. "Been jamming hard," he said on one occasion. "Black Dog is tired too. He'll be glad when the book is over and so will I. But, by Christ, I'll miss it for a while. Just wrote a goddamn wonder chapter, the man says modestly. Got it all, to break your heart, into two pages. Yesterday Roberto counted. He hates to count but counts accurately, and through this morning it is 43,745. This is so you know what you have as effectives. Think it should go sixty or just under.

"About the monies, please advise me. We ought to make a contract before it is finished. It is really the best book that I have written, I think, but I am prejudiced, of course. Have only two more innings to pitch and I plan to turn their caps around."

Cosmo's reply about the contract was that Ernest was such an old and valued friend of the Hearst organization that he was to name his own price; when I telegramed him that remarkable information he phoned me about it. He wanted to know the most *Cosmopolitan* had ever paid for a serialized novel. I told him seventy-five thousand dollars. "Okay," he said, "I figure I ought to top that by ten. Please tell them I've been throwing in my armor worse that Georgie Patton ever did and there isn't a plane on the ground that can fly. Brooklyn Tolstoys, grab

your laurels and get out of that slip stream. I even throw in
the taking of Paris for free. Will probably never live to finish
the long book anyway. So what the hell?" Irwin Shaw, Brook-
lyn-born—an enduring target for Ernest's shafts—had just published *The Young Lions.*

Although I did not know it at the time, since I had not known
him for long, this rather frequent use of the telephone was
highly unusual for Ernest. He later explained to me that there
were only a few people he felt comfortable with on the telephone. Marlene Dietrich was one. Toots Shor was another.
Ordinarily Ernest advanced upon a telephone with dark sus-
picion, virtually stalking it from behind. He picked it up
gingerly and placed it to his ear as if to determine whether
something inside was ticking. When he spoke into it his voice
became constricted and the rhythm of his speech changed,
the way an American's speech changes when he talks with a
foreigner. Ernest would invariably come away from a telephone conversation physically exhausted, sweated, and driven
to stiff drink. But he liked to phone Toots Shor from Paris or
Málaga or Venice and throw a few lefts at him before placing
a bet, through Toots' auspices, on an impending fight or a
World Series. Ernest liked to phone Dietrich because, as he
said, they had loved each other for a long time and they always
told each other everything that happened and they never lied
to each other except when very necessary, and then only on a
temporary basis.

Later on, when I got to know Marlene quite well, she told
me: "I never ask Ernest for advice as such but he is always
there to talk to, to get letters from, and in conversation and
letters I find the things I can use for whatever problems I may
have; he has often helped me without even knowing my problems. He says remarkable things that seem to automatically
adjust to problems of all sizes.

"For example, I spoke to him on the telephone just a few
weeks ago. Ernest was alone in the *finca;* he had finished
writing for the day, and he wanted to talk. At one point he
asked me what work plans I had—if any—and I told him that

I had just had a very lucrative offer from a Miami night club
but I was undecided about whether to take it.

" 'Why the indecision?' he asked.

" 'Well,' I answered, 'I feel I should work. I should not waste
my time. It's wrong. I think one appearance in London and
one a year in Vegas is quite enough. However, I'm probably
just pampering myself, so I've been trying to convince myself
to take the offer.'

"There was silence for a moment and I could visualize
Ernest's beautiful face poised in thought. He finally said, 'Don't
do what you sincerely don't want to do. Never confuse movement with action.' In those five words he gave me a whole
philosophy.

"That's the wonderful thing about him—he kneels himself
into his friends' problems. He is like a huge rock, off somewhere, a constant and steady thing, that certain someone whom
everybody should have and nobody has.

"I suppose the most remarkable thing about Ernest is that
he has found time to do the things most men only dream
about. He has had the courage, the initiative, the time, the
enjoyment to travel, to digest it all, to write, to create it,
in a sense. There is in him a sort of quiet rotation of seasons,
with each of them passing overland and then going under-
ground and re-emerging in a kind of rhythm, refreshed and
full of renewed vigor.

"He is gentle, as all real men are gentle; without tenderness,
a man is uninteresting."

"The thing about the Kraut and me," Ernest said after I
told him what Marlene had said about him, "is that we
have been in love since 1934, when we first met on the *Ile
de France*, but we've never been to bed. Amazing but true.
Victims of un-synchronized passion. Those times when I was
out of love, the Kraut was deep in some romantic tribulation,
and on those occasions when Dietrich was on the surface and
swimming about with those marvelously seeking eyes of hers,
I was submerged. There was another crossing on the *Ile*, years

after that first one, when something could have happened, the only time, but I had too recently made love to that worthless M——, and the Kraut was still somewhat in love with that equally worthless R——. We were like two young cavalry officers who had lost all their money gambling and were determined to go straight."

Chapter Two

New York ◆ 1949

Ernest came up to New York at the end of October, 1949, with the manuscript of *Across the River and into the Trees*. New York City was just a way station for Ernest, a place to stay for a week or so on the move to or from some serious place. There was a small core of New York regulars whom he invariably contacted on arrival and a large peripheral group who contacted him. For years his favorite hotel was the Sherry-Netherland (he liked their "good protection"—no name on the register, phone calls all screened, newsmen and photographers thrown off the scent); but in 1959 he gave up the Sherry-Netherland for a three-room *pied à terre* at 1 East Sixty-Second, a once-fabulous town house which had been divided into not-especially-fabulous apartments.

Ernest was always uneasy in New York and liked being there less than in any other city he frequented. Mary loved it, and I suspect that he came as often as he did as a favor to her. He did not like theater, opera or ballet, and although he liked to listen to music he rarely, to my knowledge, attended a concert or any other musical presentation, longhair or jazz. He would only go to a prize fight that paired really good boys, and sometimes he made a special trip for a first-rate championship fight. Otherwise not. He avidly followed professional football on television when he was in the States (there was no

United States television in Cuba), but he did not go to the games. He loved baseball and would go to any game; and occasionally he came to New York just to see a World Series.

The only bars Ernest liked were Toots Shor's, the Old Seidelburg, and Tim Costello's. I asked him about the story I had heard of the time that he got into a dispute with John O'Hara about their respective hardnesses of head, the dispute having been put to an abrupt end by Ernest's taking a shillelagh which Costello kept behind the bar, raising it up with an end in each hand, and cracking it neatly in two over his own head. I asked Ernest whether the story was apocryphal. He laughed. "Good story not to deny," he answered.

One of the few things about New York that Ernest unreservedly enjoyed was the visits of the Ringling Brothers Circus. He felt that circus animals were not like other animals, that they were more intelligent and, because of their constant working alliance with man, had much more highly developed personalities.

The first time I went to the circus with him, he was so eager to see the animals he went to Madison Square Garden an hour before the doors were scheduled to open. We went around to a side entrance on Fiftieth Street and Ernest banged on the door until an attendant appeared. He tried to turn us away but Ernest had a card signed by his old friend John Ringling North, which stated that the bearer was to be admitted to the circus any time, any place. We went below, as he always did before the circus began, and made a tour of the cages. Ernest became fascinated with the gorilla; although the keeper was nervous as hell and warned him not to stand too close, Ernest wanted to make friends with the animal. He stood close to the cage and talked to the gorilla in a staccato cadence and kept talking, and finally the gorilla, who appeared to be listening, was so moved he picked up his plate of carrots and dumped it on top of his head; then he started to whimper; sure signs, the keeper said, of his affection.

By now, all the keepers had assembled around Ernest, anxious that he try a few words with their charges, but he said that the only wild animal with whom he had any true talking rapport was the bear, whereupon the bear keeper cleared a path for him.

Ernest stopped in front of the polar-bear cage and closely watched its occupant swing back and forth across the small area. "He's very nasty, Mr. Hemingway," the bear keeper said. "I think you're better off talking to this brown bear, who has a good sense of humor."

"I should get through to him," Ernest said, staying with the polar bear, "but I haven't talked bear talk for some time and I may be rusty." The keeper smiled. Ernest edged in close to the bars. He began to speak to the bear in a soft, musical voice totally unlike his gorilla language, and the bear stopped pacing. Ernest kept on talking, and the words, or I should say sounds, were unlike any I had ever heard. The bear backed up a little and grunted, and then it sat on its haunches and, looking straight at Ernest, it began to make a series of noises through its nose, which made it sound like an elderly gentleman with severe catarrh.

"I'll be goddamned!" the keeper said.

Ernest smiled at the bear and walked away, and the bear stared after him, bewildered. "It's Indian talk," Ernest said. "I'm part Indian. Bears like me. Always have."

Although Ernest liked to watch movies in his living room in Cuba, the only ones he went to see in New York were those based upon his books and stories, and then he went in a spirit of self-imposed duress. For days before taking the plunge, he would talk about his onerous duty of going to see such a movie and would circle the project as a hunter circles his quarry before moving in for the kill. He made his decision on *A Farewell to Arms* following lunch at Le Veau d'Or one day, after expostulating for three days on why he was going "to give it a miss." This was the David O. Selznick remake that starred Jennifer Jones and Rock Hudson. Ernest lasted thirty-five minutes. Afterward we walked along Forty-ninth Street and up Fifth Avenue in silence. Finally Ernest said, "You know, Hotch, you write a book like that that you're fond of over the years, then you see that happen to it, it's like pissing in your father's beer."

We saw *The Sun Also Rises* the day before the start of the 1957 World Series, for which Ernest had made a special trip. When Mary asked him how he liked it, he said, "Any picture in which Errol Flynn is the best actor is its own worst enemy."

The only movie that Ernest himself had anything to do with was *The Old Man and the Sea*. He edited the script and then spent weeks with a camera crew off the coast of Peru, catching large marlins that never got hooked at the right hour for the Technicolor cameras; so like all movie marlins, they wound up being sponge-rubber fish in a Culver City tank. Ernest sat through *all* of that movie, numb. "Spencer Tracy looked like a fat, very rich actor playing a fisherman," was his only comment.

When in New York, Ernest made a point of seeing the television plays I had dramatized from his stories or novels. I would arrange for them to be shown at CBS on a closed-circuit set. Of all the shows, the one that he liked best, and the one I always declared to win with, was called "The World of Nick Adams," an episodic drama that I had based upon seven of the Nick Adams stories. It was brilliantly directed by Robert Mulligan; and after Ernest had seen it and the viewing-room lights came up, he said, "Well, Hotch, you got it on the screen as good as I got it on paper." That was the best compliment I ever received about anything. It was my good fortune that he never wanted to see "The Gambler, the Nun and the Radio," which was a disaster from beginning to end. He liked most of the three-hour *For Whom the Bell Tolls*, which I did for two successive Playhouse 90s with Jason Robards, Maria Schell, Eli Wallach and Maureen Stapleton playing the leads; he thought, however, I should have included more material favorable to the Nationalist cause. "But you got the spirit of the people, with their tempers and their true unwashed smells, and that's what counts. You see the cinema version? The big love scene between Coops and Ingrid and he didn't take off his coat. That's one hell of a way for a guy to make love, with his coat on—in a sleeping bag. And Ingrid, in her tailored

dress and all those pretty curls—she was strictly Elizabeth
Arden out of Abercrombie and Fitch."

Ernest's attitude toward New York shopping was the same
as his attitude toward movie-going; he circled for days and
then finally made the distasteful plunge. In no area was his
innate shyness more pronounced than in a store. The mere
sight of sales counters and salespeople caused him to break
out in a sweat, and he either bought the first thing they showed
him or bolted before they got the merchandise off the racks.
The one exception to this shopping syndrome was Abercrombie
& Fitch, especially its gun department and shoe department.
But even at Abercrombie's a salesman in the clothing department would have been well advised to hold Ernest by the
sleeve while turning his back to get a trench coat off the rack.

Actually, Ernest's attire was very restricted and, in a manner
of speaking, constituted a uniform; the leather vests, the knitted
tan skullcap, the GOTT MIT UNS leather belt which had been
appropriated from a dead Nazi and was religiously worn with
all raiment (it was too wide for the loops of any of his pants,
but he wore it anyway outside the loops). He owned one decent jacket, made for him in Hong Kong, two pairs of pants,
one pair of shoes and no underwear. I was with him when
he went into Mark Cross on Fifth Avenue to buy a bag. The
salesman showed him one that held ten suits and cost three
hundred dollars. "Can afford the bag," Ernest told him, "but
can't afford to buy nine suits."

But getting back to that October day in 1949 when Ernest
checked into the Sherry-Netherland with his *Across the River*
manuscript. On the morning of that day Herbert Mayes (who
had succeeded our friend Arthur Gordon as editor of *Cosmo*)
called me into his office and said that eighty-five thousand dollars was so exorbitant as to be beyond reason and I was to
tell Mr. Hemingway that, and offer fifty thousand instead. I
refused. As far as I was concerned, a solid deal had been
made and I was not going to carry the weasel. I offered, however, to bring Mayes and Ernest together so that Mayes could
tell Ernest himself. But Mayes decided, with considerable ran-

cor, to let the price stand, and I was dispatched to the Sherry-Netherland to get the manuscript.

Ernest's suite was well attended when I got there. In the center of the sitting room was a round table on which rested two silver ice buckets, each containing a bottle of Perrier-Jouet, a huge blue tin of béluga caviar, a salver of toast, a bowl of finely chopped onions, a bowl of lemon slices, a salver of smoked salmon and a thin vase containing two yellow tea roses. Around the table were Marlene Dietrich, Mary Hemingway, Jigee Viertel, Charles Scribner, Sr., and George Brown. Off to one side, with a stenographer's pad in her lap, sat Lillian Ross of *The New Yorker*. Jigee Viertel, formerly Budd Schulberg's wife, at that time married to Peter Viertel, had known the Hemingways for some time and was booked to cross on the *Ile de France* with them. George Brown was one of Ernest's oldest and best friends; the genesis of their friendship was George's demised Brown's Gymnasium, once the hangout of the boxing elite. Ernest always said that George knew more about prize fighting than all the New York managers and trainers put together. Lillian Ross, in her corner, was taking rapid shorthand notes for a profile of Ernest she was doing for *The New Yorker*. ("It was a shorter hand than any of us knew," Ernest was to say a few months later.)

Ernest introduced me to his guests and suggested that later on we all go to "21" for dinner. He said that "21" first qualified as his alma mater back in the Twenties at a time when he was living in a little room at the Brevoort. He was behind in his rent and had not eaten solidly for a week when Jack Kriendler, co-owner of "21", eased him into a posh party that was being given on the second floor of the speak-easy. During the course of the evening Ernest was introduced to an Italian girl who he said was the most beautiful girl—face and body—he had ever seen, before or since, any country, any time. "She had that pure Renaissance beauty, black hair straight, eyes round at the bottoms, Botticelli skin, breasts of Venus Rising. After the joint closed and everyone started to leave, she and I took our drinks into the kitchen. Jack said it was okay, since there were two or three hours of cleaning up to be done downstairs. So we talked and drank and suddenly we were making love there in the kitchen and never has a promise been better fulfilled. By now it was five in the morning, and she said we'd better be leaving, but we got only as far as the stairway—you know that landing as you come up the stairs of Twenty-One? That's as far as we got and then we were making love again, on the landing, and it was like being at sea in the most tempestuous storm that ever boiled up; you think you'll go under with the rises and falls, but ride it out, knowing you are close to solving the mystery of the deep.

"She would not let me take her home, but when I awoke the next day in my Brevoort squirrel cage, my first thought was to find her again. As I put on my jacket, I noticed green sticking out of the pocket—three hundred-dollar bills. I hurried back to Twenty-One, but as I came in, Jack pulled me to one side. 'Listen, Ernie,' he said, 'you better lay low for a while. I should have warned you—that was Legs Diamond's girl, and he's due back in town at five o'clock.' "

We made reservations at "21" and then Ernest led me into the bedroom, where he opened his old, battered leather briefcase and took out the manuscript of the book. "Christ, I wish you were coming along," he said. "This is going to be a jolly autumn. One of my Venice girls has written she is coming to Paris. It will be necessary to maneuver and if you were there with the proofs, we could always go into conference. And when we weren't in conference with the proofs, we could be in conference at Auteuil. Georges could keep track of the form—not this George, Georges the Ritz barman. You know him? Well, he's very classy on form and we could do the field work and I would brain and watch what happens and we could set up a bank and work out of that. Hell, the more I think of it, the more depressed I get that we'll be off on this absolutely jolly autumn and there you'll be behind a desk on Eighth Avenue, and a *Hearst* desk at that." He pulled at his mustache thoughtfully.

"Well, Papa," I said, "like Mr. James Durante says, 'It's the conditions that prevail.' "

"Conditions are what you make them, boy. Now here's what we do." He picked up the manuscript and removed a sheaf of pages from the end of it. "Now you take this to your editor and tell him that it's all there except for the last few chapters, which I'm taking with me because they need more polishing."

When I handed the manuscript to Herbert Mayes and told him that, he practically leaped out of his chair. "The last few chapters! My God, you know how unreliable he is! The way he drinks! There we'll be, going to press with the third installment and we won't have the ending! You'll have to go with him! Keep after him! Don't let him out of your sight! We *must* have these chapters by the first of January!"

When I went back to the Sherry-Netherland later that evening, Ernest was sitting in an armchair, wearing a white tennis visor and reading a book. As I walked into the room, without looking up he said: "When are you leaving?"

Chapter Three

Paris ◆ 1950

Ernest and Mary stayed in their favorite room on the Vendôme side of the Ritz. Jigee had a room two down from them, but I, out of a sense of bizarre nostalgia, stayed at the Hotel Opal, a small, cheerless establishment on Rue Tronchet, where I had been briefly quartered during the war, and whose intense discomfort had not registered at the time. They had traveled on the *Ile de France* and I had gone by air a few days later, so we arrived simultaneously. Ernest was delighted to discover that the fall steeplechase meet at Auteuil—the emerald race track in the heart of the Bois de Boulogne—was to start the following day, and he suggested that we do something he had always wanted to do but never had—attend every day of an entire meet. "You get a wonderful rhythm," he said, "like playing ball every day, and you get to know the track so they can't fool you. There's a beauty restaurant at the top, hung right over the track, where you can eat good and watch them as though you were riding in the race. They bring you the *côte jaune* with the changing odds three times for each race, and you can bet right there, no rushing up and down to the bet cages with your unsettled food jiggling. It's too easy, but wonderful for scouting a race." We each contributed a sum of money to form what Ernest called The Hemhotch Syndicate, with the understanding that we would maintain the syndicate's capital at its inception level. (In later years, when our activities became more diversified, Ernest had us formally incorporated in New Jersey as Hemhotch, Ltd.) To commemorate this liaison and to conform to the European custom of carrying calling cards in one's billfold, we had the following card struck off in a neat, smug type:

> *Mr. Ernest Hemingway & Mr. A. E. Hotchner, Esquires*
> *announce the formation of a partnership,*
> *Hemhotch, Ltd.*
> *dedicated to the Pursuit of the Steeplechase,*
> *the Bulls, the Wild Duck, and the Female Fandango.*

But that fall in Paris we were at the simpler partnership level of a racing syndicate. Our routine for Auteuil was to convene in the Little Bar of the Ritz every race day at noon, and while Bertin, the maestro of that *boîte*, made us his nonpareil Bloody Marys, we would study the form sheets and make our selections. Sometimes Georges or Bertin or one of the other barmen in the big bar would put some money on our mounts and we would bet it for them. Bertin was an indefatigable student of the track, more occult than scientific, and on one occasion he handed Ernest a list of eight horses which he had brained out as winners of the eight races on the card that day. Ernest studied the list and said, "Okay, tell you what I'll do, Bertin—I'll bet ten thousand francs on each and we'll split the winnings." All of Bertin's horses ran out of the money, but when we returned that day Ernest gave Bertin five thousand francs. "One of your horses got scratched," he told him, "and we saved the loss."

I do not expect ever to duplicate the pleasure of those Paris steeplechase days. The Degas horses and jockeys against a Renoir landscape; Ernest's silver flask, engraved "From Mary with Love" and containing splendidly aged Calvados; the bois-

terous excitement of booting home a winner, the glasses zeroed
on the moving point, the insistent admonitions to the jockey;
the quiet intimacy of Ernest's nostalgia. "You know, Hotch, one
of the things I liked best in life was to wake early in the morning with the birds singing and the windows open and the
sound of horses jumping." We were sitting on the top steps of
the grandstand, the weather damp, Ernest wrapped in his big
trench coat, a knitted tan skullcap on his head, his beard
close-cropped. We had eaten lunch at the Course restaurant:
Belon oysters, omelette with ham and fine herbs, cooked en-
dives, Pont-l'Evêque cheese and cold Sancerre wine. We were
not betting the seventh race and Ernest was leaning forward,
a pair of rented binoculars swinging from his neck, watching
the horses slowly serpentine onto the track from the paddock.
"When I was young here," he said, "I was the only outsider
who was allowed into the private training grounds at Achères,
outside of Maisons-Laffitte, and Chantilly. They let me clock
the workouts—almost no one but owners were allowed to operate a stopwatch—and it gave me a big jump on my bets. That's
how I came to know about Epinard. A trainer named J. Patrick,
an expatriate American who had been a friend of mine since
the time we were both kids in the Italian army, told me that
Gene Leigh had a colt that might be the horse of the century.
Those were Patrick's words, 'the horse of the century.' He said,
'Ernie, he's the son of Badajoz-Epine Blanche, by Rockminster,
and nothing like him has been seen in France since the days
of Gladiateur and La Grande Ecurie. So take my advice—
beg, borrow or steal all the cash you can get your hands on
and get it down on this two-year-old for the first start. After
that there'll never be odds again. But that first start, before
they know that name, get down on him.'

"It was my 'complete poverty' period—I didn't even have milk
money for Bumby, but I followed Patrick's advice. I hit everyone for cash. I even borrowed a thousand francs from my
barber. I accosted strangers. There wasn't a sou in Paris that
hadn't been nailed down that I didn't solicit; so I was really
'on' Epinard when he started in the Prix Yacoulef at Deauville
for his debut. His price was fifty-nine to ten. He won in a

breeze, and I was able to support myself for six or eight months on the winnings. Patrick introduced me to many insiders of the top French race-set of that time. Frank O'Neill, Frank Keogh, Jim Winkfield, Sam Bush and the truly great steeplechase rider Georges Parfremont."

"How can you remember their names after all these years?" I asked. "Have you seen them since?"

"No. I have always made things stick that I wanted to stick. I've never kept notes or a journal. I just push the recall button and there it is. If it isn't there, it wasn't worth keeping. Take Parfremont. I can see him as plainly as I see you, and hear him as I heard him the last time he spoke to me. It was Parfremont who scored the first French victory in the Liverpool Grand National astride James Hennessey's Lutteur III. That's one of the toughest steeple courses in the world and Georges had seen it for the first time the day before the race. He told me how the English trainers had taken him around and shown him the big jumps, and he repeated to me what he had told them: 'The size of the obstacle is nothing—the only danger in steeplechasing is the pace.' Poor Georges. It was his own prophecy. He was killed at the final hedge in a cheap race at Enghien, a hedge that was barely three feet high.

"The old Enghien—the antique, rustic, conniving Enghien before they rebuilt the stands in *pesage* and *pelouse* and all that unfriendly concrete—that was my all-time-favorite track. It had a relaxed, unbuttoned atmosphere. One of the last times I went there—I remember it was with Evan Shipman, who was a professional handicapper as well as a writer, and Harold Stearns, who was 'Peter Pickum' for the Paris edition of the Chicago *Tribune* at the time—Harold and Evan were relying on form and drew a blank on the day's card. I hit six winners out of eight. Harold was rather testy about my wins and asked me for the secret of my success. 'It was easy,' I told him. 'I went down to the paddock between races, and I smelled them.' The truth is, where horses are concerned the nose will triumph over science and reason every time."

Ernest stood up and turned and watched the people crowding to the bet windows. "Listen to their heels on the wet pavement," he said. "It's all so beautiful in this misty light. Mr. Degas could have painted it and gotten the light so that it would be truer on his canvas than what we now see. That is what the artist must do. On canvas or on printed page he must capture the thing so truly that its magnification will endure. That is the difference between journalism and literature. There is very little literature. Much less than we think."

He took the racing form out of his pocket and studied it a moment. "This is the true art of fiction," he said. "Well, we haven't done very well today. I wish I still had my nose, but I can't trust it any more. I can trace the decline of my infallible-nose period to the day John Dos Passos and I came out to this track to make our winter stake. We were both working on books and we needed enough cash to get us through the winter. I had touted Dos onto my paddock-sniffing as a sure thing and we had pooled everything we had. One of the horses in the seventh race smelled especially good to me, so we put our whole stake on him. He fell at the first jump. We didn't have a sou in our pockets and had to walk all the way back to the Left Bank from here."

Two touts, one of whom spoke with a cockney accent, came up and offered Ernest something juicy in the next race, but he graciously declined their offer. A handsome young man in a trench coat had been standing in the aisle, looking at Ernest; he came over rather hesitantly. "Mr. Hemingway," he asked in French, "do you remember me?" Ernest studied him for a moment, a puzzled look on his face. "I'm Richard." Ernest's face exploded in recognition. "Rickey!" He threw his arms around the boy and hugged him. "Rickey!" He took another look at the boy. "No wonder," Ernest said. "First time I ever saw you out of uniform—or should I say out of somebody else's uniform."

Ernest explained that Rickey had been in his Irregular troops, a member of the celebrated band which Ernest had assembled after the Battle of the Bulge. Although Ernest was supposed to be functioning solely as a war correspondent for *Collier's* magazine, he had in fact put himself on full combat status and he and his band of French and American Irregulars were credited with being the first Allied unit to enter Paris. In fact, Ernest and his boys had already liberated the Ritz Hotel and were properly celebrating the event with magnums of champagne at the bar when General Jean Leclerc came marching into Paris with what he thought was the first expeditionary force.

Ernest asked Rickey about the various members of his pickup unit, and when Rickey told him that one of his favorite boys was in serious trouble, Ernest wrote down his address so that he could go to his aid.

As Ernest and Rickey were talking, I recalled what Robert Capa, the combat photographer, had once told me about Ernest's Irregulars. He had traveled with them for a while and found that the men had a hard time believing that Ernest was not a general, because he had a public relations officer, a lieutenant as an aide, a cook, a driver, a photographer and a special liquor ration. Capa said that the unit was equipped with every imaginable American and German weapon, and that he had the impression they were carrying more munitions and alcohol than a division. When Capa was with them, Ernest's men were all dressed in German sergeant's uniforms, which they had decorated with United States insignia. But Capa was with them for only a short time. Much later when he came zipping into Paris in a jeep, sure that he was miles ahead of anyone else, he pulled up at the Ritz and found he was face to face with Archie Pelkey, Ernest's driver, who was standing guard at the Ritz entrance, a carbine slung over his shoulder. "Hello, Capa," Pelkey said in Hemingwayese. "Papa took good hotel. Plenty good stuff in cellar. Go on up."

After Rickey left we went into the bar, where Ernest ordered Scotch with half a lime squeezed into it and I ordered a split of champagne. "Hell of a boy, that Rickey," he said. "He did some things . . . " His thoughts took him away and he sipped his Scotch, holding each sip in his mouth to warm it and taste it before swallowing. He took from his pocket the pencil stub that he had been using to mark his racing form, and he began to write on the back of a paper napkin. The last race ended and the bar filled and got noisy, but Ernest wrote in deep concentration, oblivious to the post-race commotion. He ordered another Scotch and continued to write, balling up one napkin after another and tossing them under the table. There were only a few of us left in the bar when he finally put the pencil back into his pocket. He handed me the napkin. He had written a sixteen-line poem, "Across the Board," which interwove his remembrance of Rickey with the sounds of the track.

So affected was Ernest by Rickey's sudden appearance that other ghosts of the bygone war began to haunt him, and a few days later he wrote "Country Poem with Little Country," which was an ode to his boys who had died on the line. This sort of brief, impulsive poem, clumsily written, often served Ernest as a response to a direct hit on his emotions. The most memorable was an eleven-line eulogy which he wrote to his all-time favorite cat, Crazy Christian, on the day he was murdered by his brother cats. Ernest claimed that they were jealous of Crazy Christian because he was gay-hearted, young and handsome and knew all of life's secrets.

On days when there was no racing at Auteuil we went on excursions around the city. One cold December afternoon, with the sky a low canopy of gray muslin and the insolent wind slapping the last of the leaves off the trees, Mary, Ernest, Jigee and I made our way up the Montmartre hill to the Place du Tertre. No tourists, no post cards, not an easel anywhere. At one corner of the square, where the Rue Norvins starts, was Au Clairon des Chausseurs, the old restaurant where Ernest had sometimes eaten, when he had money to eat, during his early Paris days. Set into the building, above the entrance to the restaurant, was a marble plaque that proclaimed in gold letters: ICI ÉTAIT EN 1790 LA PREMIÈRE MAIRIE DE LA COMMUNE DE MONTMARTRE.

We were the only ones in the restaurant, and the ancient, mustached *patron*, M. François Demettre, recognizing Ernest as he entered, shouted his name joyfully and embraced him; he immediately poured *apéritifs* to counteract the outside chill. M. Demettre's hobbled basset hound, named Byrrh, after the *apéritif* we were drinking, rubbed against Ernest's leg for attention and got it.

We were seated around a large, scarred round table, as close to the room's potbellied stove as M. Demettre could manage.

After a wonderful lunch Mary and Jigee went to their appointments at Elizabeth Arden's and left us to the comforts of the glowing stove and an equally glowing Châteauneuf-du-Pape.

"Pauline and I had a flat very near here," Ernest said. "Good old Pauline. Her crack about Mike Ward—Mike was one of the toughest guys I ever knew, rather deaf, and so devoted to me that Pauline said about him, 'If Ernest killed his own mother Mike would say, "Well, it was his own mother, wasn't it?"'

"I'll never forget the time I set up operations in a box at the finish line of the six-day bike races, to work on the proofs of *A Farewell to Arms*. There was good inexpensive champagne and when I got hungry they sent over Crabe Mexicaine from Prunier. I had rewritten the ending thirty-nine times in manuscript and now I worked it over thirty times in proof, trying to get it right. I finally got it right. While I am in my box working one night, in comes Mike, his left hand swollen like the Pride of Your Garden, if you were growing squash. Mike sat down and explained that he had been at Henry's Bar the night before—that was a famous Paris bar where the walls were papered with bad checks—and Mike, who was pretty deaf, was standing at the bar when he heard two guys next to him mention my name, although he couldn't make out what they were saying. So Mike says he goes up to one of them and says, 'Are you a friend of Ernie's?' The guy says no, so Mike creams him. 'I figure he's got no right talkin' about you if he ain't your friend,' Mike says. 'But maybe I did wrong, huh, Ernie?'

"There was another tough little guy I used to know in New York around that time, name of Marty McCarty, who was a dock hustler, but he used to pretend he had an office in 'Wald Street.' He'd come in to have a drink and he'd say: 'Well, Ernie, every day I get my exercise walkin' up from my Wald Street office past the Umpire State Building and the Christer Building right on out to Coogan's Bluff.' Then he'd carry on about how the kids kept him up nights—little Marty with a stomach ache and he'd have to get up five, six times to get him a drink of water, or Betsy with a toothache—it was always something about the kids, every time he came in, and it wasn't until he died and I went to his funeral that I discovered he didn't have any although he was married for twenty years.

"But I started to tell you about Pauline—we were on safari in Africa, way out in the bush, and Pauline suddenly says, 'I miss little Patrick so, I fear we must go back.' I say, 'Where is he now, Pauline?' She says, 'I haven't the faintest idea.' She never mentioned him again."

"Did Pauline really like safari and skiing and all that, or did she only do it to please you?" I asked.

"Well, the one who liked skiing, who really liked *doing* things was Hadley. I remember one winter Hadley and I went skiing in Germany at a lodge run by a Herr Lint. I was an instructor and we earned our keep that way, but the previous season eleven of Herr Lint's fifteen guests had been lost in an avalanche—Herr Lint had warned them about the snow but they had disregarded his advice. Well, losing eleven guests is a very poor advertisment for a ski school, so the season I was there with Hadley there were no guests at all, and to make matters worse there were terrible snowstorms, one right on top of the other. During the storms there were all-night poker games, *sans voir* to open, and the principal antagonists at the poker table were Herr Lint and the proprietor of a rival ski lodge. Herr Lint lost his lodge, all the ski equipment and a piece of property he owned in Bavaria. Have an account of that in 'The Snows of Kilimanjaro.' Call him Herr Lent. Of course, Herr Lint couldn't pay me, but I was able to live on checks I got from the Kansas City *Star*—eleven dollars for straight pieces and between eighteen and twenty-one bucks for a Sunday spread complete with photos. Not much, but the kronen was seventy thousand to the dollar and for three hundred and fifty thousand kronen you lived pretty good."

On our way down the narrow streets leading away from the restaurant, trying to sideslip the cutting wind, we passed a bookstore and Ernest stopped to inspect the contents of the window, which prominently featured copies of a recently published book by a young writer. On the window was a sign that read: ALL SIGNS POINT TO A BRILLIANT FUTURE FOR THIS AUTHOR.

"You ever read this bird?" Ernest asked.

"No," I replied.

"Well, I have," he said. He took a pencil from his pocket and wrote across the bottom of the sign: "All signs wrong."

Ernest wanted me to see the neighborhood where he had first lived; we started on Rue Notre-Dame-des-Champs, where he had lived over a sawmill, and slowly worked our way past familiar restaurants, bars and stores, to the Jardin du Luxembourg and its museum, where, Ernest said, he fell in love with certain paintings that taught him how to write. "Am also fond of the Jardin," Ernest said, "because it kept us from starvation. On days when the dinner pot was absolutely devoid of content, I would put Bumby, then about a year old, into the baby carriage and wheel him over here to the Jardin. There was always a *gendarme* on duty, but I knew that around four o'clock he would go to a bar across from the park to have a glass of wine. That's when I would appear with Mr. Bumby— and a pocketful of corn for the pigeons. I would sit on a bench, in my guise of buggy-pushing pigeon-lover, casing the flock for clarity of eye and plumpness. The Luxembourg was well known for the classiness of its pigeons. Once my selection was made, it was a simple matter to entice my victim with the corn, snatch him, wring his neck, and flip his carcass under Mr. Bumby's blanket. We got a little tired of pigeon that winter, but they filled many a void. What a kid that Bumby was—played it straight—and never once put the finger on me."

Since cables had been arriving from Herbert Mayes, demanding to know when I'd be back with the missing chapters, on our way to Harry's New York Bar on the Rue Daunou, we stopped at a cable office and I sent a message that the chapters were still in work but not to worry.

Ernest had been one of Harry's earliest customers, and although Ernest did not particularly like the bar any more, be-

cause it was "over quaint," he still liked his old friend Harry
and went to pay his respects. On the frosted-glass door was
the legend: C'EST GENTIL D'ÊTRE VENU. Pennants from American colleges decorated all walls except the one in back of the bar,
which was covered with paper money; the face of the cash
register was covered with coins; a straw monkey holding boxing gloves dangled from the ceiling above the bar; and a
prominent sign exhorted: HELP STAMP OUT SPORTS CARS. "All
they need," Ernest said, under his breath, "is Noel Coward leading a community sing." He ordered Scotch and half a fresh
lime.

"Back in the old days this was one of the few good, solid
bars, and there was an ex-pug used to come in with a pet lion.
He'd stand at the bar here and the lion would stand here
beside him. He was a very nice lion with good manners—no
growls or roars—but, as lions will, he occasionally shit on the
floor. This, of course, had a rather adverse effect on the trade
and, as politely as he could, Harry asked the ex-pug not to
bring the lion around any more. But the next day the pug was
back with lion, lion dropped another load, drinkers disbursed,
Harry again made request. The third day, same thing. Realiz-
ing it was do or die for poor Harry's business, this time when
lion let go, I went over, picked up the pug, who had been
a welterweight, carried him outside and threw him in the
street. Then I came back and grabbed the lion's mane and
hustled him out of here. Out on the sidewalk the lion gave
me a look, but he went quietly.

"In a crazy way, that's what started me on *A Farewell to
Arms*—figured if I was getting that aggressive with lions, time
had come to put my juice into a book instead. All the other
writers who were sort of in my mob and living in Paris then,
had already written books about the war, and like the last girl
on the block who hasn't been married, I felt my time to write
a war book had come. But for years I had been telling these
writers most of my good war stories and I discovered they had
put them into their books. So when I finally got around to
doing my war novel, I found that the only country left was
Italy. I was safe there because few of them had been to Italy,

and certainly none of them knew anything about the war there.

"I've always had that problem—other writers pinching my stuff. During World War II, I traveled around quite a bit with a writer I had known a long time. I talked things out with him, the way you would with a friend. One day over drinks I told him how I had figured out that the best air-raid alarm was the attitude of cattle in the field. 'I can watch a herd of cows,' I told him, 'and tell you long before you hear any sounds, that planes are approaching. The cattle stiffen; they stop grazing. They know.'

"A couple of days later I saw other correspondents congratulating my writer friend whom I had told about the cattle. I asked what it was all about. 'He wrote a wonderful dispatch for his paper on how cattle react to planes,' one guy told me. I investigated and found that my pal had been picking my brain for some time and writing a series of articles based on the information that I had intended using in my own dispatches. 'Listen, you bastard,' I said to this writer, 'if you steal another thing from me, I'll kill you.' Two days later he switched to the Pacific theater of operations.

"There was another 'name' writer who used to steal my short stories as fast as I could write them, change the names of the characters and the locales and sell them for more money than I got. But I found a way to stop him. I quit writing for two years and the son-of-a-bitch starved to death."

The entrance to Le Trou dans le Mur is on the Boulevard des Capucines across from the Café de la Paix, but true to its name, you can pass by it a half-dozen times without seeing it. Ernest wanted me to see how he had positioned himself at the back of this mirrored *boîte*—more celebrated in the Twenties than now—whenever vendettas were threatening him. "The day after *The Sun Also Rises* was published," Ernest said, "I got word that Harold Loeb, who was the Robert Cohn of the book, had announced that he would kill me on sight. I sent him a telegram to the effect that I would be here in The Hole in the Wall for three consecutive evenings so he'd have no trouble finding me. As you can see, I chose this joint because it is all mirrors, all four walls, and if you sit in this booth at the back you can see whoever comes in the door and all their moves. I waited out the three days but Harold didn't show. About a week later, I was eating dinner at Lipp's in Saint-Germain, which is also heavily mirrored, when I spotted Harold coming in. I went over and put out my hand and Harold started to shake hands before he remembered we were mortal enemies. He yanked his hand away and put it behind his back. I invited him to have a drink but he refused. 'Never,' is actually what he said. 'Okay,' I said, resuming my seat, 'then drink alone.' He left the restaurant and that was the end of that vendetta.

"Brett died in New Mexico. Call her Lady Duff Twysden, if you like, but I can only think of her as Brett. Tuberculosis. She was forty-three. Her pallbearers had all been her lovers. On leaving the church, where she had had a proper service, one of the grieving pallbearers slipped on the church steps and the casket dropped and split open.

"Those days with Lady Duff Twysden ruined poor Loeb for the rest of his life. That and one other thing: he was an authentic Guggenheim but he never got one of his recommendations approved. Not one. There's rejection for you, in spades."

"Besides Loeb and Lady Duff Twysden, were any of the other characters in the book based on people you knew who had gone to Pamplona with you?"

"Sure. The whole mob. Based on. Not exact. Pat Swazey was the closest—he was Mike Campbell in the book. Bill Smith, who was an awfully good guy I used to fish with, was pretty much Bill Gorton. Jake Barnes . . . well, hell, Jake . . . when I was in the Italian army I had been nicked in the scrotum by a piece of shrapnel and had spent some time in the genito-urinary ward and saw all those poor bastards who had had everything blown off. Most of them from anti-personnel mines that were rigged to hit between the legs, on the irrefutable Hun theory that nothing takes a soldier out faster than to have his balls shot off."

"But Jake didn't have his balls shot off, did he?"

"No. And that was very important to the kind of man he was. His testicles were intact. That was all he had, but this made him capable of feeling everything a normal man feels but not able to do anything about it. That the wound was a physical wound, and not a psychological wound, was the vital thing."

"But you know, Papa, despite poor Jake and his tragic fate, I never really felt anything 'lost' about that group. Maybe it's just a reflection of my debauched state, but by the end of the book I felt a certain survival strength in those people, not at all the utter hopelessness of a 'lost generation.' "

"That was Gertrude Stein's pronouncement, not mine!" he snapped. "Gertrude repeating what some garage keeper in the Midi had told her about his apprentice mechanics: *une génération perdue*. Well, Gertrude . . . a pronouncement was a pronouncement was a pronouncement. I only used it in the front of *Sun Also Rises* so I could counter it with what I thought. That passage from Ecclesiastes, that sound lost? 'One generation passeth away, and another generation cometh; but the earth abideth forever . . .' Solid endorsement for Mother Earth, right? 'The sun also ariseth, and the sun goeth down, and hasteth to the place where he arose . . .' Solid endorsement for sun. Also endorses wind. Then the rivers—playing it safe across the board: 'All the rivers run into the sea; yet the sea is not full; unto the place from whence the rivers come, thither they return again.' Never could say thither. Look, Gertrude was a complainer. So she labeled that generation with her complaint. But it was bullshit. There was no movement, no tight band of pot-smoking nihilists wandering around looking for Mommy to lead them out of the dada wilderness. What there was, was a lot of people around the same age who had been through the war and now were writing or composing or whatever, and other people who had not been through the war and either wished they had been or wished they were writing or boasted about not being in the war. Nobody I knew at that time thought of himself as wearing the silks of the Lost Generation, or had even heard the

label. We were a pretty solid mob. The characters in *Sun Also
Rises* were tragic, but the real hero was the earth and you
get the sense of its triumph in abiding forever."

On another day that the nags were resting at Auteuil, we
walked across the Pont Royale to have lunch at the Closerie
des Lilas, which was another of Ernest's fondly remembered
haunts. On the way there Ernest pointed out a tall, narrow
building where he had once lived with Pauline on the top
floor. "It was a pleasant flat up there," Ernest said, "with a
big skylight that kept the place light. A Bohemian named
Jerry Kelley was visiting us one day—actually he was a reject
dadaist—and he went in to use the can before departing. Instead of pulling the chain for the toilet, he grabbed hold
of the skylight cord, gave it a heavy yank, and down came
the skylight in a shower of glass. I was standing directly under
it and the falling glass gashed my head open. When I saw the
blood gushing out, my first thought was to keep it off my one
and only suit. I ran into the bathroom and bent over and bled
into the bathtub so as to save the suit. At the same time I
put my thumb on the pressure point in my temple to slow
down the blood, which was pouring out like a son-of-a-bitch.
Pauline called Archie MacLeish, who got hold of a doctor pal
of his from the American Hospital, Dr. Carl Weiss—same guy
who years later shot Huey Long. He did a really terrible job on
my head, leaving me with this patch of raised skin which en-
larges when I get angry. Afterward we measured the blood
in the bathtub and it came to more than a pint. Doctor did
better job on Huey Long than he did on me.

"The next day I went to the bike races and that evening,
feeling absolutely wonderful from the loss of all that blood, I
finally began to write *A Farewell to Arms*. I had been ducking
and dodging for almost two months, but that cut on the head,
plus roughing up that lion, finally sprung me. Pauline had
fixed up a fancy workroom for me with a Mexican desk, where
I had been avoiding the start of *Farewell* by writing a long
account of life in Michigan. I guess it would have been a
novel about Nick Adams—but one day after I read through

all that I had written over a two-month period, I wrote across the cover page, 'Too misty to be real'; then I destroyed it all.

"Besides trouble with that book, was also having hell of a tough time with Pauline. Don't know if it was autosuggestion from *Sun Also Rises* or maybe reaction to having just divorced Hadley, but I was in a hell of a jam—I couldn't make love. Had had very good bed with Pauline during all the time we were having our affair, and after Hadley left me, but after our marriage, suddenly I could no more make love than Jake Barnes. Pauline was very patient and understanding and we tried everything, but nothing worked. I became terribly discouraged. I had been to see several doctors. I even put myself in the hands of a mystic who fastened electrodes to my head and feet—hardly the seat of my trouble—and had me drink a glass of calves' liver blood every day. It was all hopeless. Then one day Pauline said, 'Listen, Ernest, why don't you go pray?' Pauline was a very religious Catholic and I wasn't a religious anything, but she had been so damn good that I thought it was the least I could do for her. There was a small church two blocks from us and I went there and said a short prayer. Then I went back to our room. Pauline was in bed, waiting. I undressed and got in bed and we made love like we invented it. We never had any trouble again. That's when I became a Catholic."

Ernest stopped to listen respectfully to an old man who was playing a rasping violin with fingers barely moveable in the cold; Ernest thanked him and put a thousand-franc note in his cap. We then resumed walking.

"Once I started on *Farewell* it ran like a Duesenberg. Of course, much of it was projected from my own experiences, but a lot of it, like the Caporetto retreat, wasn't. I was never in the Caporetto retreat—despite what you may read in the lurid professorial studies of my wicked past—and someone will someday write a book to prove it; I got it from a friend and from all the talk I heard when I was hospitalized. I had discovered in writing *The Sun Also Rises* that it was easier to write in the first person because you could involve the reader immediately, so I again took that advantage with *Fare-*

well, but later in *To Have and Have Not* and *For Whom the Bell Tolls*, I used the third person; it's harder to write in the third person but the advantage is you move around better.

"The writing of *Farewell* really had quite an itinerary—after Paris, wrote on it in Key West, then Piggott, Arkansas; Kansas City, Missouri; Big Horn, Wyoming; and then back to Paris to work on the galleys. First draft took six months in contrast to six weeks of *Sun Also Rises*. But I knew I had it made with *Farewell* when I finished the first draft. Everyone who read it treated it as a special thing right from the beginning. You know you're in if you hit a ratio of ten to one—that is, if you get your writing to have a truth and a reality ten times stronger than the original reality you are drawing on. I sent the finished manuscript to Max Perkins at Scribner's and he was delighted.

"Max was a terribly shy man who always wore his hat in the office—I can't prove that the two have any connection, although maybe they have. I went back to New York to discuss the book with Max, and he said he had only one change which he wanted—the deletion of that pesky four-letter word which seems to be okay verbally, especially in the army, but *verboten* on the printed page.

"Max was too shy to say the word out loud, so he wrote the word on his calendar pad. I said it was okay to delete it and suggested that since we had completed the rewriting, we go out to lunch and enjoy ourselves. Along about three o'clock that afternoon Charlie Scribner came into Perkins' office to consult him about something, and not finding him at his desk, went over and looked at the calendar pad to see where he was. Opposite twelve o'clock, Charlie found the notation F-U-C-K. Later that afternoon, when Charlie did find Perkins at his desk, he said solicitously, 'Max, why don't you take the rest of the day off? You must be done in.' "

Ernest stopped to study a row of buildings. "In the basement of one of these buildings," he said, "was the best night club that ever was—Le Jockey. Best orchestra, best drinks, a wonderful clientele, and the world's most beautiful women. Was in there one night with Don Ogden Stewart and Waldo Peirce, when the place was set on fire by the most sensational woman anybody ever saw. Or ever will. Tall, coffee skin, ebony eyes, legs of paradise, a smile to end all smiles. Very hot night but she was wearing a coat of black fur, her breasts handling the fur like it was silk. She turned her eyes on me—she was dancing with the big British gunner subaltern who had brought her—but I responded to the eyes like a hypnotic and cut in on them. The subaltern tried to shoulder me out but the girl slid off him and onto me. Everything under that fur instantly communicated with me. I introduced myself and asked her name. 'Josephine Baker,' she said. We danced nonstop for the rest of the night. She never took off her fur coat. Wasn't until the joint closed she told me she had nothing on underneath."

Our wanderings had taken us onto the Rue Bonaparte, and now as he talked Ernest occasionally glanced into the windows of the antique stores. He had stopped to study a set of pearl-handled dueling pistols. "When they published Gertrude Stein's *Autobiography of Alice Toklas*," he said abruptly, "Picasso and I were very disappointed."

"Why?" I asked.

"Because it was so full of lies."

He gave his full and serious attention to the antiques the rest of the way to the Closerie des Lilas, where we settled ourselves comfortably in the dim, quiet bar. One of the barmen remembered Ernest, but everyone else was new. "Joyce came here with me a few times," Ernest said. "I knew him from 1921 till his death. In Paris he was always surrounded by professional friends and sycophants. We'd have discussions which would get very heated and sooner or later Joyce would get in some really rough insults; he was a nice man but nasty, especially if anyone started to talk about writing, nasty as hell, and when he really had everything in an uproar, he would suddenly depart and expect me to handle the characters in his wake who were demanding satisfaction. Joyce was very proud and very rude—especially to jerks." Ernest took a drink of his Pernod. "He really enjoyed drinking, and those nights when I'd bring him home after a protracted drinking bout, his wife, Nora, would open the door and say, 'Well, here comes James Joyce the author, drunk again with Ernest Hemingway.' "

He sat quietly, sipping his drink and thinking about Joyce, and then he said, "He was mortally afraid of lightning."

The maître d' came over with two menus and requested autographs on behalf of a couple of clients. After he had left, Ernest said, "They were good to me here when I needed it. Like that time with the Miró. Miró and I were good friends; we were working hard but neither of us was selling anything. My stories would all come back with rejection slips and Miró's unsold canvases were piled up all over his studio. There was one that I had fallen in love with—a painting of his farm down south—it haunted me and even though I was broke I wanted to own it, but since we were such good friends, I insisted that we do it through a dealer. So we gave the picture to a dealer and, knowing he had a sure sale, he put a price of two hundred dollars on it, damn steep, but I arranged to pay it off in six installments. The dealer made me sign a chattel mortgage so that if I defaulted on any payment, I would lose the painting and all money paid in. Well, I skimped and managed okay until the last payment. I hadn't sold any stories or articles and I didn't have a franc to my name. I asked the dealer for an extension but, of course, he preferred to keep my dough *and* the painting. That's where the Closerie comes in. The day the dough was due, I came in here sad-ass for a drink. The barman asked me what was wrong and I told him about the painting. He quietly passed the word around to the waiters and they raised the money for me out of their own pockets."

"You mean that's 'The Farm' that now hangs in your house in Cuba?"

"Yep. Insured for two hundred thousand dollars. You can see why I'm fond of this joint. Another time, I wanted to rent a flat near here, but not having any furniture or finances I was what you might call a wobbly risk as a tenant. The landlord was out of town and the concierge, who was a pal of mine, let me stay until he returned. The day before the landlord was due back, one of my friends, who was well positioned, went around to people he knew, most of whom had good art collections, and borrowed two Cézannes, three Van Goghs, two Van Dycks and a Titian. Told them it was for a charity exhibit. We hung all that art on the walls of my room, and even though I had no furniture in the joint, the landlord was so impressed with my 'collection' he gave me a lease for a year.

"I was very happy in that flat and had no trouble until the time Scott Fitzgerald came to visit me. Scott was staying at the Ritz, as usual. He brought his daughter, Scotty, with him. While we were talking, Scotty announced she wanted to make pee-pee, but when I told Scott the W.C. was on the floor below, he told Scotty that was too far to go and to do it in the hall. The concierge observed the trickle coming down the steps and went upstairs to inquire. 'Monsieur,' he said to Scott very politely, 'would it not be more comfortable for Mademoiselle to use the W.C.?' Scott said, 'Back to your miserable room, concierge, or I will put your head in the W.C.' He was mad as hell. He came back into my room and began stripping off the wallpaper, which was old and starting to peel. I begged him not to because, as always, I was behind in my rent, but he was too mad to listen. The landlord made me pay for repapering the entire room. But Scott was my friend and you put up with a lot in the name of friendship."

"But how can you say Fitzgerald was your friend when he behaved like that?"

"Well, I was speaking of our overall relation and in that respect he certainly was a loyal and devoted friend who at that time was truly more interested in my career than in his own. It was Scott who insisted that Max Perkins, who was his editor at Scribner's, read my story 'Fifty Grand.' Scott was one of their leading authors so he pulled a lot of weight. The story had already been rejected by Ray Long, editor of *Cosmopolitan*, because it was mainly about boxing and had no love interest. Max Perkins liked the story and sent it to the editor of *Scribner's Magazine*, who said he would pay me two hundred and

fifty dollars for it if I would cut five hundred words. I said
I had already cut it to its minimum size but if they wanted to
they could lop off the first five hundred words. I had sometimes done this with a story and improved it; it would not
have improved this story but I figured it was their ass, not mine,
and I would have it published properly in a book. But they
assigned a young editor to it who cut little snips here and
there all through the story so that when he got through it
made no sense. That was the end of the *Scribner's* experience, and where it finally wound up, all in one piece, was the
Atlantic Monthly. After that I had a lot of requests to write
fight stories but I have always tried to write only one story
on anything if I got what I was after the first time, because
there was a hell of a lot I wanted to write about and I knew
even then that the clock runs faster than the pen."

"Papa, I wanted to ask you . . . I know it's hard to answer for
someone else . . ." I was embarrassed and wished I hadn't
started this. "Well, I lived here for a while after the war, but
that was just having fun and spending my severance pay.
Now, though—these weeks we've been here—the more I see of
Paris with you, the more I feel I should give up job and country and seriously live here and find out if I can be a writer—
that's a pretty half-ass pronouncement, but I think you know
what I mean. So many men I know in New York work at jobs
they say they don't like and they're always promising themselves that one day they will quit and do whatever it is they
really want to do. Writing is one of their favorite Canaans.
They tell you the plots for their novels and plays which the
world is waiting for. Well, I don't want to belong to that fraternity—Alpha Gamma Frustration—but at the same time I can
see that chucking an editorial job and rushing off to a Left
Bank garret with beret and portable may be overly romantic.
It's just that I'm young now and I remember the equation
you once mentioned—'hesitation increases in relation to risk
in equal proportion to age.' "

Ernest looked down into his drink; then he looked up and
studied our reflections in the speckled mirror behind the bar

and talked to my mirror-self. "Well, it's tough advice to give. Nobody knows what's in him until he tries to pull it out. If there's nothing or very little, the shock can kill a man. Those first years here when I made my run, as you say you now want to make yours, and I quit my foreign correspondent job with the Toronto *Star* to put myself on the line, I suffered a lot. I had finally shucked off the journalism I had been complaining about and I was finally doing all the good writing I had promised myself. But every day the rejected manuscripts would come back through the slot in the door of that bare room where I lived over the Montmartre sawmill. They'd fall through the slot onto the wood floor, and clipped to them was that most savage of all reprimands—the printed rejection slip. The rejection slip is very hard to take on an empty stomach and there were times when I'd sit at that old wooden table and read one of those cold slips that had been attached to a story I had loved and worked on very hard and believed in, and I couldn't help crying."

"I never think of you crying," I said.

"I cry, boy," Ernest said. "When the hurt is bad enough, I cry." He stirred his drink meditatively. "So, Hotch, just as you wouldn't give a friend advice on whether or not to play the wheel, you can't on this, except to quote the odds, which are a damn sight worse than roulette. And yet . . . " He turned away from my mirror-self and spoke to me directly, in that special way of his that made the words come to you through a corridor of intimacy. "Yet, there's this to consider as a guide, since it's a thing I truly know: If you are lucky enough to have lived in Paris as a young man, then wherever you go for the rest of your life it stays with you, for Paris is a moveable feast."

Later, when I got back to my hotel room, I carefully wrote those words on the fly leaf of my Michelin, and years after when Mary Hemingway was searching for a title for Ernest's posthumously published Paris memoirs, which he had left untitled, I remembered those words, "a moveable feast," and gave them to her for his book. They also appear in *Across the*

River, when the colonel refers to happiness as a moveable feast, but, of course, in Ernest's lexicon, Paris and happiness were synonomous.

The last week of the Auteuil meet we audited the Hemhotch books and found we were running slightly ahead, but considering the time, skill, emotion and energy which had gone into our Steeplechase Devotional, "slightly" was hardly proper compensation. Two days before the end of the meet, however, on December 21st to be exact, as it sometimes happens to horse players, our fortunes dramatically surged upward.

It began with a phone call at six in the morning.

"This is Hemingstein the Tout. Are you awake?"

"No."

"Then get awake. This is a big day. I have just had word from Georges that there is a good horse in today's race, the first one that Georges really believes in, and I think we better meet earlier than usual and give it our special attention." Ernest was referring to Georges, the Ritz's *chef du bar*, who was a very cautious track scholar, so this development had to be treated seriously.

The Ritz's elevator lights up "*entendu*" when you press the button, which was also my reaction to being summoned to this urgent meeting. Ernest was in his old wool bathrobe, secured, naturally, with the GOTT MIT UNS belt, sitting at a small antique desk, already at work on some form sheets. "When Georges called at six," he told me, "I'd already been up a couple of hours. I got up at first light because I was dreaming the actual stuff—it sometimes happens to me—dreaming the actual lines, so had to get up to write it down or would have dreamed it all out. Closed the bathroom door and sat on the can and wrote it down on toilet paper so as not to wake Mary."

"You better get dressed, lamb," Mary said.

Ernest told me that the name of the horse was Bataclan II, that the word was that he had previously performed under wraps but was now going to be given its head for the first time; the odds were twenty-seven to one. He had already gathered and studied every available piece of information about Bata-

clan's past performances, had checked him out favorably with
his jockey-room contacts, and had come to the conclusion that
we should shoot the entire contents of our treasury and whatever other capital we could raise on the nose of this jumper.

"Papa, you promised to meet Georges at eleven, and it's
eleven now. You better get dressed," Mary said.

"Kitner," Ernest said sternly, "don't count over me. The big
problem is I can't find my goddamn lucky piece. This is a hell
of a day to lose my lucky piece."

"I'll help you look," Mary said.

"So will I," I said.

"It's a champagne cork from a bottle of Mumm. During the
war, what I had for lucky piece was a red stone my son Bumby
had given me, but one morning in England when I was scheduled to fly a mission with the RAF, the floor maid at my hotel
brought back my pants from the cleaners and I realized that I
had left the stone in one of the pockets and the cleaner had
thrown it away. The RAF car was already waiting for me downstairs to go to the airfield, and I was really sweating over hitting
a mission to Germany without the lucky piece. So I said to the
maid, 'Give me something for a lucky piece—just anything and
wish me luck on it and that will do it.' Well, she didn't have
anything in the pocket of her uniform but she picked up the
cork from a bottle of Mumm I had drunk the night before and
gave me that. Damn good thing I had it—every plane on that
flight got chewed up except ours. Best lucky piece I ever had
and now it's been spirited away. You guys won't find it—I've
checked out the whole joint. Tell you what, Hotch. While you're
out raising capital, bring me back something. Anything, as long
as it's pocket size. I once asked Charlie Scribner and he brought
me a horseshoe. I said, 'It's a nice, tidy lucky piece, Charlie,
but why did you take off the horse?' "

My Paris sources for steeplechase fund-raising were, to say
the least, limited, but by the time I checked in at the Ritz Bar
at the appointed hour, I had managed to scrounge some additional capital from a former girl friend, an old Air Force buddy
who now worked at the transportation desk of American Express, the play-writing (nonproduced) wife of a French pub-

lisher, a young lyric soprano I knew who sang at the Opéra, the proprietor of a *bistro* where I was an established eater, and the business manager of *Newsweek*, to whom I had sold my French Ford when I left Paris in 1947. I had never solicited funds before and I felt like one of those small round women who shake cans at Broadway theater intermissions. I also felt the ghost of young John Dos Passos sitting heavily on my shoulder.

Ernest was deep in consultation with Georges when I arrived. Bloody Marys to one side, the table top was a morass of charts, forms, scribbles and whatnot. The "thorough briefing" was one of Ernest's most salient characteristics, and it applied to everything he did. His curiosity and sense of pursuit would send him swimming through schools of minutiae which would flow into his maw and emerge crystallized on the pages of *Death in the Afternoon* or "Big Two-Hearted River" or in his flawless techniques for deep-sea fishing and big-game hunting. Now he was in pursuit of Bataclan II.

Apologetically I placed my rather meager collection of franc notes on the table. Ernest pulled a sheet of paper out from under the others and added my amount to a list. "We have more contributors," he said, "than a numbers drop in the Theresa Hotel on a Saturday afternoon. Every waiter in the joint has something down, plus Georges, plus Bertin, Miss Mary, Jigee, the concierge at the Rue Cambon entrance, Claude the groom, and Maurice the men's-room attendant. If Bataclan doesn't perform as expected, we better check into another hotel tonight."

Jigee and Mary came to the bar to participate in this august occasion, and Jigee decided that this was the proper time for her to take her first drink. "You mean you have never had a drink of hard liquor?" Ernest asked, astounded.

"I've never wanted to until now," Jigee said.

This important news caused Ernest to suspend his race-track thinking for the moment and consider (a) whether Jigee, who was in her thirties, should terminate a lifetime of abstinence, and if so, (b) just what the first drink should be. The answer to (a) was affirmative. As for (b), Ernest judiciously considered a range of drinks from Bloody Mary to martini, and discarded each for stated reasons, until only the Scotch sour had survived the elimination. It was mixed by Bertin with the greatest of care and placed before Jigee as the court sommelier must have placed a new wine before Queen Elizabeth. Ernest told Jigee to take a good sip and hold it in her mouth long enough to taste it and warm it before swallowing it. She did, and we hung on her reaction. When her face broke into a smile, Ernest said, "It's a good omen," and went back to his track calculations.

But again he was interrupted, this time by the arrival of a short plump man in clerical robes who called out, "Don Ernesto!"

"Black Priest!" Ernest exclaimed, and he arose and embraced him Spanish-fashion. Black Priest, on a month's sabbatical, had arrived in Paris on his way to a little town in the north of France where he was about to invest his modest life's savings in a new ceramic factory that was being started by a Frenchman he had met in Cuba. He had some reservations about the trustworthiness of his new partner, as did Ernest, but Black Priest felt it was worth the risk since it was his only chance of emancipation. He sat at the table and drank a Bloody Mary and watched in wonderment as Ernest wound up our pretrack conference with a final audit of the funds to be bet. "I'm sorry to have to run off, Black Priest," Ernest said, "but we have this titanic track venture under way. Please have dinner with us tonight at eight o'clock."

"Don Ernesto," Black Priest said solemnly in Spanish, "I have been listening to the nature of your operation, and I would like to come to the track with you and invest my ceramic money in your race horse instead."

"I'm sorry," Ernest answered in Spanish, "but I could not accept the responsibility for such risk."

A rather heated discussion followed, Black Priest insisting, Ernest refusing, until a compromise was reached that Black Priest was to bet only half his ceramic money on Bataclan II.

As we moved toward the door, Ernest said to me, "I better take my lucky piece now." We always took each other's responsibleness for granted. "It fell on my head," I said, "where the Champs Elysées comes into the Concorde. It has a nice clear eye, don't you think?"

Ernest took the chestnut, examined it, rubbed some oil on it from the side of his nose, nodded, and put it in his pants pocket. "Never lose your faith in mysticism, boy," he said, and he pushed on through the revolving door.

Ernest went down to the paddock and studied our horse and the other horses as they paraded by; later, when we were in the grandstand and Bataclan came onto the track, he said, "The ones we have to worry about are Klipper and Killibi. That Killibi has a good smell. But, as you know, the thing that really spooks me is that goddamn last jump."

The cockney-speaking tout and his pal, whom we had previously encountered, now approached Ernest and offered him a guaranteed, certified mount, but he demurred. I waited until the last moment to get our bets down; we were betting so heavy I didn't want the tote board to show it before closing. The final odds were nineteen to one. I got back to the stands just as the horses broke away. Bataclan ran first, then faded to second on the upgraded backstretch; he lost more ground on the water jump, and on the turn it was Killibi, Klipper and Bataclan in that order. As they came toward us going into the last jump, Bataclan was a hopeless twenty lengths off the pace. I moaned. "Keep your glasses on them," Ernest commanded.

As Killibi took the low hedge, pressed by Klipper, his jockey reached for the bat and in so doing loosened his grip. Killibi's front legs dropped slightly and scraped the hedge, breaking his stride, and he hit the turf hard and stumbled and pitched forward with his boy jumping clear. Klipper was already through the jump at the fall; his jockey tried to clear the fallen Killibi but he couldn't make it and Klipper went right down on top of Killibi, the jock hitting the turf hard and not moving.

Bataclan's jockey had plenty of time to see what had happened and he took Bataclan to the opposite side of the hedge for his jump and came in five lengths to the good.

Nobody in our party made any effort to subdue his feelings. We started a jubilant exodus to the bar, but along the way Black Priest suddenly stopped and refused to budge. He just stood there, looking determined. "Not yet," he kept saying. "Not yet." When the stands around us had emptied, he gave a quick look around and then moved his foot off a Bataclan win ticket it had been covering. "No doubt about it," Ernest said, "God is everywhere."

I took all tickets to the cashier while the others went off to the bar for champagne, and what I returned with was a Matterhorn of ten-thousand-franc notes. Ernest peeled off Black Priest's winnings and gave them to him. "Black Priest needs the bird in hand," he said. "He's been in the bush too long." As always Ernest was wearing his special race-track jacket, a heavy tweed coat that had been made for him when he was in Hong Kong, and which contained a very deep inside pocket that had an elaborate series of buttons which reputedly made it pickpocket proof, even by Hong Kong standards. Into it he stuffed all our loot and it made him look like a side-pregnant bear. As Ernest was stacking the money, the two touts who had approached us earlier went by. "Ah," one of them said to Ernest, tipping his hat, "one can see that Monsieur is of the *métier*."

Black Priest stood at one end of the bar, his eyes aglow, his winning wad grasped in his left hand, while with his right forefinger he lovingly counted the money. At this moment a man, in passing, raised his hat and said "Good evening, Father," and Black Priest, not taking his eyes off the money, made a quick sign of the cross with his money-counting forefinger and then immediately put it back to work.

Most of the Bataclan winnings, coming as they did on December 21st, were plowed back into France's Christmas economy. Packages filled both beds in the Hemingway room and spilled onto the floor. We celebrated Christmas on December 23rd, and after all the presents had been opened and we were engulfed in wrapping paper, Ernest said, "Never have so few bought so much, but I'm happy and proud to say that not one thing anybody gave to anybody is useful." We drank quite a bit of

champagne to celebrate that accomplishment, and as a final
obeisance to the Yule spirit, Ernest decided to send one of the
chapters to Mayes, whose latest cables were a touch frantic.

On December 24th we finally set out, two months behind
schedule, for our original destination—Venice—in a chauffeur-
driven hand-tooled outsized rented Packard. Ernest sat in front
next to Charles, the chauffeur, a position Ernest regarded as
de rigueur in an automobile. His knowledge of local terrain,
weather, customs, history, battles, grain, grapes, orchards, song
birds, game birds, wines, dishes, cattle, wild flowers, morality,
architecture, irrigation, government and accessibility of local
women to outsiders was prodigious, and he commented on
these topics frequently and cheerfully.

His intense interest in the passing countryside, however,
tended to make voyaging with him a bit slow. Paris to Aix-en-
Provence is normally a day's run, but it took us five. Mary and
Jigee sat in the rear seat, and Peter Viertel (who had joined us
the last day in Paris) and I sat on the commodious jump seats.
The things that slowed our progress were the morning fogs,
the long lunches and the street fairs in the little towns. The
shooting booths at these fairs offered as their most difficult
target a cardboard pigeon that had a red eye about the size of
a ball bearing. If the shooter, using a dilapidated .22, completely
eradicated the red of the eye with three or four shots, depending upon the generosity of the proprietor, he would win the
booth's grand prize, a bottle of champagne.

Ernest and I ruined a lot of cardboard pigeons during that
trip, and Mary scored very well in her specialty—shooting
through a hanging string. Ernest always presented the champagne, which was of questionable vintage, to members of the
audience that invariably assembles at shooting booths.

Thus we journeyed through Auxerre, Saulieu, Valence, Avignon, Nîmes, Aigues-Mortes, Le Grau-du-Roi, Arles, Cannes and
on to the Alps, eating exquisitely, drinking Tavel *rosé* almost
exclusively, and blasting the cardboard pigeons. The Viertels
left us in Cannes and we continued on to Venice. It was my
first visit there, and as I stood on the quay, looking at the Grand
Canal, Ernest said, "Well, Hotch, the name of the town is

Venice. You don't know it yet, but it will be your home town, same as it's mine."

It didn't happen that trip, for I soon had to return to New York with the last three chapters of *Across the River*. They were hand-written and Ernest's only copies, and I was to have them typed by Mme. Gros, his Paris typist, before returning to New York. I took the Simplon-Orient Express from Venice to Paris. Ordinarily there was little or no border customs-inspection on the Express, but that trip the *douane* was on some kind of special alert and all bags were carefully inspected and turned upside down.

It was not until I had checked into my hotel and called Mme. Gros that I realized I did not have the envelope that contained Ernest's manuscript. I trace my ability to speak fluent French from that moment, for there followed a nightmare of rigmarole with Paris railroad officials, yard foremen, security officers, porters and maintenance supervisors, all of whom were determined that I comply with The System, which was to wait and patiently check Lost and Found. The manuscript had not yet appeared there, but the records showed that my car had already been cleaned and dispatched to the terminal yard, so it was highly unlikely, they said, that as large an object as a nine-by-twelve manila envelope would have been overlooked *if* it had been in the compartment.

But even the iron hegemony of French bureaucracy can be cracked by a frantic and persistent American, and finally, at two in the morning, I found myself in a vast, grimy railroad yard, being led by an elderly gimpy-legged torchbearing watchman, searching for the car I had occupied that day. There were hundreds of cars along miles of terminal tracks, in no order, and it was necessary to inspect the number of each car to determine if it was the one I had occupied.

Finally, at four, we found my car but now came the worst of it, for the odds were that the missing envelope would not be there. I had already gone over all the different ways I would break the news to Ernest, and all of them sounded awful. I took the watchman's torch and began a minute search of the compartment but found nothing. I repeated the search, again fruitlessly, and was prepared to give up when the watchman spotted it. On the walls of the compartment were framed photographs of tourist scenes in France, and the envelope had lodged in the frame of a photograph of Avignon.

I never told Ernest. Once or twice I started to, but I never quite made it. If I had, I don't think our relationship would have been quite the same again. In Ernest's book an act of recovery did not overcome an act of negligence or untrustworthiness—if your gun goes off while you're going over a fence, it doesn't matter that you luckily did not hit anyone; it went off, didn't it?

So I never told Ernest.

Or anyone else.

Chapter Four

Havana ♦ 1951-53

In the spring of 1951, just before I was to depart for Cuba to discuss my ballet version of Ernest's short story "The Capital of the World," * I received a letter in which he warned me that he was Black-Ass. He furnished no details indicating the nature of this affliction but it had an ominous ring to it, and I was prepared for the worst.

As he came down the steps of the *finca* to greet me, I saw no outward signs of whatever had beset him. Later in the day, however, I realized he was a bit more subdued and contemplative than usual, and these, I was to learn, were significant Black-Ass symptoms.

After dinner that evening Mary turned in early, but Ernest and I continued to sit at the dining-room table, drinking red wine while two of the cats prowled among the remaining dishes, polishing them off. "Sorry about the Black-Ass," Ernest said. "Usually am a cheerful, as you know, but this time have maneuvered myself up the creek without paddles or oar locks. What started it was an accident I had on the boat. Was going good and busier than a one-armed South Korean when I took a beauty spill up on the flying bridge—very heavy weather, and I was just relieving Gregorio at the wheel when he put her in

---

* Subsequently performed by the Ballet Theatre at The Metropolitan Opera House, and on the program Omnibus on television, with music composed by George Antheil, choreography by Eugene Loring.

the trough. Got a good sound concussion complete with fireworks; not stars, but the ascending type, and it was arterial
and spouting. One of the clamps that hold the big gaffs went
all the way into the skull bone.

"This is the thing I always thought helped a writer the least.
I had held onto the rail when I hit, broke the fall as well as
I could with my shoulders (spine hit the big gaffs), but *Pilar*
is fifteen tons, the ocean more, me two hundred ten, and I hit
hard. But was up at the count of one and when I saw that
bright red spurting, I told Gregorio I had to go below and for
him to anchor and let Roberto come up astern. Roberto was
fishing alongside in 'The Tin Kid.' Then I told Mary to get a
roll of toilet paper and put big folded packs on and I would
hold them down. She was very good and fast and unpanicked,
and when Roberto came up we dug out gauze and tape and
made a tourniquet alongside the left eye. This way we contained the hemorrhage and made the *finca* okay.

"Very gory story. Ought to sell it to the *A.M.A. Journal*. If
Roberto hadn't been there I probably would have bled out. But
vision okay now, and on three dressings she got clean and the
hurting stopped, but they said it was too deep to take the
stitches out. Am always bored shitless when am hit or smashed
up. Never like to be in bed without a woman or a good book
or the *Morning Telegraph*, so this time decided not to go to
bed at all except very late at night. I can tell you I am getting
tired of being smacked on the head. Had three bad ones in the
1944–45 period, two in '43, and others going back to 1918.
Despite what you hear, they do not come from carelessness or
my celebrated death wish. At least none I remember did, and
I think I've got recall on all of them. Anyway, that spill on
Pilar was the beginning of the Black-Ass.

"Maybe we should antidote Black-Ass by another tour at
Auteuil. We did have lovely times racing, didn't we? Aided or
unaided by that ancient and faithful retainer, Calvados. Want
to go over when Auteuil and Enghien open in the spring?
Georges will have kept track of the form." I said that would be
splendid and I started to talk steeplechasing, but Ernest was
still bent upon explaining the Black-Ass.

"Then to solidify the Black-Ass," he was saying, "there's Korea. This is the first time my country ever fought that I was not there, and food has no taste and the hell with love when you can't have children."

"I noticed you were limping a little. That come from the fall you took?"

"Developed a few days later. I began to get pains in both legs, really bad, and when somebody around the joint, who shall be nameless, started referring to it as my 'imaginary pains' I demanded a count. Took x-rays and the photos showed seven pieces of shell fragments in the right calf, eleven in the left, and parts of a bullet jacket also in the left. One piece was resting on a nerve. Doctor wanted to cut it out. But it started to travel and is hung up for the moment and now they think it is encysting again in a good place. The calf of your leg is a good place to encyst in if you ever want to encyst. Offer that as thought for the day—correction, night.

"But otherwise am okay. Have knocked blood pressure down to one forty over seventy and don't have to take any medicine. Refuse to read any reviews on *Across the River*, not for blood pressure but they are about as interesting and constructive as reading other people's laundry lists." *

"John O'Hara's review in *The New York Times* called you the greatest writer since Shakespeare," I told him.

"That would have sent the old pressure up to around two forty. I have never learned anything from the critics. In this book I moved into calculus, having started with straight math, then moved to geometry, then algebra; and the next time out it will be trigonometry. If they don't understand that, to hell with them."

"Mr. William Faulkner got into the act by observing that you never crawl out on a limb. Said you had no courage, never been known to use a word that might send the reader to the dictionary."

"Poor Faulkner. Does he really think big emotions come from

* The reviews of *Across the River* had been predominantly unfavorable, the first setback Ernest had received since the publication of his first book, *in our time*, in 1924, and it occurred to me that this was probably the leading cause of his Black-Assedness.

big words? He thinks I don't know the ten-dollar words. I know
them all right. But there are older and simpler and better words,
and those are the ones I use. Did you read his last book? It's
all sauce-writing now, but he was good once. Before the sauce,
or when he knew how to handle it. You ever read his story
'The Bear'? Read that and you'll know how good he once was.
But now . . . well, for a guy who runs as a silent, he sure talks
a hell of a lot. Okay, now, let's write off Black-Ass as a subject. The moderator will please change the discussion. How goes
it with your writing? You making out all right since you left
Mayes' Citadel of Literature?"

"Doing fine. Did five magazine articles the last three months,
and now I've sold a couple of short stories."

"That's wonderful. But remember, free-lancing is like playing
sand-lot second base—the ball can take some awful hops—so if
you ever get pressed for eating money, I want to know about it.
We know where we had and will have fun and I always think
of you as my sound and true friend and am sorry for any bad
luck I caused you and always ready to fight our way out of
anything we get into. Yes, gentlemen, that comment is a bit
sentimental—very well, maudlin if you like, but the wine is
Châteauneuf-du-Pape, a bit maudlin in itself."

Roberto arrived and Ernest poured him a glass of the maudlin wine. Roberto had just come from a jai-alai game in Havana
and Ernest discussed it with him in Spanish. While they were
talking, I picked up a copy of *The New Yorker* in which E.B.
White had written a parody of *Across the River*, calling it
"Across the Street and into the Grill."

When I finished reading, Ernest interrupted talking to Roberto and said, "The parody is the last refuge of the frustrated
writer. Parodies are what you write when you are associate
editor of the Harvard *Lampoon*. The greater the work of literature, the easier the parody. The step up from writing parodies
is writing on the wall above the urinal." It was incredible to
me that while Ernest was carrying on his animated conversation with Roberto he had simultaneously been able to run a
re-con on what I was reading. I was to learn that for him this
was an effortless accomplishment, the ability to assimilate simul-

taneous occurrences. In a room full of people he would give
complete attention to the person he was talking to and yet
monitor other conversations. It was never safe to assume that
Ernest was either distracted or out of earshot.

When I came into the living room early the next morning Ernest
was already busy writing letters at his stand-up typewriter. He
called me into his bedroom. He was cheerful, as he always was
in the early morning, and the Black-Ass of the night seemed
to have been put to rout.

"This portable you brought last time," he said, "is being used
by a number of people, all of them extremely nice, but each
time I go to work on it something new is lacking. I have a cat
named Sun Valley who can hit five keys at a time. Am composing letter you may find interesting."

The letter in the typewriter was addressed "Your Arrogance:"
and it contained Ernest's vitriolic reaction to one of the big
news events of the day, Francis Cardinal Spellman's going
through a gravediggers' picket line. The letter had Ernest's
peculiar spacing characteristic; when he was at work on a
manuscript or writing letters that "counted," he spaced three or
more times between words   so   that   the   page   looked
like   this.   Ernest   did   this   to   slow   himself   down
and   emphasize   the   importance   of   each   word.

The letter in the typewriter was a masterpiece of invective.
"I don't think he will have any doubts about how you feel,"
I said.

"It doesn't sound too friendly?"

"Only to a gravedigger."

"Did you get a chance to read Carlo's fable?"

The night before, Ernest had handed me a manuscript to
read before going to sleep. It was a fable written by one of
his Venetian friends, Count Carlo di Robilant. When we were
in Venice, Ernest had written two fables for children of his
friends, and with his approval I had sent the fables to Ted
Patrick, the editor of *Holiday;* they were about to be published
and Ernest had asked me whether I thought *Holiday* might
also publish Count di Robilant's offering.

Where his friends were concerned, Ernest's generosity with his money, his possessions and his time, which to him was much more valuable than the other two, was boundless. Lillian Ross's career with *The New Yorker* was founded on the success of her profile of the bullfighter Sidney Franklin; she told me that when she first started it she consulted Ernest, whom she scarcely knew, and he edited, rewrote and advised every step of the way.

When his young Venetian friend Gianfranco Ivancich decided to try his hand at writing a novel, Ernest invited him to stay in the guest house at the *finca*, gave him advice and sustenance, and tried strenuously to place the book with Scribner's.

There were a half-dozen old pals, down on their luck, who received regular remittances from Ernest, and he responded with dispatch to any cry of emergency emanating from any friend who "mattered," a category that embraced several hundred people.

Late that night Ernest came into my room, carrying a clip board which had a sizable sheaf of manuscript trapped in its metal jaw. Ernest seemed tentative, almost ill at ease. "Wanted you to read something," he said. "Might be antidote to Black-Ass. Mary read it all one night and in the morning said she forgave me for anything I'd ever done and showed me the real goose flesh on her arms. So have been granted a sort of general amnesty as a writer. Hope I am not fool enough to think something is wonderful because someone under my own roof likes it. So you read it—and level with me in the morning."

He put the clip board down on my bed table and left abruptly. I got into bed, turned on the lamp, and picked up the manuscript. The title was written in ink: *The Old Man and the Sea*. Night bugs popped against the screen, huge brilliant moths buzzed insistently, sounds drifted up from the village below, but I was in the nearby port-town of Cojimar and then out to sea, having one of the most overwhelming reading experiences of my life. It was the basic life battle that had always intrigued Ernest: a brave, simple man struggling unsuccessfully against an unconquerable element. It was also a religious poem, if absolute reverence for the Creator of such earthly wonders as the sea, a splendid fish and an old man's courage can be accepted as religious.

"I will keep it as part of the big book," Ernest said the next morning, after I told him my reaction. "The sea part. I'll do the other parts, land and air, before I publish it. I could break it into three books because this one is self-contained. But why do it? I'm glad you agree it can go out on its own. There is at the heart of it the oldest double *dicho* I know."

"What's a double *dicho?*" I asked.

"It's a saying that makes a statement forward or backward. Now this *dicho* is: Man can be destroyed but not defeated."

"Man can be defeated but not destroyed."

"Yes, that's its inversion, but I've always preferred to believe that man is undefeated."

Mary told me she had typed *The Old Man and the Sea* day by day and that more than any other of Ernest's books, it seemed to originate virtually letter-perfect, the pages devoid of Ernest's usual intensive editing.

Late that afternoon Juan drove me to the airport to go back to New York. As the car pulled away from the *finca*, I looked back at Ernest, who stood on the steps, leonine against the massive house, renewed by the power of his new writing accomplishment.

Outside the gates of the *finca*, watching the passing rows of tin-roofed shacks which represented the residential section of San Francisco de Paula, I began to think about *The Old Man and the Sea*, and I realized it was Ernest's counterattack against those who had assaulted him for *Across the River*. It was an absolutely perfect counterattack and I envisioned a row of snickering carpies bearing the likenesses of Dwight Macdonald and Louis Kronenberger and E.B. White, who in the midst of cackling, "Through! Washed Up! Kaput!" suddenly grab their groins and keel over. It is a rather elementary military axiom that he who attacks must anticipate the counterattack, but the critics, poor boys, would never make General Staff. As Ernest once said, "One battle doesn't make a campaign but critics treat one book, good or bad, like a whole goddamn war."

. . .

In the early fall of 1952 Ernest asked me to fly down to discuss an ambitious television project which one of the networks had proposed. I was surprised to discover that he was already at work on a new book; it was the first time I had been at the *finca* when Ernest was book-writing and the change in him was dramatic. The discipline of morning work was absolute. The door of his bedroom was inviolate until one o'clock, when he would emerge and mix a drink to cool out before lunch. While having his drink he would read newspapers and magazines because, he said, he was too empty to talk. In the afternoon he would nap, having started work at five or six in the morning, but by late afternoon he was ready for the drinking and companionship he enjoyed. Toward the end of dinner, however, he would begin to withdraw into himself, for his mind had turned to the creative problems of the morning, and by the time he went to bed, which was always early when he was working, he knew the people, the events, the places and even some of the dialogue he would encounter the following day.

I apologized for being an interruption—I had not known he was working and the television project could surely have waited. "Wouldn't have asked you down," Ernest said, "if I couldn't handle interruption, but never think of you as an interruption. As you know, Leland Hayward talked me into publishing *The Old Man* in *Life* now and not wait for the long book, so what I'm working on is another sea part for the land, sea and air book. But I've got to stop the TV hordes invading from the north. They sweep down like the Huns with their deals and residuals; you tell them not to come when they write or phone but they come anyway, and you tell them no again when they get here, but they all want their dime's worth of publicity and they wire to Miss Louella or Miss Hedda that they have you under contract. Last week I was put under siege by a wet-palmed press agent named Richard Condon, who came out and drank gin by the yard and sweated so heavy I thought he'd pass out, all the time trying to con me into a deal he'd dreamed up. The way I am being bombarded these days with television wheeler-dealers, was thinking this morning maybe it's something you could handle. You're in New York where you can screen the dross from the brass and I'd be willing to go on your nod."

I had never written for television, but as a result of this simple suggestion—and we never had any agreement beyond it—over the following years I dramatized many of Ernest's works, among which were "The Battler," "The Snows of Kilimanjaro," "The Killers," "The World of Nick Adams," "The Fifth Column," "Fifty Grand," and *For Whom the Bell Tolls*.

"Now to begin with," Ernest said, "there's this series CBS wants me to do that I wrote you about. It would be a series based on my stories and I would introduce each one. They say they would shoot sixteen of these introductions at a clip right here at the *finca*. Very big income being mentioned, and for a writer who's always in debt, it is music for tired ears. After I got your letter suggesting I record a few things, I made three wire reels on three days straight, and the first two were worthless. This is the third. In the first my throat wasn't sore but the soft palate swollen and sort of a hangover from the really choked-up sore throat I had when it was so sore you couldn't swallow. Then I did forty-eight hundred words week before last and forty-nine hundred this last week and I was pooped.

"But I'm spooked about the whole thing, Hotch. If there was some way we could sell the stories without me talking or mugging, I would give anything. I'm going so damn good now, and in a real *belle époque*, and every morning I wake up worrying about TV and all its angles. The money would be a nice cushion, but as long as I'm hitting around a thousand words a day of the really good, it is okay to borrow to eat from Charlie Scribner. I pay him interest and there is three and a half times as much book as I would be justified in borrowing on.

"Charlie has an 876-page book by a 135-pound writer named 'Colonel' James Jones, who according to his own publicity went over the hill in 1944 (not a vintage year for that), and it recounts the 'colonel's' sufferings and those of his fellow inmates in the Army of the United States to such a paranoic degree that it gets almost sad if you are a type who saddens up easy. I don't believe 'Colonel' Jones will be around for long. But maybe

he will be with us forever. Maybe you could cover by obtaining
the services of 'Colonel' Jones to, say, exclusively belch on television. Anyway, it is Charlie's idea of a book next to something
by Taylor Caldwell. But I will just write on as good as I can.
There is an old Spanish proverb that says if you have a twenty-
dollar gold piece, you can always get change for it. If any of
this is too metaphysical, knock me on the head with your own
mallet."

Despite the potential security which the television money
represented, Ernest's distaste for the microphone, the camera,
and "public" performance conquered all, and the series was
never done.

I phoned Ernest in the late spring of 1953 because he had
not answered any letters for many months; he apologized and
explained that there had been a big pile-up of *merde* after
Pauline's death and that had put letter writing and all other
writing out of commission.

"How are you really, kid?" he asked. "I wish we could see
you. I don't have a real pal down here—you know what it's like
—and I sure wish you were here for what fun there is. But I
think we're about to stir ourselves. Plan to go to Africa next
summer. Been away too long."

"Is your safari all set?"

"Yes, even got my old pal Philip Percival to un-retire and be
our White Hunter. Mary's looking forward to it like her first
Christmas. Will you be able to join?"

"I don't think so, Papa. I have this new eater, name of Holly,
who's just enrolled, and the former one, Tracy, is now off the
bottle and onto filet mignon, so it looks like a year close to the
typewriter and the supermarket."

"You can bring them along. Kids love gazelle milk. Very
nutritious."

"Will you come through New York on your way?"

"Sure. I'll see you before we leave, either New York or here
if we by-pass New York. Going back to Africa after all this
time, there's the excitement of a first adventure. I love Africa
and I feel it's another home, and any time a man can feel that,

not counting where he's born, is where he's meant to go."

It was in that mood of poetic optimism that Ernest set out, in the summer of 1953, from Marseilles for Mombasa. Unfortunately, after a good beginning, it turned into an adventure of misfortune that was destined to plague him to the end of his days.

Part Two

You expected to be sad in the fall.
Part of you died each year when the leaves fell
from the trees and their branches were bare
against the wind and the cold, wintry light.
But you knew there would always be the spring,
as you knew the river would flow again
after it was frozen. When the cold rains
kept on and killed the spring, it was as though
a young person had died for no reason.

A MOVEABLE FEAST

Chapter Five

Venice ◆ 1954

The portière from the Gritti Palace was waiting for me as I emerged from the dry darkness of the Venice railroad station onto the brilliant quay of the noon-busy Grand Canal.

"How was your trip?" he asked, removing his visored hat and smiling.

"Just fine."

"Signor Hemingway is waiting for you at the hotel."

"How is he?"

"In good spirits."

"But what about the crashes? Is he all right?"

"Well, it seems he sustained certain injuries, but he is strong and, as always, a joyful man."

He loaded my bags onto the Gritti launch, and as we started down the canal I stood in the stern, looking backward, and considered how different this Venetian arrival was from the one before. Four years had passed since our first Venice trip with *Across the River and into the Trees.* In contrast to that good time, coming as it did on the heels of our splendid triumph in Paris, this was a relatively somber occasion. Ernest had arrived a few days before, as a passenger on the S.S. *Africa,* after a series of violent misadventures in the dense jungle near Murchison Falls in Uganda; and he had told me on the telephone that he was much more seriously hurt than anyone knew. There had been two crashes, the first less serious than the sec-

ond, but it had been the first that set off the universal mourning
and the obituaries, which had abruptly changed to cheering
and, in fact, disbelief when Ernest had suddenly emerged from
the jungle at Butiaba (press dispatches had described him as
carrying a bunch of bananas and a bottle of gin, but Ernest
disclaimed such elegant salvage). To the startled newsmen who
had rushed to interview him, he had characteristically announced: "My luck, she is running good."

A few hours later, though, his luck had run not so good. A
rescue plane, a de Havilland Rapide, had been sent to fly the
Hemingways back to their base in Kenya, but it had crashed
on take-off and burst into flames, and this was the crash that
left its marks on Ernest.

I learned of his arrival in Venice from a cable I received in
Holland, where I had been preparing an article on the royal
scandale of the day—Queen Juliana's admission that she con-
ducted her affairs through the occult guidance of a fortuneteller
who was in residence with her at the palace. The cable from
Ernest had asked me to call him at the Gritti.

Over the scratchy long-distance phone Ernest's voice had
sounded surprisingly strong and vibrant. "How long you going
to be lounging around that palace?" he had asked.

"I think I've lounged out my welcome," I had told him. "The
palace guards have begun fingering their weapons when I approach. Does that strike you as unfriendly?"

"Yep. I think you should flee the royal life and come down
here. You've got to see that Venice hasn't been damaged since
we left her. I'm going to leave in a couple of days to meet Mary
in Madrid and I thought you might like the ride. I have a
beauty Lancia and a good driver who can race it or not. I
perfer not, as we have plenty of time before the start of the
Feria of San Isidro in Madrid. I could make the run alone but
I'm pretty beat up from those kites falling all over Africa. We've
kept it out of the funny papers, but what I drew as cards when
we burned in the second kite was a ruptured kidney and the
usual internal injuries, plus full upstairs concussion, double
vision and so on. Now the left eye has cut out and we had a
very bad brush fire down on the coast, which I had to fight,

and I burned the hell out of the left hand—the good hand—
and because I was weaker than I figured, I fell over and so
burned belly, some of legs and forearm. Genitals okay. But,
Hotch, times are just faintly rough now. To top it all off, with
these few disabilities I hired on to write fifteen thousand words
for *Look*. I don't mean to sound like a morbid, but I'd sure as
hell like you to be along for this ride so I could cheer up."

The launch pulled alongside the dock of the Gritti, once the
palazzo of Italian royalty, now a serenely elegant hotel which
was Ernest's permanent Venetian headquarters. When I came
into his room he was sitting in a chair by the windows, reading,
the inevitable white tennis visor (ordered by the dozen from
Abercrombie & Fitch) shading his eyes. He wore his crumpled
wool bathrobe and the GOTT MIT UNS leather belt.

I stood for a moment in the open doorway, shocked at his
appearance. I had last seen him in New York in the fall of 1953,
shortly before he had left for Africa. What was shocking to me
now was how he had aged in the intervening five months. What
there was of his hair (most of it had been burned off) had
turned from brindle to white, as had his beard; and he appeared to have diminished somewhat—I don't mean physically
diminished, but some of the aura of massiveness seemed to
have gone out of him.

At a table in one corner of the room sat a thin, hawk-faced
man who was snipping items from a pile of newspapers. Ernest
looked up as I came into the room and smiled broadly. "Hotch!
Goddamn, I'm glad to see you!" He took off the tennis visor.
"Help me up."

I got a grip on his arm and he slowly and painfully pulled
himself up from the chair. "I feel like something coming up
from the deep," he said. Then when he was solidly on his feet
we shook hands Spanish-style, our left arms around each other's
shoulders, pounding a few times on the back. "I hope I didn't
pull you away from your work."

"No," I said, "you probably rescued me from a miserable
fate."

We talked for a while and as the familiar enthusiasm and
energy began to return to his speech, my apprehension lessened.

"Papa," I said, "I'm sure as hell glad to see you on your feet. That couple of days when all the papers were running your obituaries—well, they shook my confidence in the firm a little."

"Forest Lawn was already submitting bids. Very reasonable. I presume I was to be featured as a loss leader. Now over there we have Operation Obit." He led me over to the hawk-faced man, whom he introduced as Adamo, a first-class driver who was also a prominent undertaker in Udine. Adamo, it seemed, had been spending his days going through newspapers from various countries, cutting out obituaries of Ernest, which had been run at the time of the crash, and pasting them in a large scrapbook. Ernest said that he greatly enjoyed reading his obits and that his newest vice was a regular morning ritual of a glass of cold champagne and a couple of pages of obituaries. To give me a sample of their entertainment value, he picked up a clipping from a German paper which pronounced that the fatal crash was simply a fulfillment of Ernest's well-known death wish. In *Götterdämmerung* prose the article connected Ernest's supposedly dismal end with the metaphysical leopard he had placed on the top of Mt. Kilimanjaro in his story "The Snows of Kilimanjaro."

Ernest finally tore himself away from the obits to pour some champagne from a bottle of Piper-Heidsieck, and while he was doing so I noticed several long, narrow wooden boxes leaning against the wall; I asked about them. "Spears," Ernest said. "Was trying to learn the spear. Mary's gun-bearer, Charo, thought I could kill anything but elephant with it and could learn to kill elephant if I worked at it. But would have to work hard in the gym for that. What I had as score were wild hunting dog, hyena and leaping hare for speed. You use it like a boxer's left hand and right, and you keep punching and get inside right away.

"Christ, I wish you had been there when the going was good," Ernest said. "I wanted to write you about it but there were complications. The game ranger had left me in charge of the district, made me honorary game ranger, gazetted and commissioned as such, with duty to protect crops but kill nothing that is not a real destroyer of the necessary to live. They should have had great sheriffs like Cooper to play my part. Wish you could have seen me giving them justice without rancor. Keeping everything clean. No torture. Nobody guilty who wasn't guilty. I know it's a sin but, Christ, it is lovely to command.

"Anyhow, every time I sit down to write old Hotch, some character comes in and says, 'Bwana, the elephants are destroying my *shamba'*—that can be his planting or his home—or the police boy, who is twenty-two and who runs the area and does not know his ass from Adam and is full of too much zeal, arrives, completely destroyed, and says, 'Bwana, we must block the passes. They are coming through, running arms with Masai donkeys. How many men can you commit?'

"I know it is ten to one to be ballroom bananas, but I always know there is that one, so I say, 'I have six fighting men with service in K.A.R. or in the Scouts'—not Boy Scouts—'whom I can arm, and four spears. How many passes are you blocking?'

" 'Four,' he says. 'I'll brigade my twelve men with yours.'

" 'Who will block the two unknown roads to Amboseli?'

" 'You.'

" 'Shit-maru,' I say, having my pen in my hand to write to old Hotch, but he doesn't get written to. This type of operation takes all night. Three nonarms carrying donkeys are intercepted. But I do it for our Queen. The men stand at attention. God bless our Queen. God bless Miss Mary. God bless old Hotch-maru.

"Cut to the next incident, when not writing to old Hotch but exhausted and in bed. We hear the noise of the Land-Rover of the police; he is beat up, confused and overdisheveled. 'Bwana, there is a lion terrorizing Laitokitok!"

" 'How many lions? Sex of same?'

" 'A single male lion. He has just killed a goat one-half mile from town.'

" 'I will pay for the goat.'

" 'No, Bwana. As honorary game ranger you must kill the lion.'

"I buckle on the equipment and we go. When I get back to the tent, Miss Mary says, 'Papa, you must really stop chasing lions in the middle of the night. Do you realize you have not

taken any rest since August twenty-seventh?' Since it is then
the beginning of December, I do not know what type of rest
I took on that specific date. Probably packing to get off the
boat." Ernest's back suddenly seemed to bother him and he
reached back and massaged it.

"How are you, Papa? I mean really?"

"Well, leave us consult the evidence." He started toward the
bathroom and I followed. On a table near the door was a large
bottle of rubbing alcohol—Ernest rarely bathed in water, preferring alcohol sponge-baths. On another table in the corner
between the tub and the sink were a half-dozen glasses containing urine. Ernest picked up one of them and studied its
dark contents in the light. "Couldn't piss for two days on account of plugged somewhere with kidney cell material. Finally
passed it okay. Look at the damn stuff—you can see it in there
floating around like quill toothpicks. The color spooks me.
Prune juice. The doctor on the boat was very good. Gave me
some stuff for the kidneys and scissored away all the dead
flesh from the burns—very classy doctor—but, listen, Hotch . . ."
He picked at his beard for a moment, seemingly ill at ease;
then he smiled. "Goddamn, but I'm glad to see your freckled face."

He hesitated a bit and then began again—more seriously.
"What I was thinking about this trip . . . listen, sit down . . ."

I sat down on the toilet seat; he had suddenly transformed
the bathroom into an office. "Now that I've leveled with you
on how beat up I am . . . you know how I've always held back
on the stuff I was going to write, inventory stuff, insurance
against the dry-up . . . but the way I'm feeling, I thought we
might take it easy. It's beauty country, and I could tell you
some of it so that if I never actually got around to it, then
someone would know. I don't mean to sound like a morbid, but
every time you take out insurance it's an act of morbidity, isn't it?"

"Hell, Papa, give yourself time to heal. Don't worry about
that inventory. You'll get to it all right."

"Well, don't make book on it," he said, "till you get a reading
on the odds." He led the way out of the bathroom and was
happy to see a fresh bottle of champagne in the cooler. As he
uncorked the champagne, which was one of Mary's favorites,

I asked about her.

"Mary's all right now, but life at the *finca* got a little rough just before we left for the Dark Continent." He tasted the champagne and nodded approval, one quick nod, as a pitcher approves a sign from his catcher. He described the incident that had landed him in the doghouse—a doghouse, he said, whose dimensions pass description.

"I was running as a straight sad with built-in head wind," he said. "Mary was being tough but good. No matter what they tell you, tough dames are the only ones that matter. Tenderness is the way to handle them. When you least feel like it, be tender. Only three things in my life I've really liked to do—hunt, write and make love. You can give me advice on any of these—shooting or writing or making love—but you can't tell me how to enter a harbor."

"I trust you inched your way back into Mary's heart?"

"I'll tell you—there are a lot of womens in this highly disorganized world, but the thing that actually got me out of the doghouse is that I love Miss Mary truly. She knows this and it helps her to forgive me when I am in the wrong. She ended that incident by telling me that I was not taking life seriously. Someday I might take it seriously and a lot of characters will hang by their necks until dead.

"When I was young I never wanted to get married, but after I did I could never be without a wife again. Same about kids. I never wanted any but after I had one I never wanted to be without them. To be a successful father, though, there's one absolute rule: when you have a kid, don't look at it for the first two years." He thought for a moment, pulling at the mouth-corners of his beard. "Only one marriage I regret. I remember after I got that marriage license I went across from the license bureau to a bar for a drink. The bartender said, 'What will you have, sir?' And I said, 'A glass of hemlock.'

"Mary is pretty damn wonderful, you know. She loves Africa and is at home there. She's in London now, shopping with Rupert Belville; she sent you her love and said to tell you to roll with the punches and that at the fair in the Piazza San Margherita the merry-go-round has gondolas instead of horses. I don't know whether or not this is code. It is transmitted as received."

There was a sharp rap on the open door, immediately followed by the exuberant entrance of a man whom I recognized from our previous visit to Venice. He was Count Federico Kechler and he was a polite, amusing, chic, nimble Venetian who on this occasion was wearing suède shoes, matching suède gloves, an *almost* matching suède jacket, and a severely weathered, misshapen snap-brim fedora which took the curse off all that matching suède. He spoke perfect Cambridge English and was considered one of Venice's top marksmen and all-around sportsmen. He and Ernest greeted each other energetically, and Ernest made him a present of a pearl-handled knife he had received for Christmas.

"I gave my Christmas boots to Jackie," Ernest said, "my Christmas tie-holder to Bertin and my money clip to some infant. I like to start new every year. Anyway, you don't own anything until you give it away." Ernest was forever giving away his possessions to make sure he would never be possessed by them; outside of his hunting equipment and his paintings, he kept very little of value. "You can have true affection for only a few things in your life," he once told me, "and by getting rid of material things, I make sure I won't waste mine on something that can't feel my affection."

Ernest was now briefing Count Kechler on his African hunting. "You would have enjoyed some of the shoots, Kech. One time Mary and her trusty gun-bearer, Charo, aged around sixty and the same height as Miss Mary, were photographing buff with the wind perfect toward them and steady, and a beautiful approach made. In back, and backing up like the Unione Siciliano and invisible, were Mr. Papa and N'Gui, my gun-bearer, who was about thirty, and my bad and wicked brother. While Mary was photographing—I bought her a Hasselblad with a fourteen-inch lens that looks like a sixty-millimeter mortar and costs a little less than a Jaguar—N'Gui and I saw a pack of wild hunting dogs under the same tree as Miss Mary and Charo. Miss M. and Charo were photographing, and the hunting dogs were counting the buffalo calves. Neither group had seen the

other. Then the hunting dogs heard the click of the camera, and
seeing Miss Mary and Charo, decided they would just as soon
take them as buffalo calves. It was really something to see a
wolf pack work. But Miss Mary kept on photographing, and
N'Gui and I broke it up with our powerful old Vincent Coll
approach, picking off the dogs without spooking the buff."

Ernest then told us about his startling nuptials: during one
of Mary's trips into Nairobi, he said, he had taken an eighteen-
year-old Wakamba bride and, as local custom dictated, in-
herited her sister, a widow of seventeen. The three of them
slept on a goatskin bed fourteen feet wide, Ernest said, and
when Mary returned she was very solicitous about the event
and impressed with the lofty position Ernest had attained in
the tribe by virtue of his matrimony.

One of Ernest's mischievous pleasures was the practical-joke
fantasy, and this matrimonial escapade may well have been
just that, even though he backed it up by showing us photos
of his African bride. It reminded me, however, of the time he
had recorded for posterity an account of his sexual encounter
with the celebrated spy Mata Hari.* He told a well-wined
group of us that he did not know her very well, since he was
a simple sublieutenant and she was consorting with general
officers and Cabinet ministers, "but one night I fucked her very
well, although I found her to be very heavy throughout the
hips and to have more desire for what was done for her than
what she was giving to the man." I had been very impressed
with this cool appraisal of the talents of Mlle. Hari until it
dawned on me that the lady in question had been executed
by the French in 1917, and Ernest had first gone abroad as a
Red Cross ambulance driver on the Italian front in 1918. After
that, I was always on the lookout for the practical-joke fantasy
but I could never determine whether Ernest's African nuptials
was one of them.

"Very good show on Mary's part, wasn't it?" Federico asked.
"Average woman might have been miffed."

"Mary was lovely the four months on safari, really wonderful,

* This account is on an LP record, "Ernest Hemingway Reading," dis-
tributed by Caedmon Records in 1965.

and most of the time quite brave. But after the first crash, when we were down in the jungle with the elephants pretty thick, she got a little testy—refused to believe I could tell the males from the females by the smell. Her other failings were that she never really considered lions dangerous and that the really bad fight we had with a leopard—when I had to crawl on my face into bush thicker than mangrove swamp and kill him with a shotgun—was stunting. Leopard was hurt bad and very dangerous, and I had a piece of shoulder bone in my mouth to keep my morale up. I had to fire at the roar because it was too thick to see. So that was stunting. Actually, what I'm saying is not against her because she was in a state of shock from the crashes, but she doesn't know about shock nor believe in it and she thinks when I am removing impacted feces from a busted sphincter, I am dogging it. But mostly she is loving and wonderful. And, as I say, very brave. But I wish she had some Jewish blood so she would know that other people hurt. But you can't have everything and I married a woman who is one-half Kraut and one-half Irish and that makes a merciless cross but a lovely woman. She is my pocket Rubens."

"You know, when you were announced dead," Federico said, "your friends here took it very hard. Adriana begged me to take her to Cuba so that she could burn down your *finca*, so no one would ever sleep in your bed, sit in your chair or ever go up into the white tower. She was seriously going to destroy the swimming pool. Poor damned blessed girl."

Adriana Ivancich was a tall, nineteen-year-old aristocratic beauty with long black hair and a curiously shaped but not unattractive nose that Ernest said was true Byzantine. Ernest had known her since early 1949; she came from a fine old Venetian family, wrote delicate poetry, painted, and skied expertly. She designed the book jacket for *Across the River and into the Trees*, and the length of time Ernest knew her corresponded roughly to the period that Colonel Richard Cantwell of the book knew the young Contessa Renata.

"I haven't told Hotch yet," Ernest said, "but we are going to Adriana's *palazzo* on the Grand Canal tonight for dinner. It

seems that the husband of Adriana's sister, an officer in the
Italian navy, is attached to an American naval unit in Norfolk,
Virginia, where he has fallen in love with The Hamburger.
He's coming home next week and there is great anxiety in Adriana's household because of their total ignorance of The Hamburger. I've been prevailed upon to demonstrate the construc-
tion and execution of The Hamburger, but now that Hotch is
here, I'll defer to him."

After Federico had left, Ernest said, "What a damn classy
gent he is. Italians are wonderful people. Probably have had
the worst press in the world."

"I'm damn glad to be back here. Our trip in '49 was the best
time I ever had anywhere," I said.

"Don't despair," Ernest said. "There's more where that good
time came from." Ernest's confidence in the unending order of
good times was founded on a very disciplined point of view
toward the hours of his days and weeks. Each day was a challenge of enjoyment, and he would plan it out as a field general
plans a campaign. That did not mean that there was no flexi-
bility—two days in Paris quite often meant two months, as I
had found out to my delight in 1949. But each of those Paris
days was set up carefully before it dawned or, at the very
latest, at its dawning. "When in Paris," Ernest had said to me,
"the only thing you leave to chance is the Loterie Nationale."

That day in Venice, Ernest was as usual helping things happen. His plans consisted of a visit to his jeweler's, Cogdognato
& Company, to look at some emeralds, then a visit to Harry's
Bar to see his old friend Cipriani, the enterprising Italian who
is, in fact, Harry. At Harry's we were to pick up a ten-pound
tin of béluga caviar to bring to the hamburger dinner. "We
can't eat straight hamburger in a Renaissance *palazzo* on the
Grand Canal," Ernest said. "The caviar will take the curse off
it." After Harry's we were to meet some of Ernest's duck-
shooting Torcello pals whom I had met on my previous trip.
The plans seemed an ordeal for a man in Ernest's condition, but
when I mentioned this he said, "They've slowed me down, but
they haven't stopped me. They'd have to chop off both legs

at the knees and nail me to the stake for that—but even then
I could probably still get them with my reflex action."

A hostile Adriatic wind had command of the Piazza San Marco
as Ernest and I hunched our way toward Harry's Bar. We had
already seen the ten-emerald display at Cogdognato's (Ernest's
rating: one possible, three passables, two questionables, four
absolute rejects), sent flowers and regrets to a duchessa's dinner
invitation, and supervised the grinding of the evening's hamburger meat at a butcher shop on the Calle Barozzi. Now
Harry's was refuge and reward.

We stood at the bar and drank a Bloody Mary but it was
not in the same league with Bertin's. The barman asked Ernest
what he thought of the previous night's prize fight, a contest
that had pitted Tiberio Mitri of Italy against Randy Turpin of
England. Ernest gave the barman a detailed analysis of that
one-punch fifty-second encounter, and then went on to discuss
his own exploits in and around the ring.

"Any time I was in New York I used to work out at George
Brown's Gym," he recalled. "I was working out there one time
with George when *The New Yorker* asked if they could send
over St. Clair McKelway to do a 'Talk of the Town' on Hemingway the Boxer. Well, George and I talked it over and decided
McKelway ought to have some good authentic color for his
piece. At the entrance to George's place there was a big photo
blowup of an Abe Attell fight, two faces like raw liver, so
bloody you couldn't see the features; when McKelway shows
up I say, 'See those guys, Mr. McKelway? They weren't really
trying.'

"Then George and I start to work out in the ring. George
kept calling out, 'Maurice!' (The ring boy was named Morris.)
'Maurice! Mr. Hemingway wants to toughen his feet.' (I didn't
own boxing shoes, so boxed in my stocking feet.) 'Bring down
some pebbles from the roof.' Morris got some pebbles and
sprinkled them around the ring. McKelway took notes. We
boxed a little; then George yelled, 'Maurice! Strew some broken
glass.' McKelway is writing a mile a minute. 'Mr. Brown,' Morris says, 'we ain't got no broken glass.' 'Then break some,'

George says. Finally we belted each other a few times for show.
McKelway was very impressed. Don't know if *The New Yorker*
ever published the piece."

Cipriani, a compact, energetic gentleman, all in gray—hair,
face, suit and eyes—came in and was delighted to see Ernest.
"I have been to Torcello," he said, "and the ducks are beyond
description. Ernesto, you must stay a few days longer and
shoot."

"I couldn't raise a gun, much less hit anything," Ernest said.

"How's your hand?" Cipriani asked.

Ernest showed him the hand that had been badly burned
in the African brush fire. "The new skin is beginning to gain
confidence," Ernest said. "I wish I could say the same for the
vertebrae, the kidney and the liver."

"I didn't know about the kidney," Cipriani said.

"Ruptured," Ernest said. "Do you mind if we sit at that table?
Christ, you ever know me to sit at a table when there was a
bar to stand at?"

"What injured you?" Cipriani asked.

"Crash number two. We went right to fire on that one. When
I picked myself up off the floor of the plane I felt busted inside.
The rear door was bent and jammed. My right arm and shoulder were dislocated but I used my left shoulder and my head
and had good pushing room to get it open. Ray Marsh was up
front with Miss Mary. I yelled to him, 'I have it open here.
Miss Mary okay?' He yelled back, 'Okay, Papa. Going out the
front way.' Was glad to see Miss Mary without a scratch on
her and carrying her vanity case. Never been in a crisis yet
that a woman forgot her jewels.

"We stood there, helplessly watching the de Havilland burn
up, and I made several scientific notations that might interest
you, Cipriani, as a student of the alcoholic occult. First noted
there were four little pops, which I chalked up as belonging to
our four bottles of Carlsberg beer. Then there was a more sub-
stantial pop, which I credited to the bottle of Grand MacNish.
But the only really good bang came from the Gordon's gin. It
was an unopened bottle with a metal top. The Grand MacNish
was corked and besides was half gone. But the Gordon's had

real *éclat*. I did sixteen thousand words about the crashes for *Look*, but it wasn't easy. Sometimes I wish I had a ghost writer. By Ernest Hemingway as told to Truman Capote."

A large, tawny cat came up to the table and Ernest picked her up and snugged her against him, rubbing in back of her ears. "I got a letter from René yesterday that Friendless and Ecstacy had a serious fight and completely disappeared." Ernest continued to rub the tawny cat's neck and told her in a low, sincere voice how beautiful she was.

A blue tin of caviar the size of a small hatbox was brought to the table, and Ernest patted Cipriani on the shoulder in approval. Then he held up the cat, looked at it thoughtfully for a moment and gently placed it on the table.

Again we crossed the Piazza San Marco, its blanket of pigeons barely parting for our feet. There were only a few tourists buying corn from the elderly vendor. Ernest watched the pigeons as they strutted about our feet. "One thing about a pigeon," he said, "he's always ready to screw."

As we passed the corn vendor, Ernest said, "You see that old fellow? Well, he had a fifty-four-year-old parrot that caught cold one day and said 'I'm going to heaven' three times over and died."

Two young men wearing fur hats and giggling passed us. "One thing I've learned," Ernest said, "never hit a fairy—he screams." One of the pigeons flew up and perched on Ernest's arm for a moment. Ernest stopped and gentled him. "I once had a room at the St. James et Albany in Paris," he said, "and at the bottom of the porcelain toilet bowl there was a pair of blue lovebirds. Made me constipated."

The hamburger dinner at the Ivancich *palazzo* was a great success. It was easy to see that Adriana was someone special in Ernest's life. I later discovered that Ernest often inducted into his coterie a striking young girl whom he apotheosized as he did the heroines of his novels. This Romantic Girl was never a clandestine affair but always an open consort, someone for whom Ernest could preen.

After the hamburger dinner, Adriana returned to the Gritti with us for the getaway party; Federico and a group of well-wishers were already waiting. Although I could tell he was occasionally in pain, Ernest stretched out on the couch and managed to enjoy himself. There was plenty to drink and someone had thoughtfully brought a portable phonograph. Along about midnight, for what reason I cannot now remember, I was called upon to demonstrate American baseball. It had something to do with a discussion Ernest was having with a British friend who was a cricket nut. Ernest suggested that a pair of his wool socks be rolled up and used as the baseball, and it was my bright idea to use the ornamental doorstop as a bat. The doorstops at the Gritti, like everything else there, are very elaborate. They are hand-carved mahogany with a heavy leaded base and a thin upright shaft that resembles a table leg. This shaft, when grasped at the end, with the round base at the top, made an excellent bat. Federico, who had seen baseball played, undertook the pitching assignment and I stationed myself at an improvised home plate.

I smacked the first pitch on a deadline to center field, and to my shocked surprise the baseball socks went sailing through the highly arched glass window and out into the Venetian night. The glass broke with a terrible clatter, and from the sidewalk below we heard angry voices. For a few minutes I basked in the glory of having belted a pair of wool socks so hard that they had shattered a glass window, but then we discovered that what had really happened was that the leaded base of the doorstop had come loose and gone flying out of the window along with the socks. I still have a piece of that glass, autographed by everyone who was there.

That was the end of the party; the next day when we checked out Ernest offered to pay for the broken glass.

"Ah, yes, the window," the manager said. "The flying saucer barely missed the nose of a gentleman who unfortunately is a member of the City Council. This gentleman, trembling with rage, came in with the disk, but we calmed him successfully. As for paying for the window, in the three-hundred-year history of the Gritti, no one, to our knowledge, has ever played baseball in any of its rooms, and in commemoration of the event, Signor Hemingway, we are reducing your bill ten percent."

Ernest invited the manager into the bar to have a glass of departure champagne; we clinked glasses all around and Ernest looked very sad. He often said he was reluctant to have to leave any place and this was especially true of Venice.

Ernest boarded the motor launch slowly and painfully, Adamo helping him. As we started along the canal on our way to pick up the Lancia, he said, "How can anyone live in New York when there's Venice and Paris?"

I watched the squat cargo barges and the graceful gondolas crisscrossing against the majestic background of Santa Maria della Salute, the air filled with the warning cries of the boatmen emerging from the Rio del Albero onto the Canale Grande, and I realized that Ernest's prediction had come true—it was my home town, all right—thanks to him.

"Gritti was pretty damn chic about that window," Ernest mused. "Reminds me of the time I fired a pistol shot through my toilet at the Ritz—they were just as chic. Which just goes to prove that it pays to stay at the best places."

Chapter Six

The Riviera ◆ 1954

The route to Madrid was to take us first to Milan, via Padua and Verona, for a visit with Ingrid Bergman. Adamo drove smartly and proudly, but to our growing dismay we learned that he had absolutely no sense of direction. We were only a few miles out of Venice when he started making wrong turns, although the road was clearly marked, and from then on, for the entire six days of the trip, Ernest, who had an excellent sense of direction, and infinite patience, had to operate as full-time navigator—a post that he always relished.

As we drove along the autostrada past Verona, Ernest watched, or rather *tried* to watch, the countryside but with growing annoyance. "This would be pretty scenery if you could see it," he said, referring to the signboards that solidly cluttered the sides of the road, "but you can't even see the signs because of the signs. Back in the days when American billboard-advertising was in flower, there were two slogans that I always rated above all others: the old Cremo Cigar ad that proclaimed, 'Spit Is a Horrid Word—but Worse on the End of Your Cigar,' and 'Drink Schlitz in Brown Bottles and Avoid that Skunk Taste.' You don't get creative writing like that any more. All the geniuses are gone."

As we approached Milan, Ernest began to talk about Ingrid Bergman. "The Swede's battling her way out of it," he said, "but in the beginning, when she had first thrown in with Rossellini and was really taking her lumps, it did not occur to Signor Rossellini to do anything more chic and gallant than to read my private letters to her to the press. When the famous become infamous it's pathetic. But Miss Ingrid has taken everything they could throw at her and that always mollifies the angered mob."

"What is she doing in Milan?" I asked.

"What she's always doing—playing Joan of Arc. You'd think she would have run out of Joans, having done her in the movies and on Broadway, but Signor Rossellini has found a novel way of squeezing the turnip for a last drop. He has written the libretto for an opera version, with music by Honniger, and directed same at La Scala."

"But can Bergman sing well enough for La Scala?"

"Of course not, but Maestro Rossellini has even got around that—everybody sings but the Swede, whose entire role is spoken in Italian, which she has mastered."

Although we got to Milan in the early afternoon, Adamo's keen sense of direction kept us in constant circlement for an hour and a half, searching for the Hotel Principe & Savoia, where Ingrid and Rossellini were staying. Since Adamo considered asking directions an irreparable loss of face, there was nothing to do but circle and hope for the best.

Around four-thirty, after Adamo had made three complete tours of the city, he finally found the hotel; Ingrid was waiting for us in the hallway as we stepped off the elevator. She was radiantly beautiful in a high-necked white silk blouse, the top six buttons of which were undone. Her Jeanne d'Arc haircut was very becoming. She hugged Ernest and they were very happy to see each other. We went into the living room of her suite, where every possible surface was ablaze with long-stemmed red roses.

"You are riddled with roses, Daughter," Ernest said.

"They were sent by an official on the Stock Exchange. I have never met him but he was so moved by the performance he sends roses every day. There is so much wealth in this city. The homes I have been in, Ernest, why, in comparison the houses in Beverly Hills are shacks. Even the ash trays are by Renaissance masters."

Ingrid Bergman was one of the few women in his life whom Ernest called "Daughter" who refused to call him "Papa" in return. "I don't have Papa feelings about him," is the way Ingrid explained it. But Mary called him Papa, and so did Ava Gardner and Marlene Dietrich. Some of his old cronies like Toots Shor called him Ernie, but for the most part the name "Ernest" in spoken form, was anathema to him. He was very rough on people who called him Papa without meriting such intimacy.

"Where is Signor Rossellini?" Ernest asked.

"In there having a nap."

"You going to make any more Hollywood pictures?"

"No, no more Hollywood. Not that I'm not grateful; I am. I loved much of Hollywood while I was there and I know how much I owe them. But life is short and the years run away and you must do everything you really want to. The only part I ever had with dialogue that was all there was in *For Whom the Bell Tolls*. I would like to perform elsewhere now, places I have not been to. I get movies to read all the time, same old plots bent a little this way or that."

"They plan to redo *A Farewell to Arms*," Ernest said. "I will receive nothing for it since it was sold outright. They are also about to make *The Sun Also Rises*, which was long ago sold for a pittance, and another version of *To Have and Have Not* and maybe *The Killers*, for which they'll also pay nothing, so my hand is virtually palsied from not receiving any monies."

"I read about the movie version of 'The Snows of Kilimanjaro,' " I said, "and how there was only one minor alteration— the man lives instead of dying."

"We must look on that as a very minor change, don't you think?" Ernest asked. "Now all we need is to have some Hollywood gag-writer take that poor bloody colonel of *Across the River* out of the back of that Buick and let him hike back to Venice and walk down the middle of the Grand Canal (this is a symbol, natch) and into Harry's Bar dry-shod. They will probably call it *Across the Selznick and into the Zanuck*."

"Once they make a purchase," Ingrid said, "they don't care how they defile the thing they've purchased. They only care about box office but they don't know what creates that. They buy a book that has sold a huge number of copies and they don't have faith in its content. And the last person they value is the writer."

"True. But sometimes you can peg them," Ernest said. "There was the time we were living in a remote ski cabin in Sun Valley. We had been out skiing all day and had just come back, very tired, feeling wonderful, taken off our clothes in front of a beauty fire, the drinks just being stirred, when there was a knock on the door. It was the man who ran the little general store, who had trudged up on snowshoes because there was a very important Hollywood call; been calling all day. So I shelved drink, got dressed and dragged my sagging ass over the drifts. It had started to snow like a son-of-a-bitch.

"A very excited operator's voice told me that Darryl F. Zanuck himself of Twentieth Century-Fox was going to speak to me. And by golly he did! 'Hello, Ernest?' he said (you could tell it was Hollywood because here he was calling me Ernest and we only knew each other from having exchanged my story for his dough). 'Ernest, we are in executive session here in my conference room, and we've been wrestling all day with a crisis that only you can resolve. We have made a truly wonderful picture of your wonderful story "The Short Happy Live of Francis Macomber" and we're ready for distribution but we feel that the title is too long for the average movie marquee, so we would appreciate it very much if you could change it to something short with eye appeal—you know, a title that would create on-sight excitement—something that'll appeal to both sexes and make them feel they *have* to see the movie."

"I told Zanuck to hold on while I gave the matter some thought. The storekeeper mixed me a drink and every once in a while I'd go back to the phone to tell the operator not to cut us off because I was engaged in emergency thinking. Finally, when I felt my A.T. and T. stock had gone up at least three points, I said that I thought I had just what the doctor ordered. Zanuck said he had his pencil at the ready. 'Now,' I said, 'you want something short and exciting that will catch the eye of both sexes, right? Well, then, here it is: *F* as in Fox, *U* as in Universal, *C* as in Culver City and *K* as in R.K.O. That should fit all the marquees, and you can't beat it as a sex symbol."

Ingrid laughed.

"How do things go?" Ernest asked, looking at her closely. "How do they really go?"

"Oh, when I think how it was a few years ago and how it is now! If only in a crisis one could learn to have patience, everything would be fine. Look at my children . . . " She took a picture from her handbag. "Robertino, four; the twins are now two. Did you ever see such beautiful children? Oh, how I love little children when there are a lot of them. To have only one, like my first child, is sad by comparison."

"It's a good blood mixture," Ernest said, "Swedish and Italian."

Rossellini came in from the bedroom. He was a short man, going to paunch and baldness; he had a small, reluctant smile on his face. Ernest told them how we had been joking about invading La Scala and rescuing Ingrid from the stake, and Ingrid laughed happily, but Rossellini halved his smile.

"Perhaps Ernest would like a drink," Ingrid suggested.

Rossellini opened a large antique sideboard which had been converted into a bar, and revealed, lurking in one corner, a partial pint of Black and White Scotch. He poured a drink for Ernest, but not wanting to put him out of business, I declined.

"Have you been skiing much?" Ernest asked Ingrid. Then he said to me, "She's a beauty skier."

"Haven't been skiing at all. I love it so, and I miss it but I've been pregnant ever since I came to Europe. I was going to go last winter during my one nonpregnant lull, but I figured up what it would cost to outfit the children and the nurse, and it didn't seem worth it."

"It certainly didn't," Rossellini said with conviction.

"A few seasons ago when we were skiing in Cortina," Ernest said, "Miss Mary broke her leg when she was running beautifully but hit some heavy wet snow she didn't understand. Skiing now, with the lifts and all, is about like roller-skating. Nobody has any strength in his legs because nobody ever climbs any more, and the best concession around a ski joint is the x-ray and plaster-cast booth."

I asked Ingrid whether she had a picture lined up. "No," she said, "but I really don't care. S. Hurok wants to tour the St. Joan opera—Paris, London, New York, South America—but the way things are now I could just concentrate on being a housewife and be perfectly happy because I have a husband who is in the theater and talks movies, and artists are around all the time and that would be enough for me. I could not be happy being a housewife married to a merchant, but to Roberto, yes."

"Where would you live?" Ernest asked.

"There is only one place to live forever, Paris, but it is so expensive now. I loved Naples; the people there were so loving and friendly, but for full-time living, Rome, I suppose. People are always calling who are friends of friends and I like that. I try to see everyone, not out of duty, but because I *love* people. I love to talk to them, and be with them . . . "

Ingrid made a date to have dinner with us that evening— there was no performance and Rossellini was making a speech before some civic group. Ernest was delighted to hear that and went to his room to rest—his kidney and his back were giving him trouble. An hour or so later, however, Ingrid phoned to say that Rossellini had decided she should hear his speech, and we all understood what that meant. But Ingrid did manage to come to Ernest's room to have a drink before going off to listen to Rossellini.

We got an early start the next morning but the signboards on the way out of Milan made Ernest just as unhappy as those on the way in. A few kilometers outside Milan, however, they began to thin out and Ernest's cheerful interest in the country-side was restored.

When we passed through Torino, he said, "I almost married a girl here. Red Cross nurse. I was laid up here in the base hospital because of the leg. I used to keep a bowl by the side of my bed, full of the metal fragments they took from my leg, and people used to come and take them as good-luck souvenirs.

They had a good track here and I got tips from a jock and from
a certain Mr. Siegel of Chicago, who was permanently on the
lam. I went to the races as an outpatient but I always left by
the end of the fifth race."

"Is it true they took two hundred pieces of steel from your
leg?"

"Two twenty-seven. Right leg. True count. Got hit with a
Minenwerfer that had been lobbed in by an Austrian trench
mortar. They would fill these *Minenwerfers* with the goddamnedest collection of crap you ever saw—nuts, bolts, screws, nails,
spikes, metal scrap—and when they blew, you caught whatever you were in the way of. Three Italians with me had their
legs blown off. I was lucky. The kneecap was down on my
shin and the leg had caught all that metal but the kneecap was
still attached. They say I was hit with a machine gun afterward
and that's when the kneecap went, but I think the *Minenwerfer*
did the whole job."

"How did you ever carry one of the Italians back to the
trench in that condition?"

"Christ, I don't know, Hotch. When I think of that leg—I
doubt that I did. But you shock out and what they tell you, you
think you remember. The big fight was to keep them from saw-
ing off the leg. They awarded me the Croce al Mèrito di Guèrra,
with three citations, and the Medaglia d'Argènto al Valore Mili-
tare—I threw them in the bowl with the other scrap metal."

"This Torino girl you almost married, did she go into *A Farewell to Arms?*"

"Sure. Everything that happened to me in Italy went into it,
one way or another. The Torino girl was Catherine Barkley,
and so were some others. You invent fiction, but what you invent it out of is what counts. True fiction must come from everything you've ever known, ever seen, ever felt, ever learned.
The way Lieutenant Henry felt when Catherine Barkley let
down her hair and slipped into his hospital bed was invented
from that girl in Torino—not copied, *invented*. The real Torino
girl was a Red Cross nurse. She was beautiful and we had
a wonderful love affair while I was hospitalized during the
summer and fall of 1918. But she never had a Caesarean nor

was pregnant. What happened between the Red Cross nurse
and me is pretty much as I wrote it in 'A Very Short Story.'
Who really had the Caesarean was Pauline. Happened while I
was writing on *Farewell* in Kansas City. So that's part of Catherine; and Hadley is part of Catherine. But the Red Cross nurse
was most of Catherine, plus some things that were of no woman
I had ever known."

This was a curious and exciting revelation—laying bare, as
it did, the process Ernest used for romanticizing his heroine,
filtering out the nonromantic, as sludge is refined from oil. The
romance with the Red Cross nurse had ended sordidly if, as
Ernest said, "A Very Short Story" was its chronicle. In that
story, which is exactly two pages long but manages to com-
press the essence of what was to be *A Farewell to Arms*, the
young American returns to the States after recovery, having exchanged vows with Luz (the nurse) that he will bring her
over shortly and they will be married. However, Luz falls into
an affair with an Italian major and writes the American that
she had never known an Italian before, so would he forgive
her, but it was obvious that theirs was just a boy and girl
affair and she was going to marry the major in the spring.
Then Ernest ends the account with: "The major did not marry
her in the spring, or any other time. Luz never got an answer
to the letter to Chicago about it. A short time after, he contracted gonorrhea from a sales girl in a Loop department store
while riding in a taxicab through Lincoln Park."

This was the realistic sludge of his relationship with the
Red Cross nurse that was refined out of the romantic concept
of Catherine. After their hospital affair the nurse was replaced
with the romantic times he had had with Hadley during their
trips to Switzerland, and it was Hadley who then became Catherine, only to give way to Pauline to provide the Caesarean
that brought on the dramatic end of Catherine's life.

"I have always found being in a hospital rather romantic,"
Ernest was saying. "I was in a London hospital one time after
a severe auto accident and when I came out of the ether the
first person I saw was a nurse standing by the bed. She was a
very plain, old-maidish nurse, but I was so glad to be back

among the conscious, I pulled her arm to my lips and kissed
her on the elbow. 'Oh, Mr. Hemingway,' she exclaimed, 'that's
the only romantic thing that's ever happened to me!' Couple of
weeks later, on the day I was being discharged, she came to
my room, shy and embarrassed, and asked me whether I'd do
it again. I did. Same elbow."

"Did you get to Italy during the Second World War?"

"No, just England and France. Of course I had the antisub
operation going in Cuba, but Miss Martha did not think that
qualified since it was not in a theater of operations, and she
wasn't happy until I became a fully gazetted and uniformed
war correspondent for *Collier's* magazine. I wrote them some
good straight pieces from the inside, since I had thrown in
with the troops and did not do my stuff from P.R. handouts in
the Officers' Club; but *Collier's* was chickenshit from the word
go. During the whole time I was abroad for them I had not
received any mail and I cabled them quite often about it, since
they were my mail drop, but they said there wasn't any; then
when I got back I found an entire desk drawer crammed full
of letters addressed to me.

"Also, there was the expense account. I lived good and I
spent a lot of my own dough to get the kind of stuff I used
in my pieces, but I figured I should only charge them one-
third of my actual expenses. They dismissed the one-third as
exorbitant and paid nothing. So that's what we had as our war-
time alma mater. Well, after the war there were a lot of changes
in the editorial staff so that by the time *Collier's* built its new
building on Fifth Avenue the editor I had had my troubles with
was gone. The new *Collier's* editor came to me and said they
were asking a selected list of the 'world's most important living
people' to contribute messages which would be buried in a
time capsule in the cornerstone of their new structure. This
capsule has an atomic ejector that will automatically spring it
in the year 1975 or thereabouts and there will be a big cere-
mony at which all the messages would be read. So I wrote them
a message. I said that I hoped that Mary and my three sons
were all well, that my friends had prospered and that the
world was at peace. I also said that I hoped that by then the

guy who had been my editor, whom I named, would have gone out and hanged himself by the neck to save everyone else the trouble. Hope I'm around in 1975 when they read it."

"I remember one piece you did for them about the three G.I.'s in a café and one of them, who had sung with a band before the war, was worried about his wife."

Ernest began to laugh. "That character! He sat there getting drunk on cider and complaining that his wife was unfaithful to him and wanted a divorce but he would not give it to her and that's why he wasn't a bombardier. She wouldn't sign his papers for bombardier school because he would not sign her divorce papers, and every day she wrote him who she had been unfaithful with the night before."

"*Collier's* got its money's worth."

"They were the first ones to use tape-recorders for interviews. All my life I had been struggling to perfect my ear to record exactly what I heard and I was a sad son-of-a-bitch when I discovered they had invented a machine that put all my training out of business. But I'm glad we have our machine now."

We were climbing through the Alps, going due south on our way to the French border. Ernest had been sipping wine from a bottle of Valpolicella, but when we came to Cuneo, an Alpine town of about twenty-five thousand, he decided to get a bottle of Scotch. A girl in the liquor store asked Ernest for his autograph, and by the time we left the store, news of his presence had raced around the little town; before he could reach the car, Ernest was surrounded by a large group of townspeople, which quickly grew into a mob. They stormed the local bookstore, which was right next to the liquor store, and quickly bought out all the Hemingway books in stock, and then all other books in English. Ernest autographed everything from *Of Human Bondage* to *Casserole Cookery*. The pressing crowd was closing in on him completely, and he had to strain to keep them from crushing him. I tried to reach him but the crowd was too solid and unyielding. It was suddenly a very serious situation, and I do not know what would have happened to Ernest, beat up as he was, if a small detachment of soldiers from the local army post had not appeared at that moment to make a path for him to the car.

Ernest was very shaken; Adamo got away fast and Ernest took a large drink of the Scotch to steady down. "A thing like that spooks you," he said. "Must be this goddamn beard; while being crushed, was also aware was patsy for having my pocket picked, so every time I was jostled I checked myself. Only compensation, I pinched one of their ball-point pens."

As the Lancia continued on its way toward the border, Ernest's relief at having been rescued from a fate that had begun to shape up as pretty miserable, turned to anger. "All that goddamn publicity! Not just the crash, but before that. Malcolm Cowley's thing in *Life* and Lillian's in *The New Yorker*. They made me sick. Not the phrase. Truly *sick!* Lillian's thing was my fault. I should never have allowed her to do it. Shouldn't have let Cowley either. Did you read his piece? Sure is a lot of difference between *Life* and life. Not to mention liberty and the pursuit of a modicum of happiness. I try to be a good character and keep all promises, good or bad, keep deadlines, not abort on missions, hit it on the hour you say you will, be where you say you will even if you have to move other people out of it. But I don't think Cowley or Lillian know anything about whatever material people like me are made of. All the time I was reading Cowley's piece I felt like I was being formed into his image. He has me in World War II a martini addict with a canteen of gin on one hip and a canteen of vermouth on the other—mixed fifty-fifty, I presume. Can you imagine me wasting a whole canteen on vermouth? The piece is riddled with other interesting items, like calling my son Jack 'Bumpy' instead of 'Bumby'—I suppose because Cowley thinks he's had a rough life.

"As for Lillian, Christ, she didn't understand anything, did she? She's a good girl who should have been practicing 'deadman's float' in the shallow water and had no business on the high dive. After you finish a book, you're wiped out. As a writer herself I thought she'd know that. I had just finished *Across the River* and New York was a release. But all she saw was the irresponsibility that comes after the terrible responsibility of writing. So she put down dialogue in her shorthand without understanding that I get so bloody tired of sounding like me that I invent ways of not sounding like me. Sometimes I leave out the nouns. Sometimes the verbs. Sometimes the whole goddamn sentence. As a writer I put them all in, but when I've just finished a book and come to New York for a few days to see friends and have fun and be irresponsible, I can do what I want and say what I want, but Lillian doesn't know any of that, so cartoons you into a gin-crazed Indian."

"Did you read John O'Hara's reaction to her profile?" I asked. "Appeared in *The New York Times*."

"No."

I found the clipping in my wallet—I had been meaning to send it to Ernest. I gave it to him and he read it aloud:

> "The most recent, and most disgusting, example of the intrusions into Hemingway's private life was made by a publication that reported on Hemingway's drinking habits somewhat in the manner of a gleeful parole officer. It also included some direct quotes, in tin-ear fashion, of what were passed off as Hemingway's speech, but sounded more like the dialogue written for the Indian chief in *Annie, Get Your Gun*.
>
> The inability to write the way people talk is a common affliction among writers. But for Eustace Tilley to raise an eyeglass over anybody's drinking is one for the go-climb-a-lamp-post department. The magazine had printed numerous little attacks on Hemingway by a semianonymous staffman who has gone to his heavenly reward, just as it printed attacks on Faulkner by a critic who has returned to his proper chore on the radio. With the long piece on Hemingway the magazine achieved a new low in something."

"That's damn nice of John. Is it all right if I keep this?"

"Sure. Lillian told me she sent you the proofs and you approved them."

"Sure she did. They arrived in Cuba on a Monday morning when the piece was already locked into the next issue. Ask Mary. But, anyway, what was there to correct? The whole damn thing was awful. *Awful.* Everything telescoped to fit into *The New Yorker* distortion machine. I'm never going to have another piece about me ever if I can help it. I had a nice private life before with a lot of undeclared and unpublished pride and now I feel like somebody crapped in it and wiped themselves on slick paper and left it there. I ought to move to Africa or stay at sea. Can't even go into the Floridita now. Can't go to Cojimar. Can't stay home. It can get on your nerves really badly, Hotch. I know some of it is my fault, but some of it isn't too. If I had had any brains, once Miss Mary was safely out I should have stayed in that second kite at Butiaba. Anyway, that's how I feel after that Cuneo mob has raked me over. Sorry to be Black-Ass. I'll look at the scenery and try to cheer up."

"Marlene phoned me the day *The New Yorker* came out," I said, "in an absolute fury. She was incensed that no one had told her who Lillian Ross was and that she was doing a piece, and then more incensed that it was so distorted."

"Can you imagine," Ernest said, "that after having spent the whole night with the Kraut and me, hearing all the things we discussed, all Lillian could write about was that the Kraut sometimes cleaned her daughter's apartment with towels from the Plaza. Hope you talked Kraut out of lawsuit."

"She's over it."

"So am I," Ernest said. "Lillian writes well—I thought her Hollywood pieces were superior, didn't you? And the piece on Sidney Franklin—well, I judged her on that—but my judgment blew up in my face."

In my opinion, what had happened was this: when Lillian had begun the Sidney Franklin profile, Ernest had told her she was as unqualified as anyone he could think of, since she knew nothing about bullfighting or bullfighters, had never been to Spain and did not even have any interest in American sports. She was equally unqualified to write about Ernest, for she knew as little about this kind of man as she did about bullfighters, but the difference was that in writing about Sidney Franklin she had Ernest to guide her, and in doing Ernest she had no one.

By the time we reached the Limone check point at the border, Ernest had restored his spirits with the pleasures of the Alp-

winding scenery. The Limone customs guards, however, gave
us the kind of reception they must reserve for the more obvious
gold-runners. They ordered us out of the car, and we stood in
the road while they went through the baggage, checked the
upholstery of the car, probed the tires, and even examined the
contents of the spare cans of oil that Adamo carried in the
trunk. The name Hemingway meant nothing to the chief guard,
who quite obviously couldn't read and who was convinced that
the pillow Ernest had been using to give support to his lame
back contained shredded plutonium.

Ernest was amused by the performance. "You can't blame
them," he said. "Did you take a good look at the three of us?
Adamo in that oversized pink safari jacket of mine, me in my
stocking cap and beard, and you in your gangster slouch?
Three of the gamiest bastards I ever saw. If I were the guard,
I'd line us up against the nearest wall and shoot us."

The trip over the Alps into Nice was exhilaratingly beautiful.
The Lancia took the corkscrew turns with the rhythm of a fast
pendulum, which Ernest enjoyed greatly.

"When I first came to France from Italy," Ernest said, "I
came third-class on the train. There was a pretty Swiss girl in
my car, and since the train was going very slowly on the ascent,
I decided to solidify my position with her by jumping off the
train and picking some of the beautiful mountain wildflowers
that were growing by the track, while running alongside the
train. But what I didn't know was that there was a tunnel a
short distance ahead around a curve, and also didn't know it
was the custom to lock the train doors when going through
tunnels. So I couldn't get back in and I had to cling to the side
of the train all the way through that black tunnel. There was
very little clearance and I was all skinned and bleeding and my
clothes were torn when the conductor finally unlocked the doors
and I climbed back in. Through it all, somehow managed to
hang onto the bouquet of flowers. Despite blood, soot and rips,
Swiss girl very impressed. Dressed my wounds. Made out okay."

In Nice we checked in at the Ruhl, a magnificent seaside
hotel. Ernest immediately sent for the barber and instructed
him to shave off his beard, trim his mustache severely and

shape up what postburn hair existed. "It might avert another Cuneo," Ernest explained.

We had planned to overwhelm Monte Carlo that night, but Ernest's injuries, particularly his back, were troubling him so much that he asked me to handle the wheel while he planned to set up headquarters in the Casino's bar. We each put up ten thousand francs and Ernest suggested the number seven if that was okay with me. "Play it with red and *impair*," he said, "and make them fear us the way they now fear us at Auteuil."

Adamo brought the car around after dinner; Ernest asked him if he knew the way to Monte Carlo (foolish question). He said yes, yes indeed, he had driven there many times. "Would it be all right," he asked, "if I opened it up this once to show you what she can really do?" Ernest said okay. Monte Carlo is about thirty kilometers from Nice, and Adamo had his foot on the floorboard the whole way. It was a wild ride. With a screech of brakes he pulled up at what he thought was the Monte Carlo seaside, but in reality we had made a giant loop and landed right back at the Ruhl. Adamo looked up at the hotel, blinked, and said, "What do you know about that? They have a Hotel Ruhl in Monte Carlo too!"

Seven was the number all right, usually in combinations, and *impair* did all right, but red was cold from the start and I laid off. Around eleven-thirty, with about a hundred eighty thousand francs in front of me, I could feel the board begin to go so I cashed in. I went into the bar. Ernest was asleep in a leather chair, an unfinished drink on the table beside him. I gave him his split and he was very pleased, as he always was with good performance against heavy odds.

On our way out of Nice the following morning we passed a road direction to Cap d'Antibes, and Ernest said, "One June I was at Cap d'Antibes with a group that included Charley MacArthur and his wife, Helen Hayes. It was the custom then for the Riviera to shut down for the summer, considered too hot, but Charley and I persuaded some of the places at the Cap to stay open for the first time. Charley was wonderful fun and we had a fine time. He was the master of the baroque practical joke and there was nothing from mother's milk to

Pope's ring that Charley held sacred. First-class gent. Well, one balmy evening Charley and I staged a prize fight, all in fun of course, with seconds in each corner and buckets of champagne instead of water. We had a pact not to hit at heads.

"But Charley, in a flurry of champagne and mistaken strength, tried to cream me. Twice while we were in clinches I warned him to cut it out, but two more times he threw roundhouse rights to my head. I then dumped him for keeps with a right chop. We had to carry him out of the ring. Well, I didn't see Charley much after that, but one day in Cuba, years later, I received a cable from him asking whether he and Helen could stop by to see us. Naturally I invited him. Poor Charley was by then very sick and knew he was going to die. We had lunch and it was pleasant, but sad. Mary took Helen on a tour of her vegetable garden, leaving Charley and me alone. 'Hem,' he said, 'it's not true that we were just passing through. I came down here especially to see you. Listen, Hem, something's been bothering me for a long time. You remember that night at Cap d'Antibes? Well, they've got me on pretty short rations and I wanted to ask you something—sort of a last favor—that prize-fight of ours—would you promise me never to write about it?' That was Charley for you—came all the way to Cuba to ask me that."

We stopped in Cannes, which is about twenty minutes from Nice, because Ernest was feeling rocky; he said he doubted whether, the pain being what it was, he could make it to Aix-en-Provence, which was our day's destination. He had two Scotches, two fried eggs, unbuttered white toast and a piece of pickled herring; that lifted him enough for us to continue.

The window of a *charcuterie* caught Ernest's eye when we were passing through Bourgogne, and he asked Adamo to stop. "If I'm not mistaken," he said, "they're showing tins of Capitaine Cook's mackerel in white wine. Haven't seen Capitaine Cook since 1939." Ernest invested all his Monte Carlo winnings in tins of the Capitaine's mackerel, containers of *pâté de fois gras*, bottles of Cordon Rouge champagne, and jars of pickled mushrooms and pickled walnuts. We could barely fit all of it into the Lancia.

That night in Aix-en-Provence, Ernest and I dined at the four-forked, one-flowered Vendôme, where the *spécialité* was *carré d'agneau arlésienne;* afterward we sat for a long time over coffee and wine; Ernest consumed more wine than I had ever before seen him drink. He talked steadily and with a curious immediacy as if the talk somehow alleviated his pain, which I knew intensified at night. He was talking about books, how many worthless ones he had read on the boat.

"Did you read John O'Hara's *A Rage to Live?*" I asked. "I thought it was very good. First book of his I've liked in a long time."

"No, haven't read John's book yet. Mean to. When I first read him, it looked like he could hit: *Appointment in Samarra.* Then, instead of swinging away, for no reason he started beating out bunts. He was fast and he had a pretty ear but he had the terrible inferiority complex of the half-lace-curtain Irish and he never learned that it doesn't matter a damn where you come from socially; it is where you go. So he kept beating out bunts instead of trying to learn to hit, and I lost interest. Am awfully glad if he has a good book. I'd written him off and am always happy to be wrong. The writing Irish cannot stand either success or failure, so if book is good we can expect him to become fairly insufferable, but we can always keep away from his joints and if he writes good, that is all that matters. It was damn pretty the way he put the shiv in *The New Yorker.*

"But look at what's being written. The guy who wrote *The Naked and the Dead*—what's his name, Mailer—was in bad need of a manager. Can you imagine that a general wouldn't look at the co-ordinates on his map? A made-up half-ass literary general. The whole book's just diarrhea of the typewriter. The only truly good novel, maybe great, to come out of World War II is *The Gallery.* I say 'maybe great' because who in the hell can tell? Greatness is the longest steeplechase ever run; many enter; few survive.

"I logged a lot of reading time on the S.S. *Africa* and reread *Huckleberry Finn*, which I have always touted as the best American book ever written and which I still think is. But I had not read it for a long time and this time reading it, there

were at least forty paragraphs I wished I could fix. And a lot of
the wonderful stuff you remember, you discover you put there
yourself."

"Do you think you'll write another book about the last war—
with that background?"

"No, I don't think so. *Across the River* is my book. I only
write once on any one theme; if I don't write it all that one
time, then it is not worth saying. You know that old Greek gent
Heraclitus? 'One cannot step twice in the same river, for fresh
waters are forever flowing in upon you.' I never start out with
a plot in mind, and I've never yet set out to write a novel—
it's always a short story that moves into being a novel. I always
make it prove that it can't be written short. There's only one
requirement to being a successful writer if you have talent—
stay healthy."

"Also to work every day, or damn near every day, don't you
think?"

"Yes. That's why I like to start early before I can be distracted by peoples and events. I've seen every sunrise of my
life. I rise at first light—the wars ruined my sleep, that and my
thin eyelids—and I start by rereading and editing everything
I have written to the point I left off. That way I go through a
book I'm writing several hundred times. Then I go right on, no
pissing around, crumbling up paper, pacing, because I always
stop at a point where I know precisely what's going to happen
next. So I don't have to crank up every day. Most writers slough
off the toughest but most important part of their trade—editing
their stuff, honing it and honing it until it gets an edge like
the bullfighter's *estoque*, the killing sword. One time my son
Patrick brought me a story and asked me to edit it for him.
I went over it carefully and changed one word. 'But, Papa,'
Mousy said, 'you've only changed one word.' I said, 'If it's the
right word, that's a lot.'

"I like to write standing up to reduce the old belly and because you have more vitality on your feet. Who ever went ten
rounds sitting on his ass? I write description in longhand because that's hardest for me and you're closer to the paper when

you work by hand, but I use the typewriter for dialogue because people speak like a typewriter works.

"But I've had my writing problems; don't think I haven't. When I asked Mary to marry me, I had a gaping hole in my head from having smashed a car into a water tower during a London blackout and I didn't know if I could write again, or do anything else. I had tried to write but no go. Mary gave up her career as a London *Time* correspondent, and in two and a half months everything began to fall in place. Except the writing. Tried for one year, but still no go. The turning point was out in Sun Valley when we were tracking a big elusive buck for Miss Mary, and for eight days we trudged through the deep snow from first light to dusk. On the eighth day Mary shot him, and the next day I started to write.

"There are only two absolutes I know about writing: one is that if you make love while you are jamming on a novel, you are in danger of leaving the best parts of it in the bed; the other is that integrity in a writer is like virginity in a woman— once lost, it is never recovered. I am always being asked about my 'credo'—Christ, that word—well, credo is to write as well as I can about things that I know and feel deeply about."

"Papa, you've often talked about maybe writing a book with an American locale . . ."

"I always wanted to, but had to wait till after my mother's death. You understand? Now I don't know. My father died in 1928—shot himself—and left me fifty thousand dollars.* There's a paragraph in *For Whom the Bell Tolls* that . . . well . . . took me twenty years to face his suicide and put it down and catharsize it. The thing that bothered me the most was that I had written him a letter that was on his desk the day he shot himself, and I think if he had opened that letter and read it he wouldn't have pulled the trigger. When I asked my mother for my inheritance, she said she had already spent it on me. I asked her how. She said on my travel and education. What

---

* I have not been able to find substantiation of this bequest. Ernest was left a sum of money by an uncle, and it may be that on this particular evening he transferred the source of his inheritance.

education? I asked her. Oak Park High School? My only travel,
I pointed out, had been taken care of by the Italian army. She
didn't answer, but instead took me to see the lavish new music
wing she had built on the house. Of course, that's where the
fifty G's had gone. My mother was a music nut, a frustrated
singer, and she gave musicales every week in my fifty-thousand-
dollar music room. When I was in school she forced me to
play the cello even though I had absolutely no talent and could
not even carry a tune. She took me out of school one year so
I could concentrate exclusively on the cello. I wanted to be
playing football out in the fresh air and she had me chained
to that knee-box. Even before her music-room period she was
in constant pursuit of musical personalities, trying to lure them
to her soirées. On one such occasion I found myself being
dawdled on the knees of Mary Garden. Since I was big for my
age, it was a tossup just who would dawdle who, but she
dressed out at one eighty-five and got the nod.

"Well, as for that fifty-thousand-dollar music salon, I got a
small return on my inheritance by putting up a punching bag
in the middle of it and working out there every afternoon until
I left Oak Park. And that time when I left, it was for keeps.
Several years later, at Christmastime, I received a package
from my mother. It contained the revolver with which my father
had killed himself. There was a card that said she thought I'd
like to have it; I didn't know whether it was an omen or a
prophecy."

Along toward midnight, all the other diners having left a
good hour before, I mentioned to Ernest that the waiters wanted
to close up. He had begun to repeat stories he had told me that
afternoon—a thing he had never done before—but there was no
other manifestation of how much he had been drinking.

He insisted on finishing the bottle of wine. "I was healthy
and in really good shape," he said, "before they banged me up in
this one. Was down to two hundred six and had pressure down
to one sixty over seventy. Before that, had it down to one forty
over sixty-five but Doc said was too low. Now it's all shot to
hell and how can you write out of that? Or do anything else?"

"Papa," I said, indicating the two forlorn waiters who

were maintaining a vigil, "I think they want to go home."

"Boy," he said, "you have to learn to drink under the withering fire of the fixed stare or the guided missile. During the war I had set up headquarters for my Irregulars in a farmhouse that was smack on the front line. It was designated at command headquarters as Task Force Hem. The Germans frequently sent patrols right into our front yard. Well, you know the artist John Groth? He came one night on his way to some assignment and we put him up. During dinner the German eighty-eights opened up and hit around us pretty good, shattering plaster and window glass; when it cleared, Groth crawled out from the potato cellar, where he had dived with the other eaters when the first pieces of plaster started flying around, and he said, 'Mr. Hemingway, how could you sit there eating cheese and drinking wine when they had us under fire?'

" 'Groth,' I said, 'if you hit the deck every time you hear a pop, you'll wind up with chronic indigestion.' You going to finish your wine?"

I pushed my half-filled glass over to him. His speech was getting slurred at the edges.

"They shot a lot of our good guys in the war but the beauty of our country is that there's a good guy born every minute. You know what the French call war? *Le métier triste*. You're looking at a man who's been shot at two years longer than General Grant. The sad goddamn science."

"The wine's gone, Papa."

"What month is it?"

"May."

He counted on his fingers. "September I will have an African son. Before I left, I gave a herd of goats to my bride's family. Most overgoated family in Africa. Feels good to have African son. Never regretted anything I ever did. Only regret things I didn't do. Bob Benchley once suggested we should maybe take it easy. That he and I were criticized because we didn't slow down. I said, 'Okay, Bob, we'll slow down.' 'When?' he asked. 'When we are old and full of other people's sleep,' I told him. Good old Bob . . . and Maxwell Perkins . . . and Charlie Scribner . . . I miss Charlie badly. Goddamn! Who is left that ever stuck together when things were really impossible? You are who is left. The reppo-depot is empty, and there are no replacements."

He got up and started toward the two waiters. "I am sorry I kept you so long," Ernest said in his facile, Midwestern French, "but it was necessary." He tipped each of them a week's salary, shook their hands and went out.

Going up in the hotel elevator, he said, "I heard Carl Brandt died. Was never my agent. Never had an agent. But always heard good things about him. Well, the grave's a fine and secret place but from there it's hard to collect ten percent." He got off the elevator tentatively, not completely trusting his feet, but his room was near the elevator and he did not have far to go. He hesitated at his door for a moment; his eyes narrowed in thought. "You know the real *métier triste?*" he asked. "Writing. There's a *métier triste* for you." He opened the door to his room and I started down the hall toward mine, but a moment later he called to me and came down the hall as I turned back. "What you should know, because we level with each other," he said, "is what my mother said that time I went back for my inheritance. 'Don't disobey me,' she said, 'or you'll regret it all your life as your father did.' " His eyes were fixed on a point at the end of the hall, where his mother stood in the doorway of the big frame house in Oak Park. He started to say something more about her, but his eyes left Oak Park and returned; he punched my arm and said, "See you in the morning," and this time he went into his room for keeps.

The next day, traveling through Arles, Ernest talked about the grapes and the cultivation of the vines and explained why all expensive wines grow on hills. He did not, that morning, mention the previous night; nor did he ever. It became, therefore, the one and only time he assessed our friendship, which, until then, I had only regarded from my point of view; that is, it had never occurred to me that he esteemed my friendship as highly as I held his. His life was so full of events and people that the fullness had obscured the fact that most of the meaningful individuals of his life had, one by one, disappeared. Certainly when I first met him in 1948 there was none of the need that now expressed itself in 1954. *The Old Man and the Sea* had been published with wide acclaim, and he had recently won the Pulitzer Prize for it, but acclaim, I was discovering, could not provide those who "stuck together when things were impossible." This unquestioning loyalty was what Ernest prized most highly, to be given and to be received, and it was a trait common to all those with whom he had long and lasting relations. But now they were few. The mortality rate was as high as Ernest's standards, and if you inquired about someone who had fallen by the way, Ernest would simply tell you that he or she "didn't measure up."

Perhaps part of the explanation could be found in his dictum: "The way to learn whether a person is trustworthy is to trust him." But then Ernest's measure of trustworthiness and the lack of it could certainly not be explained in conventional terms. It seems to me, in analyzing this mystique, that the real clue to his lasting friendships could be found in the fact that the people who stuck were straight and unphony and formed in their own image. Dietrich; Toots Shor; Waldo Peirce, the painter; Philip Percival, the White Hunter; Matador Ordoñez; Sylvia Beach, of the famed Paris bookshop; Gary Cooper; Willie Walton, the artist; Bud Purdy, the Ketchum rancher; Leonard Lyons, the columnist; Bill Davis, the Málaga expatriate; Winston Guest, the sportsman; Evan Shipman, the poet and track expert; Maxwell Perkins. People who in Ernest's estimation were true to their own identity and whose performance was consistent. That was what Ernest demanded, and it was a virtue he prized above all others.

Those who failed were drummed out with anger and scorn and sometimes sorrow, often drummed out in public, although the incident which Ernest picked for the break was usually a matter of expediency and not the real reason the subject was being "excommunicated." Thus, Kenneth Tynan was brutally executed on the terrace of the Hotel Miramar in Málaga before a tableful of witnesses for having disagreed with Ernest over whether the matador Jaime Ostos had killed well that afternoon. Peter Buckley, the photographer and writer, was run through and destroyed in the lobby of the Royal Hotel in Valencia for having interviewed Antonio just before the afternoon *corrida*, against Ernest's hotly expressed disapproval. Slim Hayward was summarily guillotined on the sidewalk in front of the crowded Bar Choko in Pamplona for having had dinner with David Selznick. Peter Viertel was shot down in the Imperator restaurant in Nîmes for whining about his feet, which had become chilled when we were all shooting pigeons at the street fair while waiting for Ernest and Jigee to join us. Spencer Tracy and Leland Hayward were simultaneously executed one afternoon in Peru for having delayed Ernest's marlin fishing in connection with the filming of *The Old Man and the Sea*.

Ernest often maintained subsequent relations with the violently jettisoned. Although the jettison removed them from the list of Those Who Counted, that did not necessarily mean that Ernest would not continue to see them. Thus, he subsequently helped Peter Buckley with a book about bullfighting, and hired Peter Viertel to work on the screenplay for *The Old Man and the Sea*. But his basic attitude toward The Fallen was irrevocably curdled.

On this clear, sunny Riviera morning, however, traveling through the vineyard country outside Arles on our way to Nîmes, Ernest had dismissed the rancors of the previous night and was remembering with pleasure the bicycle trips he had made through this region. "I know the vineyards of this region by heart," he said. "I used to bicycle through here with Scott in the days when he wasn't a crazy, at least not a bona-fide crazy. We had wonderful, carefree times. The bike is the only way to truly learn the contours of a country, since you have to sweat up the hills and coast down them. I wish I could remember just the good times with Scott and forget all the rest; but it was too painful, I guess. Like the time I went to visit Scott and Zelda outside Baltimore. They had a beautiful mansion there and they invited me for the week end; I said I could only come for dinner, as had to get back to New York because I was working on galleys with Max Perkins. I was met at the station by their chauffeur, Pierre, who was driving a custom-built Hotchkiss, one of the most elegant and expensive French cars of its day. Soon after we started out, I noticed black fumes rising from the engine; when I brought it to Pierre's attention, he told me this sad story:

"He said he had been a taxi driver in Montmartre when one night Zelda came out of a night club and hailed him to take her back to the Ritz. She stopped somewhere to pick up Scott, and when they got to the Ritz, Scott made arrangements with Pierre to drive them to Le Havre the following morning. Next day when they arrived at Le Havre, where they were boarding a boat for America, Scott was seized with a brilliant idea. He had just purchased a new Hotchkiss, which was being loaded onto the boat; what better than to have a true Frenchman drive it in America. Pierre pointed out that he spoke no English and had no clothes or passport with him, but, as usual, Scott's enthusiasm and persuasiveness prevailed and Pierre abandoned his taxi at the dock; some kind of temporary papers were issued, enabling Pierre to debark.

" 'But Monsieur Hemingway,' Pierre told me, 'from the moment I arrive here life has been a nightmare. This beautiful car, Monsieur Fitzgerald will not allow me to change the oil and the grease. He insists they are *French* oil and *French* grease and they must not be changed. So this beautiful car is burning up. Look at it! Right before my eyes. I show him the black smoke; he knows what is happening but still he will not let me put in any oil or grease. Please, can you not influence him?'

"It was a beautiful mansion, right on the water, rolling green lawn, but the big trees made it kind of melancholy. Scott and Zelda were being dressy and grand and were bearing down heavy on the sauce. Scott knew I liked burgundy so he had six bottles of wonderful vintage on the table, all uncorked. Turned out they were drinking Moselle and the burgundy was just for me. Six bottles *uncorked*. Can you imagine? There was a very attractive colored maid serving dinner, and every time she passed a dish Scott would say, 'Aren't you the best piece of tail I ever had? Tell Mr. Hemingway.' The girl never answered him and kept her composure. He must have said it to her ten times. 'Tell him what a grand piece of pussy you are.' Like that, over and over.

"After dinner Scott started up about Gertrude Stein. It was

a thing he never let up on. Gertrude had once said that Scott's flame and my flame weren't the same. Scott was so damn insecure he decided she meant I had a bigger or brighter flame than he did. When he first brought it up, I said all the talk about flames was Stein horseshit since we were both serious writers who would write the best we could until we died and there was no competition between flames or anything else. But he kept on. And on, and on.

"When it came time for me to catch my train, Scott had passed out and Zelda had disappeared; since no one knew the whereabouts of Pierre and the Hotchkiss, I had to stay overnight, obviously the way Scott planned it.

"Next morning Scott appeared in a blue blazer and white flannels, clear-eyed and vigorous, and wanting to play forced games like croquet. There was only one train a day so I went along with the activities until it got near train time, when I made it clear that I was going to catch this one. Scott and Zelda insisted on coming to the station with me, but delayed leaving the house so that making the train would be a tight squeeze, if not impossible. Scott rode with his feet sticking out of the window. He was being churlish about my not staying and when we got near the station he suddenly swung his feet around and kicked out the windshield, cutting his foot in the process. He told Pierre to drive to his doctor's. *I* told Pierre to keep on to the station, and *then* to the doctor's. Scott turned savagely abusive and hysterical and I had to slap his face hard to quiet him down. Zelda huddled in a back-seat corner, sobbing. There was glass and blood all over. Poor lovely Scott."

Ernest watched a string of passing carts, still thinking about Scott. "After I left, I wrote Scott that I'd like to see him again when he was sober enough to talk and not stinking all the time. I told him that neither of us was a tragic character, that we were writers who should write and that's all we were, and he should give up the false and worthless pose of being tragic. Of course, his marriage to Zelda was tragic, and I told him that someone as jealous of his work as Zelda was, was always competing with him and out to wreck him—I told him it was obvious to me the first time I met her that Zelda was a crazy. But

Scott was in love with her and did not see the obvious. Being
a rummy made him very vulnerable—I mean, a rummy married
to a crazy is not the kind of pari-mutuel that aids a writer. I
told Scott that because I thought the brutal truth might shake
him out of himself, and then I tried to set him up by pointing
out that Joyce was as bad a rummy as he was and that most
good writers were rummies. How the hell can you bleed over
your own personal tragedies when you're a writer? You should
welcome them because serious writers have to be hurt really
terrible before they can write seriously. But once you get the
hurt and can handle it, consider yourself lucky—that is what
there is to write about and you have to be as faithful to it as
a scientist is faithful to his laboratory. You can't cheat or pretend. You have to excise the hurt honestly. That's what I told
Scott. And I told him that at this point in his life, hurt as he
was, he could write twice as well as he ever could, booze or no
booze. Zelda or no Zelda. Tried to build him up. Light a fire.
Didn't work. He resented my telling him and he was angry
and it didn't work at all."

Ernest and I were now driving through beautiful Van Gogh
country, and we arrived in Nîmes in time for lunch. "You remember the last time we were here?" Ernest asked. "With the
Viertels? From Paris to here was fine, but I started to lose a
little faith when we couldn't get them out of the car to see
the Maison Carré there in Nîmes that beautiful morning. I
think you and I were the only ones who went in. Did Mary?
You know, for a dime they wouldn't have seen the arena, and
to Peter, Aigues-Mortes was a place to take a picture. Well,
what can you expect from a guy who by his own admission had
had only two sleepless nights in his entire life. Count 'em,
gentlemen, two. Probably all those eighteen-month no-tax chaps,
including Herr Irwin Shaw, the Swiss banker, and other charter
members of the Klosters Kaffeeklatch will be the founders of
the next great American fortunes. The former fortunes were
founded by the people who didn't fight in the Civil War."

As we drove along, Ernest was reminded of many things.
Of the time at Aigues-Mortes when he and Hadley stained
themselves with walnut juice so they could crash a gypsy dance;

they were broke and the vision of free-flowing wine was their inspiration, but there was nothing to drink at the dance and it took a week for the walnut stain to wear off.

When we passed through Lunel, we stopped to admire a monument in the center of town, a black, life-sized bull mounted on a white stone pedestal. "This is the home town of Sanglé," Ernest said, "one of the greatest bulls that ever lived. They used to tie a rose between his horns and paid a prize of three thousand francs to anyone who could pick it off."

We stopped for the night in Montpellier, where a big street carnival was in progress. We drove slowly past the wheels of fortune, the weight-guessers, the shooting galleries, the games of skill and chance; Ernest wanted to rekindle our attack on the red-eyed pigeons, but when we stopped and got out of the car he had to beg off. "If I tried to take aim I'd be as likely to shoot myself as the pigeon."

The following day our route took us through Béziers to the walled city of Carcassonne in the shadow of the Pyrenees. In Béziers we stopped to ask directions (Adamo never forgave us) of an ancient gentleman who was sunning himself on the steps of the Cathédrale St. Nazaire. As we continued on our way, Ernest said, "Have you noticed that toothless people the world over, regardless of language, sound the same?"

In Carcassonne we stayed at the Hôtel de Cité, which is one of the most unique and beautiful hotels in Europe. It has a medieval atmosphere and all its rooms look upon the ramparts of the town. "Most of the wall and the towers of the city are faked," Ernest said, "but the restoration is so wonderful, who gives a damn?"

When we went down to dinner, Ernest was surprised and pleased when an old New York friend came over to the table to greet him. Ernest invited him to dine with us and over drinks inquired about the gentleman's wife, whom, it seemed, Ernest had liked. The man explained that they were separated and Ernest said he was genuinely sad to hear it. There were three children. "The thing I've got to decide, Hem," the man said, "is whether to make another stab at it or tell her to go to Reno. She'd like to try again, but she says she'll go to Reno if that's what I want. Frankly, I don't know. I miss the kids . . ."

"How long you been separated?"

"Four months."

"You got dough laid away?"

"No. Hell, who can save anything? I live on what I make, and you know what I make."

"Well, Barney, one thing you have to remember is that the economics of people having bust-ups is almost fatal. You not only lose the children, no matter what you're promised, but you go straight into economic slavery, and what's left, unless you hit jackpots, is never enough to satisfy anybody else. Maybe I just read all this in an article by Hotch here, who had a piece on the subject in a magazine. But if you ask me, any sort of *modus vivendi*, if you can keep from fighting, can be better. The last time with Miss Martha it was a break to break up, on account no children, no love, she was making more money than I was and convinced she had a much better future without me and was probably right since our interests and tastes were not the same and I liked to write and could not match her in ambition. Nobody can advise anybody. I don't want to try."

"What concerns me more than the economics," Barney said, "are the kids. I have a good relation with them. That means a lot to me. If I could see them regularly and keep that . . . well, I know how tough it will be supporting two houses on the same income . . . but . . . aw, I don't know . . ."

Ernest then discussed his own sons in terms of his relations with them after his divorces. He told about Patrick, who had been living with Pauline in Key West, and how on one occasion when he came to visit Ernest in Cuba he had come down with meningitis. The meningitis induced a delirium in Patrick that made hell out of everyone's life at the *finca*, but with the help of Sinsky Dunabeitia, Roberto Herrera, Taylor Williams, who was staying in the Little House, and Ermua, the great pelota player, Ernest had pulled Patrick through the crisis and nursed him back to good health. Ernest said there was one stretch when

Ermua had to sleep with his arms wrapped around Patrick to keep him from harming himself. For four weeks, Ernest said, he had averaged less than four hours sleep a night.

Patrick, of course, had no memory of these delirious months after his recovery, so that when his mother told him that he had fallen ill in Cuba and Ernest had abandoned him and she had taken him back to Key West and claimed to have done all the things for him that Ernest had actually done, the boy believed her, and it was a long time before Ernest could reestablish himself with Patrick.

"This is only to tell you," Ernest said, "that you can't figure on retaining much of children these days if you split up. But the real thing about Pauline is that when women have any feeling of guilt, they tend to get rid of it by slapping it onto you."

Barney asked how Ernest got along with his sons now that they were grown. "Pretty gcod, I think. We see each other when we can and we like each other pretty good. The boys haven't developed, though, the way I thought they were headed. The number-one son, Bumby, who was O.S.S. and parachuted behind the German lines and who I had pegged as career Army, is now a West Coast stockbroker. Gigi, who was the adventurer, crack shot, rider, roper and hell-raiser, is pre-med and set on doctoring.

"Patrick, who has the nickname Mousy, is the one I told you about, Harvard *cum laude*, married a Baltimore socialite. Figured to be the Thinking Man's Hemingway, but he's the one set himself up in Africa, licensed White Hunter and a damn good one, and is conducting a big experiment in plantation corn."

"Do they consult you about their work and plans?"

"Yes, we all keep in touch. Just answered Bumby, who asked advice on salary arrangements with new firm. Wanted to know about a drawing account. Told him drawing account was the enemy of man, and expense account was its evil little brother."

The next morning arrived in a shroud of wet fog. We delayed leaving and when we finally did leave we traveled cautiously

along the partially obscured road to Toulouse; Ernest refused
to stop in Toulouse, even for coffee. "This town has the ugliest
people in the world," he said. "As a matter of fact, you can
drive all the way from Nîmes to Paris and never see a pretty
girl."

Twenty kilometers south of Toulouse, where apparently pul-
chritude took a sudden surge upward, Ernest said it was okay
to stop for lunch in the little town of Muret, where we dined
very well on *champignon de bourgogne* and a bottle of Sancerre.
The bar was cheerful; the kitchen aromas were good. "One
good thing about France," Ernest said, "you don't get any rummies around." His eyes had lost some of their ominous yellow
color and I could tell that his pain had lessened somewhat.
Our waitress was blessed with non-Toulousian features, and
breasts that bubbled over the top of the circular cut of her
dress. Ernest asked her to have a glass of wine with us, which
she did, and she would have driven with us to Biarritz if her
boy friend, who was the local mailman, hadn't bicycled up as
we were paying the check.

We arrived in Biarritz, which is just north of the Spanish
border on the Bay of Biscay, toward evening, the mist solid all
the way and the beauties of the Pyrenees to our left totally obscured. We checked into the Hôtel Palais, which had once been
the summer palace of Napoleon III, and as far as I was concerned still was. My room was high-ceilinged sumptuous splen-
dor with a balcony that seemed to touch the spray of the
ocean as it cascaded against a formidable stand of offshore black
rock. Ernest said he was so moved by his accommodations
that he had changed his shirt.

We went across the street to Sonny's Bar, which Ernest had
often talked about as one of his favorite places in the days when
he and Charley MacArthur and Fitzgerald and the others were
first discovering the joys of the Riviera. In those days Sonny's
Bar handled Ernest's mail, extended him credit, served him his
favorite dishes at his favorite corner table, and covered for
him with girls and creditors. It had a proper, leather air about
it, with a mahogany bar and padded-leather bar stools and

chairs. This was early season for Biarritz and there were only
a few customers. The barman handed Ernest a letter which
had been there for three years.

After Sonny's Bar we drove to the contiguous town of Saint-
Jean-de-Luz, where we visited another of Ernest's old haunts,
the Bar Basque. We had a drink, standing up at the bar. Beside
the bar were tables and chairs. Ernest stood with his back to
the bar, sipping his drink and studying one of the empty tables.

"This is where I was standing," he said, "the day Charley
Wertenbaker came in with the most beautiful girl I ever laid
eyes on. They sat here, at this table. Bar was crowded, so
don't think Charley saw me; anyway, he was too concentrated
on girl. Was not eavesdropping but Charley began to raise
his voice and I heard him say, 'I'll kill her,' so naturally from
then on I strained my ears to listen. Girl said, 'Does it do any
good to say I'm sorry?' Charley said, 'No, did no damn good.'
Girl said she loved him very much. Charley said, 'If only it
was a man,' and that let me in on the whole thing."

" 'The Sea Change,' " I said, "so this is where it happened."
It had never occurred to me that the short story was anything
but fiction.

"In the story I called the man Phil, but it was Charley and
the girl was some beauty."

"Did he really tell her to go?"

"Actually he begged her not to, but the way it is in the story
it amounts to the same thing."

"And she said she loved him and would come back to him?"

"Yes."

"Did it happen that way? Did Charley take her back?"

"I don't know. But one afternoon I saw Charley's girl walking
along the beach with the girl she had gone to. Had expected
other girl to be a typical bull-dyke: pompadour hair, tweed suit,
low oxfords. But she was as pretty as Charley's girl. Those two
beauties walking hand in hand on the beach."

Chapter Seven

Madrid ♦ 1954

In San Sebastián, our first stop in Spain on our way to Madrid, Ernest hunted for a certain café, the name of which he had forgotten (this was one of the few times that I had known Ernest's memory to fail him on such a detail; he kept no notebooks or journals but his phenomenal recall kept places, names, dates, events, colors, clothes, smells and who won the 1925 six-day bicycle race at the Hippodrome, on orderly file).

Ernest was anxious to find the café because it was the only way he knew to get in touch with his old friend Juanito Quintana, whom he describes in *Death in the Afternoon* as one of the most knowledgeable *aficionados* in Spain. Quintana had been an impresario of means in Pamplona before the Civil War, when he ran the bull ring and owned a hotel. But Franco had stripped him of both and left him to scrounge, which is a very overcrowded occupation in Spain. As an old comrade-in-arms, Ernest was loyal to him and sent him a monthly stipend, as he did to several other of his old Spanish friends.

We finally found Juanito, a short smiling man in need of dentistry, who had an overruddy complexion; he quickly packed a few belongings and joined us for the trip south.

In the northern town of Burgos, Ernest asked Adamo to stop at the cathedral, which is one of the grandest in Spain. "Wherever you see a big cathedral," Ernest said, "it's grain country." With my help Ernest pulled himself torturously from the car and went slowly up the cathedral steps, bringing both feet together on each step. He touched the holy water and crossed the murky deserted interior, his moccasins barely audible on the stone floor. He stood for a moment at a side altar, looking up at the candles, his gray trench coat, white whiskers and steel-rimmed glasses giving him a monkish quality. Then, holding tightly, he lowered his knees onto a prayer bench and bent his forehead onto his overlapped hands. He stayed that way for several minutes.

Afterward, descending the cathedral steps, he said, "Sometimes I wish I were a better Catholic."

We spent the night in an *albergue* near Logroño on the Madrid road. When Ernest and I entered the bar of the *albergue*, which was crowded, we could hear an Englishman saying to his two companions, "You know, this is where *Fiesta* took place [the title for *The Sun Also Rises* when it was published in England]. Wouldn't it be a scream if old Hemingway was in here having a drink?"

Ernest walked up to the men and said, "What will you have, gentlemen?" I think he enjoyed that moment more than anything else on the trip, and he referred to it many times over the following years. While Ernest was talking to the men, a tall, fleshy Pinocchio-nosed man approached me and introduced himself as John Kobler of Westport, Connecticut. He said he had been stranded at the motel for two days because mosquitoes had clogged the radiator of his Buick, which was in the local garage for declogging. He asked whether I thought it would be all right for him to take pictures of Mr. Hemingway with his movie camera. I told him to ask Ernest.

Kobler went over and broke in on Ernest's conversation, which is a maneuver Ernest liked about as much as breaking into his house. Kobler started to ask him about posing for his camera, but Ernest interrupted to ask Kobler where he got the jacket he was wearing, saying he thought it was the most sensational jacket he ever saw; and then he checked out the Englishmen's opinions on its cut and color, wanted to know if it shed, and on and on; Kobler preened and answered dutifully and felt very proud of his jacket. (This form of relentless attack upon the plumage of an interloper was one of Ernest's commonly used weapons. I especially recall such an assault at the Ritz upon a pair of chandelier earrings worn by an overbearing, overbreasted autograph-seeking matron from Steubenville, Ohio.)

"Jacket made by Johnson and Johnson from reject Band-aids," Ernest confided to me when he saw Kobler later that evening in the dining room. "What's he doing here?"

"Mosquitoes have clogged his Buick."

"It figures," Ernest said.

As we approached Madrid, Ernest pointed out the mountain top where Pablo's band had hid out in *For Whom the Bell Tolls*. "We'll drive up there one day with Mary," he said, "and have a picnic by the bridge."

Ernest checked into the Palace Hotel (le Capitaine Cook and the other comestibles filled a closet), which, like all Madrid, was very crowded because the Festival of San Isidro, Spain's number-one bullfight spectacle, was to start the following day, May 15th. Mary was driving up from Seville with Rupert Belville, who was an old and valued English friend, although he had been a pilot on Franco's side during the Civil War.

We went to have a drink at the Cervecería Alemana on the Plaza Santa Ana, a favorite hangout for matadors and bullfight impresarios, and many of the men came over to greet Ernest. We drank beer and ate delicious shrimp and *langosta*. Then Ernest ordered an absinthe; his eyes were yellow again. He began to talk about Madrid events during the Civil War, and I asked him how much of *For Whom the Bell Tolls* had come from actual events.

"Not as much as you may think. There was the bridge that was blown, and I had seen that. The blowing of the train as described in the book was also a true event. And I used to slip through the enemy lines into Segovia, where I learned a lot about Fascist activity which I carried back to our command. But the people and events were invented out of my total knowledge, feeling and hopes. When Pilar remembers back to what happened in their village when the Fascists came, that's Ronda, and the details of the town are exact.

"All good books have one thing in common—they are truer than if they had really happened, and after you've read one of them you will feel that all that happened, happened to you and then it belongs to you forever: the happiness and unhappiness, good and evil, ecstasy and sorrow, the food, wine, beds, people and the weather. If you can give that to readers, then you're a writer. That's what I was trying to give them in *For Whom the Bell Tolls*.

"Toward the end of the war, when things were going very badly for the Loyalists, I took time out to return to the States to try to raise money; when I got back to the front I sought out the Polish general who was then in command, a man I respected very much, and asked him how things were going.

" 'And how is Mrs. Hemingway?' was his answer.

"A French colonel came running into the command post. 'We've got to do something!' he shouted. 'We've got to do something! The Fascist planes are coming! Tell me what my men and I can do!'

"The general said, 'You can go out and build a very high tower that you can climb up so you can see them better.'

"It was along about this time that Dos Passos finally came to Spain. He had been in Paris the whole time, writing me notes heatedly in favor of our cause, but now he announced he was actually coming down to join us and we eagerly awaited his arrival because we were all starving and he had been instructed to bring food. He arrived with four chocolate bars and four oranges. We damn near killed him.

"He had left his wife in Paris and on arrival he gave Sidney Franklin a telegram for her and asked him to take it to censorship. The censor called me. Wanted to know if the message was in code. I asked him to read it. It was, 'Baby, see you soon.' I said to the censor, 'No, it isn't code. It just means Mr. Dos Passos won't be with us very long.'

"Dos spent his whole time in Madrid looking for his translator. We all knew he had been shot but no one had the heart to tell Dos, who thought the translator was in prison and went all around checking lists. Finally, I told him. I had never met the

translator, nor had I seen him shot, but that was the word on
him; well, Dos turned on me like I had shot him myself. I
couldn't believe the change in the man from the last time I had
seen him in Paris! The very first time his hotel was bombed,
Dos packed up and hurried back to France. Of course, we
were all damned scared during the war, but not over a chickenshit thing like a few bombs on the hotel. Only a couple of
rooms ever got hit anyway. I finally figured it out that Dos's
problem was that he had come into some money, and for the
first time his body had become valuable. Fear of death increases in exact proportion to increase in wealth: Hemingstein's
Law on the Dynamics of Dying."

We both ordered absinthe, and Ernest continued to talk
about the Civil War: "General Modesto was in love with Miss
Martha, made three passes at her in my presence, so I invited
him to step into the men's can. 'All right, General,' I said, 'let's
have it out. We hold handkerchiefs in our mouths and keep
firing till one of us drops.' We got out our handkerchiefs and
our guns, but a pal of mine came in and talked me out of it
because money was scarce and our side could not afford a monument, which all Spanish generals get automatically."

Still talking about Martha, Ernest was reminded of the night
they were asleep in bed when an earthquake struck and the
bed was thrown around. He recalled that Martha gave him a
shove and said, "Ernest, will you please stop tossing!" At that
moment, Ernest said, a pitcher slid off the table and broke and
the roof caved in on them and he was finally absolved.

"Martha was the most ambitious woman who ever lived, was
always off to cover a tax-free war for *Collier's*. She liked everything sanitary. Her father was a doctor, so she made our house
look as much like a hospital as possible. No animal heads, no
matter how beautiful, because they were unsanitary. Her *Time*
friends all came down to the *finca*, dressed in pressed flannels,
to play impeccable, pitty-pat tennis. My pelota pals also played,
but they played rough. They would jump into the pool all
sweated and without showering because they said only fairies
took showers. They would often show up with a wagon full

of ice blocks and dump them into the pool and then play water polo. That began the friction between Miss Martha and me—my pelota pals dirtying up her *Time* pals.

"God knows I do not have a definitive reading on womenies, but I do know that little things count much more than big things. And it's all a question of balance. Too little sex, neglected; too much, you're oversexed; Christ, man should get changing readings on a woman's mood like he gets the *côte jaunes* before each race. But don't try to find an untroublesome woman. She will dull out on you. What makes a woman good in bed makes it impossible for her to live alone."

We left the café and went to look for Mary, whom we found waiting at the hotel with Rupert, a tall, well-groomed, ruddy-faced perfectly dictioned constituent of the leisured, nonworking, White's-Clubbed upperest class. Mary and Ernest were very glad to see each other and Ernest hugged her against his stomach bulwark and she kissed his lips through his partially restored beard.

It rained so hard the first day of the *feria* that the bullfights had to be called off. As a substitute we had drinks and *tapas* in the Palace Bar, the nerve center of Madrid social intrigue, where every woman looks like a successful spy.

We saw several good bullfights (in Ernest's judgment) on the succeeding days, but most of the afternoons were cloudy and windy and Ernest was unhappy about this aspect of the performances. "Sun is the best bullfighter," he said. "When the day is overcast it is like a stage show without lights. The matador's worst enemy is wind." He was delighted with the performance of a short, very courageous matador named Chicuelo II ("although it is no longer stylish to tap the bull on the nose to start him"), and had great admiration for the way a matador named Cortega killed. "He goes in cleanly over the horns, holding back nothing. But he has been gored so often he is nothing but steel and nylon inside."

Ernest was still suffering from his injuries, and although he had stopped complaining, I could tell he was in considerable pain. He finally went to see Dr. Madinoveitia, an old friend and one of Madrid's leading practitioners, who told him, "You should have died immediately after the airplane accidents. Since you did not, you should have died when you got those brush-fire burns. You also should have died in Venice. However, since you are still alive, you won't die any more if you will be a good fellow and do as I tell you." He put Ernest on a strict diet and cut him down to two drinks a day and two glasses of wine per meal.

On the way back from the doctor's, an overpoweringly putrid smell suddenly invaded the car; Ernest identified it as the smell of the Madrid slaughterhouse. "This is where the old women come early in the morning to drink the supposedly nutritious blood of the freshly killed cattle. Many a morning I'd get up at dawn and come down here to watch the *novilleros*, and some-times even the matadors themselves, coming in to practice killing, and there would be the old women standing in line for the blood. Practice-killing in the slaughterhouse was prohibited by law, then as now, but if you were friends with the slaughter-house foreman, he would slip you in with your killing sword hidden under your coat and you could practice sighting and coming in over the horns to find the target in back of the neck, which is the size of a quarter. There is no way to practice killing except in the slaughterhouse. No one can afford to buy animals just to kill them, and although you can practice the cape and the *muleta* with dummy horns on wheels or at *tientas*, and even practice placing the *banderillas*, there is no way to simulate killing."

Ernest said that by watching the matadors in the slaughter-house, he really learned about killing, so that when he wrote about it in "The Undefeated," he wrote it for keeps. And, inci-dental to that, he learned about the old women, whom he put into *For Whom the Bell Tolls*. Then Ernest reminded me of an account in *Death in the Afternoon* of a gypsy brother and sister who avenged the death of their older brother who had been gored by a bull that toured the *capeas*. They went to the slaughterhouse on the morning the bull was to be slaughtered for beef, and got permission to kill him by gouging out his eyes, spitting in the sockets, and severing his spinal marrow. They

then cut off his testicles, which they roasted over a fire they
made in the street opposite the slaughterhouse, and ate them.
Ernest said he had been there the morning it happened. It
happened in Madrid but Ernest changed it to Valencia. "Sometime read about the old women in *For Whom the Bell Tolls*,"
Ernest said. "Many, many cold mornings went into that one
paragraph."

For Whom the Bell Tolls had never been published in Spain
but copies were bootlegged in English, and a British Embassy
friend of Rupert's lent me his. I thought I knew the book well,
but I could not recall the blood-drinking old women of the
Madrid slaughterhouse. They were there, all right. Pilar says
she can smell death, and Robert Jordan disputes her: death has
no smell, he says; fear maybe, but not death. If death has an
odor, what is it?

Pilar describes the smell of death: first, it is the smell that
comes when on a ship there is a storm and the portholes are
closed up. She tells him to put his nose against the brass handle
of a porthole on a rolling ship that has made him faint and
hollow in the stomach, and that is a part of that smell. The
next part of the smell she says he will find at the Puente de
Toledo early in the morning; she tells him to stand there on
the wet paving when there is a fog from the Manzanares and
wait for the old women who go before daylight to drink the
blood of the slaughtered beasts. When one of these old women
comes out of the *matadero*, Pilar tells him, holding her shawl
around her, her face gray, her eyes hollow, the whiskers of age
on her chin sprouting from the waxen white of her face
as sprouts grow from bean seeds, pale sprouts in the death of
her face; then he must put his arms around her, and hold her
against him and kiss her on the mouth and he will have the
second part of the odor of death.

After his visit to the doctor, Ernest ate sparingly, rested more,
and talked about reducing his drinking. He would invariably
get into bed after the afternoon *corrida* and stay there, reading,
until nine or ten o'clock, when he'd get up to dress for dinner.
Some nights he did not get up at all and ordered dinner in his

room, eating it off a bed tray. He resumed keeping urine specimens in drinking glasses in the bathroom, and occasionally a
sample was dispatched to Dr. Madinoveitia.

Ernest was a prodigious reader and his bed table at the
Palace, like his bed tables everywhere, was piled high with a
wide assortment of reading matter. To approach a magazine
stand with him was a unique experience. He would carefully
go down the lines of magazines on display and choose just
about one of everything, except what he called the ladies'-aid
magazines: *Good Housekeeping, Ladies' Home Journal*, etc. He
would cart off twenty or more magazines, but the amazing part
of it was that he actually read them through and would discuss
their contents. Spanish, French and Italian kiosks were treated
with equal patronage. At the *finca* he regularly subscribed to
*Harper's, Atlantic Monthly, Holiday, Field & Stream, Sports
Afield, True, Time, Newsweek* and *The Southern Jesuit;* two
British publications, *Sport and Country* and *The Field;* a Mexican jai-alai magazine, *Cancha;* and a number of Italian and
Spanish weeklies. In addition, Scribner's sent him an unceasing
supply of books in response to lists he sent them; and he received a steady flow of unsolicited books from all other publishers who hoped he might say something that could be quoted
on a dust jacket.

One evening while Ernest was propped up on his Palace
Hotel bed, deeply immersed in a Spanish bullfight magazine,
he received an unexpected visit from Luis Miguel Dominguin—
at that time Spain's number-one matador. He was a lithe, magnificently handsome man who came from a family of bullfighters; even his beautiful sister Carmen had once performed brilliantly in the ring. Dominguin had not fought for over a year,
following a severe stomach *cornada*, but he had recently received highly lucrative offers from South America and was
thinking of returning to the bullfight wars. He came to the
Palace to ask Ernest to visit his girl, Ava Gardner, who was
hospitalized with a very painful gallstone. Ava had appeared
in *The Killers*, which Ernest considered his only good movie,
and a film which he called *The Snows of Zanuck*.

After he had left, Ernest said, "Christ, but Luis looked awful, didn't he? At his peak he's a combination Don Juan and Hamlet, but now looked beat up and drained. Probably logging too much time at Miss Ava's bedside."

Ava was surrounded by hospital nuns when we went to see her. They were fixing her bed, taking her pulse, marking her chart and cleaning her room; she was on the long-distance telephone to Hollywood, talking to the head of a studio. In a commanding voice.

"I don't give a goddamn how many scripts you send. I am not, repeat not, *not*, *NOT* going to play Ruth Etting!"

Five-second listening pause.

"And you can take that contract and shove it up your heinie!"

A sister smoothed the sheets and pulled them up a bit higher on Ava's shoulders.

"Don't give me that crap about commitment and you'll get . . . and don't interrupt me; it's my call! What in Christ's name are you trying to do to me? Great part? I stand there mouthing words like a goddamn goldfish while you're piping in some goddamn dubbed voice!"

A sister plumped up the pillows behind Ava's back, and smiled upon her.

"I said a *dramatic* part, for Christ's sake, and you send me Ruth Etting! It's no wonder I've got this attack. I ought to send you the bill . . . Oh, shut up!"

Ava hung up, swept her hand out to Ernest, smiled beautifully, and said, in a soft, lyric voice, "Hello, Ernest."

"I take it the sisters are not bilingual," Ernest said, taking her hand.

"The sisters are darling," Ava said, patting one and smiling at her, whereupon all of them smiled upon Ava, "and I love this hospital so much I almost don't want to pass this goddamn stone. Sit here on the bed, Papa, and talk to me. I'm absolutely floored you could come." Their work done, the sisters withdrew. Dominguin and I sat on chairs.

"Are you going to live in Spain?" Ernest asked.

"Yes. I sure am. I'm just a country girl at heart. I don't like New York or Paris. I'd love to live here permanently. What have I got to go back to? I have no car, no house, nothing. Sinatra's got nothing either. All I ever got out of any of my marriages was the two years Artie Shaw financed on an analyst's couch."

"Tell you the truth, Daughter, analysts spook me, because I've yet to meet one who had a sense of humor."

"You mean," Ava asked, incredulously, "you've never had an analyst?"

"Sure I have. Portable Corona number three. That's been my analyst. I'll tell you, even though I am not a believer in the Analysis, I spend a hell of a lot of time killing animals and fish so I won't kill myself. When a man is in rebellion against death, as I am in rebellion against death, he gets pleasure out of taking to himself one of the godlike attributes, that of giving it."

"That's too deep for me, Papa."

Dominguin told Ernest that he had arranged a *tienta* to see what kind of shape he was in, and invited us to attend. Ava promised she'd make it even if the nuns had to push her there in her hospital bed.

The *tienta*, which is a testing of calves for bravery, was held in a glistening *plazita* (miniature bull ring) on the bull-breeding ranch of Antonio Perez, which was located in the magnificent high country at Quadusaura in the Escorial, in the lee of the Guadaramus. We left Madrid in a procession of three cars, a Vauxhall, Dominguin's custom Cadillac, and Ernest's Lancia, and arrived at the ranch around noon. Dominguin would work the calves with the *muleta*, and they would be slightly *pic*-ed to get their heads down, but there would be no killing. By testing a few of the animals, an owner can determine characteristics of the herds from which they come, enabling him to make decisions on future breeding. There was an undercurrent of excitement not ordinarily associated with a *tienta*, for Dominguin would be testing himself as well as the calves to determine whether he would continue his career.

"These calves," Ernest explained to Ava, "are sometimes more

difficult than bulls; they whip around faster and have better
co-ordination. Don't let the name 'calf' fool you. I've seen a
lot of guys run through at *tientas*."

Ava stood with Ernest at the ring wall, behind a wooden
barrera, as they watched Dominguin work the first cow that
came charging into the ring. After Dominguin's remarkably
graceful performance, Ernest turned to Ava and said, "Did you
see what Luis Miguel did to that cow? He made it into something. He convinced it. He gave it a personality and then made
a star out of it. That cow went out of here proud as hell."

"He's a lovely man, isn't he?" Ava said.

"Are you serious about him?" Ernest asked.

"How do I know? We've been together for two months now,
but I speak no Spanish, he speaks no English, so we haven't
been able to communicate yet."

"Don't worry—you've communicated what counts," Ernest
said.

At this point the cow Dominguin had been working, a mean
little beast with a three-foot horn spread, suddenly lost interest
in the *muleta* and decided to charge Ernest instead. Ernest had
been leaning against the wall, a good distance away from the
protective *barrera*. Everyone, and especially Mary, shouted at
him to break for cover, but he did not budge and as the calf
came charging into him he grabbed one of its horns with one
hand and its nose with the other and flung it away from him.
Dominguin then ran over and made the *quite*, leading the cow
back to the center of the ring. "Not bad for a guy who's supposed to be beat up," Ava said to Ernest.

"I'm beat up," Ernest answered, "but not in the clutch."

Dominguin worked five calves, and when he was finished he
was perspiring and tired. "Ah, Papa," he said, "if only I had
your arms. Feel his arm," he said to Ava, pointing, and she did,
approvingly. "Ah, the arms and the legs after so long a vacation," Dominguin said sadly.

"Use double *muletas* and a big sword," Ernest said. "That'll
build up the arms." Dominguin sat down against the wall to
rest. Ava asked Ernest how he thought Dominguin had worked.
"Never worry about him," Ernest said. "He is a prince among

matadors. He is like the great matador Maera, who never worried because he knew more about the bulls than the bulls themselves knew. There are bullfighters who do it just for the money—they are worthless. The only one who matters is the bullfighter who feels it, so that if he did it for nothing, he would do it as well. Same holds true for damn near everyone else."

I left Madrid for Paris toward the end of May, but Ernest and I spoke on the telephone before I returned to the States in June. Mary and he were in Naples, where they were about to board the *Morosiu* for a long, slow voyage back to Cuba.

Ernest said he had seen a new matador, Antonio Ordoñez, whom he liked very much. This was the first time I heard Ordoñez's name. He was married to Dominguin's sister Carmen —the beautiful one who as a teen-ager had been acclaimed for her bravura and style in the ring. Antonio was the son of the matador Cayetano Ordoñez, who in the Twenties fought under the name Niña de la Palma; Cayetano and Ernest had been good friends and he had been the prototype for Pedro Romero, Lady Brett's matador-lover, in *The Sun Also Rises*.

"I wish you had seen him," Ernest said, speaking of Antonio. "Classic. If he keeps on and doesn't get put out of action, he can be as good as his father. Maybe better. Rupert thought so too. The only thing worries me about young Ordoñez, having known his father so well and so many other fine matadors, some of whom were killed, and some who lost out to fear and other such occupational afflictions—I long ago resolved never to be friends with a matador again because the agony for me was too great on those days when my friends could not handle the bull because of fear. On any given day, any matador, no matter how great or how young, can suffer an attack of fear and be virtually incapacitated. When it used to hit my friends I suffered right along with them, but it was an idiotic torture since I was not hired for the job and its agonies. So I swore off matadors as friends. But now, with young Antonio, I am tempted—I think I have learned some things that have helped me write off fear as a personal problem. That would make it

easier to be friends with Antonio. He has such a great sense of
alegría."

"What's *alegría?*"

"It's a deep-going happiness that nothing can kill. When
you'll meet him you'll see why I'm tempted. Of course, any
given afternoon my hold over fear can be broken. Then I'll be
in the soup again. But maybe it's worth the risk. I thought
about it quite a lot during the drive to Naples after we left
Madrid."

"How was that trip?"

"Wonderful."

"How are you feeling?"

"Think will beat this rap okay if kidneys straighten out. The
right one was hurt bad. Just beginning to find out how bad.
But am following doctor's orders. Had only four drinks of
whiskey and water in fifteen days in Spain. Then had a couple
in Bayonne, a couple yesterday, six in all. No gin. It is a lousy
bore for everybody else and for me. After you left, Mary and I
skipped the fights one day and went up and picnicked at the
bridge. Next time I'll take you there."

"You mean the *For Whom the Bell Tolls* bridge?"

"Nothing's changed. Just as it was. They put it back together
after the war, reassembling all the stones that had fallen into
the river bed after we blew it."

"Tell me, Papa—did you finish up the Capitaine Cook's? And
what about the cases of champagne and the *foie gras* and
pickled mushrooms and all the rest?"

"Just left it all in the closet in the room. Told the chamber-
maid to take it home to her kids."

Chapter Eight

Havana ◆ 1954-55

Ernest had no sooner returned to Cuba in the summer of 1954 than the pressure of the Nobel Prize began to build. What should have been a quiet time to recuperate from his physical troubles became instead one of the most concentrated assaults he had ever been subjected to. And never in his life was he less able to cope with it.

When he had won the Pulitzer Prize the year before for *The Old Man and the Sea*, he had easily beaten off the publicity assaults. But now he was in no shape for this tougher Prize-combat and it took something out of him he never got back.

The assault started in September, when the newspapers began speculating that Ernest would get the Prize. He phoned me to say that he had received, among many magazine inquiries, a request from Doug Kennedy, the editor of *True*, for me to write an article about the sports he had played from boyhood on. I said I would if he wanted me to.

"No," he said. "What I'd like you to do is go see Kennedy and explain that I'm working and would like to put off such a piece until a later time. That all right with you?"

"Sure. How are you feeling? The back any better?"

"Well, for your own information, and yours only, I have not been without considerable pain ever since I saw you. My back still hurts so badly that when I move it too much it brings the sweat out. I try to be good about this and I ignore it to the limit of my abilities but I think it would get on almost anybody's nerves. It gets on mine anyway. I can make the back and head feel better by taking a drink. But if I took a drink every time I hurt or felt bad I could never write, and writing is the only thing that makes me feel that I'm not wasting my time sticking around."

He said the constant assault of visitors was brutal. He had finished a short story and was thirty-seven pages into another one when Bill Lowe showed up with a proposal to make an African documentary film in the fall. This seemed like a good idea until Lowe put out a press release to the effect that Ernest had agreed to write, act in and co-produce an original full-length feature. End of film project. Then right after Lowe left, Ava Gardner appeared, and she had no sooner left than Winston Guest arrived, and then Dave Shilling, the flyer. Next, the U.S. Air Force brought out some enlisted personnel who had won an award as Aircraftsmen-of-the-Month, which included visiting the Hemingways as part of their award. Then Luis Miguel Dominguin showed up and had been there for nine days; Sinsky turned up at the same time and was drunk for four days.

"I go into my bedroom and work no matter what," Ernest said, "but it is murder. Roberto, who as you know is my right arm, gets sick. He is now convalescing on a voyage on Sinsky's ship. Sinsky never drinks at sea. Only at our house. And I am a son-of-a-bitch who needs to be let alone to write.

"It is about as restful and favorable to the production of literature as Hürtgen Forest. But have started the counter-attack. Won't take any phone calls from anyone. Long distance neither. If we had any brains we should have been killed in Africa at Murchison Falls and come back under some other names and I could have continued to write posthumously. Will begin to write you sensible letters, soon as I get the joint cleaned out. Hope they don't clean me out of it first."

On October 28th the award was formally announced by the Swedish Academy: "For his powerful style-forming mastery of the art of modern narration, as most recently evinced in *The*

145 Havana · 1954–55

Old Man and the Sea ... Hemingway's earlier writings displayed brutal, cynical and callous signs which may be considered at variance with the Nobel Prize requirements for a work of ideal tendencies. But on the other hand he also possesses a heroic pathos which forms the basic element of his awareness of life, a manly love of danger and adventure, with a natural admiration of every individual who fights the good fight in a world of reality overshadowed by violence and death."

Ernest excused himself from attending the ceremonies in Stockholm, giving as the reason his unhealed crash injuries, but even if he had been in the best of health I seriously doubt that he would have gone. Ernest had made very few public appearances in his lifetime, attributable to his intense shyness and his smoldering hatred of The Tuxedo. "Wearing underwear is as formal as I ever hope to get," he once told me—and to my knowledge he never wore any.

But he did send an acceptance message, which was read for him at the ceremonies in Stockholm by the United States Ambassador, John M. Cabot: "Members of the Swedish Academy, ladies and gentlemen. Having no facility for speech-making and no command of oratory, nor any domination of rhetoric, I wish to thank the administrators of the generosity of Alfred Nobel for this prize. No writer who knows the great writers who did not receive the prize can accept it other than with humility. There is no need to list these writers. Everyone here may make his own list according to his knowledge and his conscience. It would be impossible for me to ask the Ambassador of my country to read a speech in which a writer said all of the things which are in his heart. Things may not be immediately discernible in what a man writes and in this, sometimes, he is fortunate, but eventually they are quite clear and by these, and a degree of alchemy that he possesses, he will endure or be forgotten. Writing at its best is a lonely life. Organizations for writers palliate the writer's loneliness but I doubt if they improve his writing. He grows in public stature as he sheds his loneliness and often his work deteriorates. For he does his work alone, and if he is a good enough writer, he must face eternity

or the lack of it each day. For a true writer, each book should
be a new beginning where he tries again for something that is
beyond attainment. He should always try for something that
has never been done or that others have tried and failed. Then
sometimes, with great luck, he will succeed. How simple the
writing of literature would be if it were only necessary to write
in another way what has been well written. It is because we
have had such great writers in the past that a writer is driven
far out past where he can go, out to where no one can help
him. I have spoken too long for a writer. A writer should write
what he has to say and not speak it. Again I thank you."

At this time I was at the Pentagon researching an article I
was writing on the Congressional Medal of Honor, but I had
been following the chaotic course of events in Cuba, and sym-
pathizing with Ernest about the inroads I knew it was making
on his work and disposition. When I got back to my Washington
hotel late one afternoon—in fact it was New Year's Day, 1955—
there was a message to call the overseas operator in Havana
for an urgent call. It took four hours to get through. Ernest's
voice was thick and he spoke faster than usual, sometimes almost running his words together. There was a steady hum of
background noise similar to what you hear when someone calls
you from a corner telephone booth. I couldn't imagine why he
was calling.

"Hotch, I called to apologize about all the damn confusion,"
he said.

"What confusion?"

"You can't know what it's been like. But I wanted to lay it
out in detail for you. We're too good friends to let a thing like
this cause any trouble."

"What trouble, Papa? I'm not aware—"

"It wasn't till September that I could crank myself up; then
I started writing maybe better than I ever have and had thirty-
five thousand words done, after two months of trying and failing
every day, and was truly going wonderfully. Then the Prize
thing began to build up and I still kept working until the day
they sprung. Had no chance to enjoy it, if any of it is supposed

to be enjoyable; just photographers, people misquoting you
and yammer, yammer, yack, yack—and my book, all I gave a
damn about, and which I had been living in day and night,
being knocked out of my head like clubbing a fish.

"Well, for two to three days there are these photographers
and all the rest and then I say there won't be any more and I
get back into the book. Then characters come down anyway,
no matter what you say. That you are writing a book means
nothing. Bob Manning of *Time* phoned Mary and said he had
to write a cover story and that he would write it whether I
saw him or not. He said he wanted to make it good instead of
bad and would I call back. Of course, when they pull that on
you, it's nothing but blackmail, but effective. I talked to him
on the phone and said I would give anything if *Time* would
not write a cover story on me, but he said they were going to
do it anyway. So I agreed to see him if he did not bring a
researcher nor a tape-recorder and if all questions on wars,
religion, personal life, wives and so forth were barred. I said
that I was working hard and it was murder to interrupt and
that to interrupt a man while he was writing a book and going
well was as bad as to interrupt a man when he was in bed
making love. He agreed on this but said the thing had to be
done and they were going to do it anyway and he wanted it
to be a good piece rather than a bad one."

"Papa, why are you telling me—"

"Because I wanted you to get the background on the *True*
thing."

"What *True* thing?"

"So I said I'd give him two days, and he came down and
stayed in the Little House and that's all he got, two days. We
talked about writing, which after all is the trade a writer is
supposed to know something about. I do not regard all this as
disloyalty to *True*, which is not, after all, my alma mater. I
would rather say 'For God, For Country and For Keeps' than
'For Yale and For *True*.'"

"Papa, listen, let me get this straight about *True*—"

"Listen to the rest of it. So you know. Manning no sooner

clears out than a London *Times* man shows up without giving
me any address where I could tell him not to come, and a
Swede with a Magnum photographer who interrogated (and
probably got all the answers wrong) and photographed for six
hours and fifty minutes, and the Japanese chargé d'affaires,
who speaks a little basic English, plus an elderly Japanese journalist who he is the interpreter for, along with a delegation
from the Rotary Club of Guanabacoa, then more Swedes
flown from Sweden, and I won't try to fill you in on all of it.
I am still trying to write through this but am going nuts fast.
And while all this is going on, some problems have come up
about reinvesting for the children's estates, and I have to check
on the five percent debentures offered in exchange for six percent preferred.

"When I finally got the children's end straightened out, I
thought I had better get the hell out before I blew up. So Mary
and I went out on *Pilar*, but I forgot how sound you have to
be to handle a rod, especially to fish in 'The Tin Kid.' So I
don't fish, can't swim, don't get any exercise. Hotch, this all
sounds like one long blab of crybabyismo, but when I get
interrupted when I'm working good it really ruins me. Now
I've got so sick of myself, of answering questions, of photographers, of making goddamn pronouncements, of pieces for and
against me, I don't want to ever hear about or think about
myself so I can get writing clean and fine the way I was going.
But how can I do that when we no sooner get back from the
boat yesterday than Mary takes a call from Mr. Douglas Kennedy, editor, who says that he had planned the whole April
issue of *True* around the story you were going to write about
me, that he had reservations to come down to consult with me
on the technical fishing part, that now all this had to be canceled, and that you were losing a chance to earn a sizable fee.
Mary told me that he said, 'I know your husband is fed up,
that he wants to get back to work. But I have just one question:
if your husband will submit to the Bob Mannings and the Swedes
and the Japs and whatnot, why won't he sit still for a magazine
that has published him and that he likes?' We have no tape

Once in a while, Ernest climbed up to the study at the top of the white tower.

Outside Finca Vigía, Cuba, 1948, the Hemingways with Black Dog, Ernest's constant companion at the typewriter.

Ernest with members of his shooting club.

Christmas, 1949: En route from Paris to Venice, the Hemingways with Jigee and Peter Viertel high up in the top turret of the walled fort of St. Louis at Aigues-Mortes.

Venice, January, 1950, wearing his indispensable Hong Kong jacket, Ernest with Mary and a favorite companion, the young Adriana Ivancich. Just out of the picture—the Bridge of Sighs.

Ernest and Mary entering the splendid Roman coliseum at Nîmes, France, during the 1949 trip.

All hell broke loose in the mountain town of Cuneo, where this autograph mob grew wildly out of hand and only an army squadron saved Ernest from being crushed.

The next day, with the Lancia and driver Adamo; Ernest had his beard shaved off the night before to avoid recognition and avert another Cuneo.

At the 1954 Escorial tienta, *Ernest demonstrated his cape technique for Ava Gardner and Luis Miguel Dominguin, Spain's reigning matador.*

Part of the 1956 Zaragoza feria *mob: Rafe Henderson, Babe Henderson, Peter Buckley, Hemingway, Rupert Belville, Polly Peabody, and Mary Hemingway (foreground).*

Ernest beams with pride at the Guardia Civil who had stoood sentinel over Mary's treasure-laden handbag.

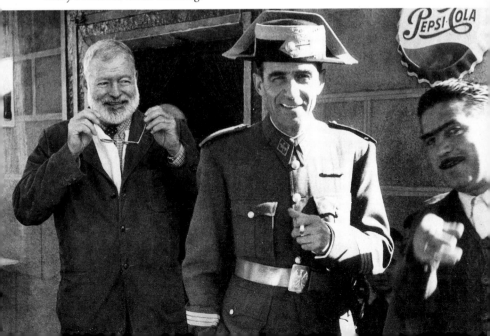

Ernest at the cold mountain stream where Pilar of For Whom the Bell Tolls *washed her feet.*

Ernest with Owl, autocrat of the Ketchum house.

Scouting mallards with Bud Purdy, the rancher, and Gary Cooper.

One of Ernest's typical luncheon mobs nearing the end of a four-hour Spanish lunch.

High up in the moss-carpeted beech-wooded Irati, Ernest found an afternoon's sweet surcease from the Pamplona tumult and was joined by this sweet hound who mysteriously came out of the forest to lie down beside him.

The 1959 birthday party at Málaga: Ernest shooting a cigarette from the lips of Antonio Ordoñez (General Buck Lanham at left).

The fire extinguished, the firemen joined the party and here Annie Davis and Beverly Bentley congratulate the fire chief, whose hat Ernest is wearing and whose boot Antonio is autographing.

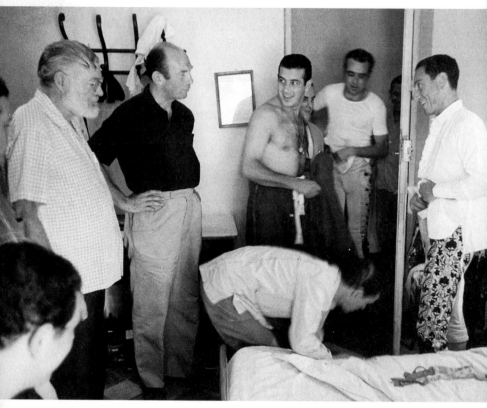

At this point the author still thought his role as sobresaliente *was a joke; it was all like a fraternity initiation. Later, standing at the bull-ring entrance with Dominguin and Ordoñez, the world's leading matadors, El Pecas was suddenly impressed with the solemnity of the occasion.*

The view from Ernest's Ketchum home.

Lunches on the 1959 Ketchum-to-Key West trip were roadside, featuring Mary's pheasant and Ernest's crackling cold Sancerre.

Ernest and Mary in the living room of the finca.

1960, Ernest's last days at his beloved finca, *the proud old house sad and crumbled, as was its master.*

The Hemingways, drinks in hand, on an evening walk from the main house down to the pool.

*This is the last photograph I took of Ernest. He is standing in the hall of his
Cuban house, backed by his two great passions—the bullfight and the hunt. But
he is strangely detached from them, as if they had never been a part of his life.*

recorder on our phone but this is what Mary told me and what
I have just gone into her room to have her confirm. She only
told me about it this morning."

"But, Papa, this whole thing is unbelievable!"

"No, it's damn believable—at least from my end of it. Now
it is a fact that I like *True* as a magazine and have it sent to
Patrick in Tanganyika, but I thought I had made it clear to
you, and you to him, that there was to be no article now. I
have been writing my closest and oldest friends, asking them
to please omit visits they had planned because I was working
and not in shape to see people. Right after I spoke to you about
True, for instance, I wrote Alfred Vanderbilt asking him not
to come down on a visit he had planned, and I have known
him since 1933."

"Papa, I phoned Kennedy right after you spoke to me and
explained it all to him, and he said would I mind if he wrote
you, asking you to reconsider. I said that was up to him but
that I wouldn't write anything without your permission and as
far as I was concerned he was wasting his time. I had no idea
that he . . ."

"Well, in case Mr. Kennedy still thinks I am seeking publicity while pretending that it is harmful to me and an interruption to me, please tell him that this week, so far, I have
turned down the chance of a piece by J.P. McEvoy in the
Reader's Digest, some six different journalists who have wanted
to come out to the house, a man from *Argosy* who, according
to the Air Attaché at the Embassy, would pay a thousand dollars if I would let him come out and take some pictures, and
just this morning I wrote a letter to Bob Edge turning down a
proposition that would have been very attractive to anyone
who wished publicity.

"Every day there are letters, phone calls and brutal interrup-
tions. It is getting on Mary's nerves and it hit mine a long time
ago. I do not want to be driven out of here in the good working
months. It is my home and my work place and I love it. But I
am not a public performer, nor am I running for office. I am a
writer and I have a right to work and also a right to make a

fight to stay alive. I like *True* and have always had good relations with them. But I should think that they could understand
how it is to write under really bad handicaps when you have
something and are going good and have to stay in it for the
whole twenty-four hours and not be interrupted. Should a guy
be asked to throw away and lose a book that is as much a part
of his life as anything can be to help any magazine get out
any given issue?"

I realized by now that Ernest was not just venting his angry
annoyance at *True*—because *True* was certainly of no importance to him—but that he was assailing the whole bloody force
that had been crushing him since the day he survived the
African crash. Although this force took the form of journalists
and photographers and broadcasters and magazine editors, the
real force was the world's insatiable curiosity about him, and
there was no way to assuage it. I found it almost unbearable
to listen to him crying out for respite, pleading for the isolation
that is a writer's blood, but knowing in his heart that he had
been put to rout.

"Nobody takes the excuse that you want to work or that you
don't want any piece or that you've gotten pathological about
pieces about you and one goddamn more and you'd never write
another bloody line. Hotch, if you can, forgive me for being so
difficult and know it comes from being beat up and also from
being spooked about destroying what I write with through all
this publicity. It really makes me sick."

"I understand, Papa. I understand everything. Honestly I do.
I'll take care of *True* so they understand. Kennedy's a good
guy—he's just made a mistake."

"Hotch, I explained to you privately that my nerves are shot
to hell with the pain, and that is not a thing I would tell anybody. You know that a first-rate writer has to have a delicate
writing mechanism. You don't write with a club or a hatchet.
You can't use junk. You have to take it cold turkey. You look
awful and the lousy pain shows on your face. So they take
photographs of you. During that hell time after the Prize somebody told me that one photographer boasted at the Floridita

after he left the house that he got four hundred twenty-five shots of me. The guy shooting all of the time, even crowding into the pantry when I was talking private on the long-distance. Then the outfit that made them sent them all to me as a present, thinking I'd like to have them. Some four hundred fourteen of them looked more or less like Chinese-torture shots. They had even thought of taking a picture of Blackie lying in front of my empty chair, just in case.

"Well, a cable just arrived this morning, New Year's Day, addressed to Robert Ruark, care of Ernest Hemingway, Finca Vigía, San Francisco de Paula, Cuba. I guess Mr. Kennedy will never be convinced I didn't invite Mr. Ruark down. Felt pretty cheerful this morning until I saw the cable. Then Mary remembered to tell me about Kennedy's call. Went to bed at ten on New Year's Eve, didn't eat supper, didn't drink anything, washed and scrubbed, put the new stuff the skin specialist gave me yesterday on the chest and on the face—had clipped off the damn beard for Christmas—and in four days my face broke out with something a little handsomer than jungle rot. The face makes impetigo look like The Skin You Love to Touch. It is sort of comic to have this all outside while you are making your main fight inside. Don't know whether it's the antibiotics' revenge cr whether somebody is sticking pins into a piece of wax in Africa."

"I'm sorry about all this, Papa. It's a lousy way to start the New Year."

"Want to hear my New Year's resolution? Not to pay any attention to any physical troubles, but just follow doctor's orders and try to train good and get my work done."

"I'll second that. You're probably going to have one hell of a year to make up for the last one."

"Don't need a big year. Just need to be left alone to write. Good luck, Hotch."

"You too, Papa." I hung up and looked at the clock; he had been on the phone for over an hour.

The following day Ernest phoned again. His voice sounded clearer, and his speech was less hurried. After some general talk about Washington and the Pentagon, and badinage over whether Batista or Eisenhower shot a better game of golf, he returned to the previous day's discussion. "Been thinking some of it's my fault for not having written sooner and more completely on the rejection to *True*. But I was forty-five thousand words into the new book, writing nothing else but checks, pouring out my stuff in some sort of race against I cannot tell you exactly what. You could call it trying to keep from going nuts, I guess. Think of it this way: injuries to the brain and the spinal cord, the kidneys, and the liver, which is the seat of valor, don't clear up by snapping your fingers and saying, 'Clear up.' You have to take it slow and easy and you can do only so much a day. I opted for writing, which cheers me up and takes me out of whatever hell I happen to be in.

"So now we have poor *True* bitched by me. I said I could not interrupt my writing but then I prove myself a liar, if not much worse, by seeing Bob Manning of *Time*, obviously seeking publicity for myself. But actually laying it on the line in the interview for poor bloody Ezra Pound and knowing all the trouble I will get into for it. No doubt about it—the editor of *True* is dealing with a first-class heel. So now we should seek a solution. Tell *True* to publish anything that has been written about my sports exploits. The only sports I was ever outstanding in were fishing and shooting. You would have to get that from people who have seen me do it. I do not know who could give you the true gen on those. It certainly should not come from me. I have had long strings of shooting in the field and on big game was hotter than Willie Mays in baseball. But am I the son-of-a-bitch to describe them? The guys who know about these things are inarticulate, reserved, and would think someone was trying to frame Ernie.

"What *True* can do is publish whatever has been written, and I'll mail you a statement that can run in a box accompanying the piece, and *True*'s troubles will be over. A visit by Kennedy is out; repeat *out*. Don't break it to him too gently."

The statement arrived in the mail a few days later. I never gave it to *True;* they eventually published a symposium of pre-

viously published biography and anecdotes about Ernest, almost
none of them about sports.

I did not hear from Ernest for a couple of months after that.
I began to worry about his physical condition, but he finally
wrote that his health was much better all the way around since
the weather had warmed enough for him to swim. He said he
had been taking a lot of exercise and had been out in the boat
twice, which loosened him up and made him feel better. He
thought his back would be absolutely okay within a few weeks.
His work was going good, too, averaging over four thousand
words a week, which he said was too much for him. I thought
that despite its attempt to sound positive, the letter had a sad
and subdued ring.

It was a time when I myself was not running as a cheerful, and
I guess my letters must have reflected it because in June of 1955
Ernest accused us of being "tandem morbids."

"I have a suggestion for alleviation of morbidity," he said.
"Mary and I are going over to the Key West house—the small
house with the pool. The pool is sixty-foot regulation, fills and
empties overnight, semisalt wonderful water. House really lovely
and charming place. Why don't you meet us there and we can
sun and swim and discuss the play you want to do? We can
use it as a consolation for not having got to Europe. The only
negative satisfaction is that I don't think Europe would have
been any fun last year. They never had a day of spring and it
was wet, cold, overcrowded and expensive as hell, and summer
never came at all. Not just a bad British summer. Everywhere.

"This winter has been miserable with floods, and in the spring
it will be overrun with tourists. When you get homesick for it,
remember the Autobahn with the signs on both sides from
Mestre to Milano and Milano to Torino. You can remember that
lovely day and how the Alps looked to have something to hold
on to. That stretch below Turin to the border. But I can get
Black-Ass about going anywhere when I remember those auto-

graph people in a remote town like Cuneo. You'll like Key West —it's the Saint Tropez of the poor."

Chapter Nine

Key West ♦ 1955

On the morning of July 3rd I flew to Miami, where I caught the small afternoon plane to Key West and took a taxi to 414 Olivia Street, the address Ernest had given me.

When the taxi stopped, I was sure the driver had taken me to the wrong place. It was a street of grimy, run-down houses with ramshackle sidewalk fences that contained yards of high weeds. When Ernest had bought his place in the 1930's, the neighborhood was sparsely settled and the few houses that were there were of a quality that matched his. (Actually Ernest had two houses: a large main house and a small, more modern house that had been constructed beside the pool.) But the years had been unkind to the neighborhood, which was now crowded and seedy, and the Hemingway property was an oasis amid the squalor. Ernest had not lived there since 1940, when he was divorced from Pauline; it had become her property as part of the divorce settlement and she had continued to reside there with their children until her recent death, when the property had passed to the children. But the children did not want to live there, nor were they around to look after it. So it fell to Ernest to try to keep it rented for them and to attend to its problems. The pool house was unrented at the moment, and in addition to his desire to get away, Ernest had come over to attend to maintenance problems and to arrange for a real estate agent to rent it.

The address I had been given was that of the pool house,
but when I knocked on the screen door, no one responded. I
carried my bag in and called out but no one was around. It
was a two-story house, the downstairs consisting of a kitchen,
through which I had entered, a small bedroom with a single
bed, and a large, high-ceilinged living room that had been
furnished with imagination and taste. Crammed book shelves
ran from floor to ceiling. The floor was a beautifully designed
tile, and the front of the room opened onto a charming terrace,
beyond which was the pool, surrounded by verdant, extrava-
gantly colored tropical plants and trees.

On the outside of the house was a winding iron staircase,
the only access to the second floor, which, I presumed, contained the master bedroom. It was midafternoon and very hot
but the shuttered interior of the living room, with its tile floor
and wicker furniture and cool vista, was quite pleasant. I had
rightly guessed that Mary and Ernest were taking a siesta, for
around five o'clock I heard descending steps on the spiral staircase and a moment later Ernest, wearing swim trunks, came
into the room.

He had gained considerable weight, most of it in his girth.
His hair had thinned and his white beard was scraggly. His
face bore signs of the white scaling which constantly abused
him, not a serious condition but an irritating one that caused
his skin to flake off as if from sunburn. The condition was one
of the reasons why, many years before, he had started to grow
a beard: to cover the look of his skin and to eliminate the irri-
tation of shaving. Ernest sometimes called his facial condition
skin cancer, but this was Ernest's pronouncement and not that
of an M.D.

He looked old. There were lines in his face I had not seen
before, especially the vertical lines between his eyes. It had
always been characteristic for him to walk lightly on the balls
of his highly arched feet, but now he walked flat-footed,
slightly favoring his right leg.

He settled me into the little bedroom, and then we both went
for a swim in the very warm, brownish salt water that had the
effect of a sulfur bath. Ernest entered the pool cautiously, stop-

ping several times on the pool steps to splash water across his
middle. He swam breast stroke very slowly, his head out of the
water, his frog-kick without force, his arms moving through the
water listlessly. As he reached each end of the pool, he would
stop and rest several minutes. Mary came down and joined us
while we were swimming.

After we had changed to dry clothes, we had drinks on the
terrace and Ernest began to shed his siesta heaviness and some
of his natural juice began to flow.

Mary prepared to go pick up a package that had arrived
from New York. Ernest was very solicitous about how she felt
and whether she had taken several varieties of medicine. "Poor
Mary," he said, after she had gone, "she's taken a bad beating;
all that Nobel Prize crap, and then her father so bad up in
Gulfport, she having to commute back and forth from Havana.
He died finally and she had to get her mother settled and handle
her. It was all an awful job. I have been trying to help her
get back into shape, help her with our income tax—it was a
complicated year to keep track of—and write on book every
day."

Mary returned with several huge cardboard boxes, the fruit
of her pickings from an Abercrombie & Fitch catalogue. Such
items could not be sent to Cuba without paying heavy duty,
so being in Key West was a rare opportunity to stock up. Mary
took a small cardboard box out of one of the big boxes and
handed it to Ernest. It contained a tiny transistor radio, which
Ernest was surprised and delighted with; he kissed Mary and
said it was his first successful toy in years. We took it outside
to get clearer reception. In a few moments Mary emerged from
the living room, carrying a high pile of Viyella shirts, pants,
shorts, socks, belts and other haberdashery. She stopped in front
of Ernest and held them out, as one would present an offering
at an altar, but Ernest just narrowed his eyes and regarded
them suspiciously.

"I feel like I've been traded and have to wear a new uniform," he said. He inspected the pile very gingerly and settled
for six shirts, a pair of shorts and a belt. Everything else was
to be returned. "Listen, Kitner," Ernest said to Mary, his voice

even and serious, "my Kraut belt has disappeared. I know I had it when I hit here and they cleaned me out fast."

"I'll look for it, lamb," Mary said. "I'm sure it's around."

"That's what the sheriff said when he got the news about Judge Crater," Ernest replied.

That evening Ernest decided to call the *finca* to find out how everything was; he approached making the call as one would approach being shot out of the Ringling Brothers cannon. On those occasions when he phoned me from the *finca*, the call was always placed by someone else, usually Roberto, so that *initiating* a call was a new experience for him and, his attitude toward phones being what it was, a very upsetting one.

To begin with, he had forgotten his phone number and had to ask Mary. Then, in communicating with the overseas operator he had all the manifestations of stage fright. When he finally got René on the phone he spoke too loudly and distinctly, the way some orators do regardless of microphone and public-address system. Ernest had made the call because he was concerned about Black Dog and a cat named Boise, both of whom were under the weather when he left. René reported that they had recovered, and Ernest was happy when he hung up. "I'm proud of that boy René," he said, "because after eight years in my employ he has learned to answer the phone and say in English, 'Mr. Hemingway is not here.'"

The next morning, while I was having breakfast in the kitchen, Ernest took sips from a bottle of cold vodka which he took from the refrigerator. He drank constantly, the most I had ever seen him drink. It was obvious that he was still suffering from his crash wounds, and liquor transfusions helped ease the pain. He washed down a large variety of pills with these libations.

"Hotchner," he said with conspiratorial earnestness, "I have stumbled across a new invention which may make us dependently wealthy. Regard!" He took two glasses, put a couple of jiggers of Scotch in each, added water and placed the glasses in the freezing compartment of the refrigerator. "While we are waiting for the *dénouement*, I will show you the joint." He took me up the winding staircase and showed me the second-floor bedroom, which was a huge, wonderfully decorated room with wide windows that gave out on a beautiful panorama of tropical greenery.

Then, returning below, he led me to a door off the living room that opened into a storeroom that contained first editions, original manuscripts, letters and unpublished materials. He picked up a first edition of *The Torrents of Spring*, his first published novel, a rare item, and the mildewed cover dropped off in his hand. Inside a small cardboard box was a working manuscript of *To Have and Have Not*. The pages were so stiff and deteriorated they splintered at his touch. Mildew and jungle rot and evil-chewing beetles had wrought havoc upon this storehouse of priceless memorabilia. "Just imagine," Ernest said, examining the crumbled remains of an early short-story manuscript, "if we worked for the Library of Congress. Well, one way or another, it all goes. Most of the first editions were thieved by uninvited guests and by God-knows-who when the house was loaned, without charge, to friends. The really rare, earliest first editions were conveniently small so could be slipped effortlessly by a guest into a pocket or handbag. Then add to thieving guests, cleaning out by womenies you live with. Periodicals that got in the way of housekeeping were pitched. All manuscripts were tidied up by removing them from rot-proof file cabinets and packing them into cardboard boxes where they furnished ideal nesting materials for mice and rats and were munched on by the king-sized Key West cockroach. This process, plus jungle rot and mildew, often caused complete disappearance of manuscripts *and* their cardboard containers. Many poems also went this route.

"Then, of course, there was the regrettable incident, in the days before I was getting my stuff published, when Hadley had in her possession everything I had ever written, original copies and their carbons, in a suitcase she was bringing me—it was Christmastime and I was covering the Lausanne conference for the Toronto *Star* and the suitcase was in a compartment on the train, which was in the Gare de Lyon. While Hadley went to get a bottle of Vittel water, the valise was stolen, and none of the stories or the first draft of a novel that were in it were ever recovered. Poor Hadley was so broken up about it, I actually felt worse for her than for having been robbed of everything I ever wrote. Only story that was salvaged was 'My Old Man,' which had been sent to a magazine by Lincoln Steffens and had not as yet been returned. After that we called it 'Das Kapital'—my total literary capital. I never really blamed Hadley. She had not hired on as a manuscript custodian and what she had hired on for—wife-ing—she was damn good at."

That was the only time I almost told him about my misadventure on the Orient Express with the *Across the River* manuscript.

Ernest opened the covers of a book, all the pages of which, he discovered, had been totally consumed by literary beetles. "Well," he said, "I've got a lot of other stuff stored in the back of Sloppy Joe's—must be in the same shape." Sloppy Joe's is one of Key West's most celebrated saloons.

"I used to be co-owner of Sloppy Joe's," Ernest said. "Silent partner, they call it. We had gambling in the back and that's where the real money was. But getting good dice-changers was difficult because if he was so good you couldn't detect it yourself, you knew he would steal from you. The only big expense in a gambling operation, ours included, is police protection. We paid seventy-five hundred dollars to elect a sheriff who, in his second year in office, went God-happy on us and closed us down, so we closed down the sheriff."

Mary and Ernest had been invited to an elaborate Fourth of July party but Ernest had begged off at the last moment and Mary was going alone. Ernest assured her that we could manage in her absence. He consulted his watch. "Past meridian," he said. "We can break out the serious drinks." He took the two glasses of Scotch from the freezer and replaced them with two others. The water had frozen around the Scotch, and when you tilted the glass, the Scotch cut a rivulet through the ice to reach your mouth, ice-cold and giving the illusion that you were drinking out of a mountain stream that had suddenly turned to Scotch. I complimented Ernest on his invention.

We put slabs of turtle meat, which Mary had cooked beautifully, on large pieces of pumpernickel bread and covered them generously with fresh horseradish; it was an absolutely wonderful lunch of mountain-stream Scotch and turtle sandwiches.

Later we listened to a transcript I had brought of a National Broadcasting Company radio tribute to Ernest for winning the Nobel Prize. It contained accolades and anecdotal remembrances by such as John Mason Brown, Leonard Lyons, Sidney Franklin, Marlon Brando, Max Eastman, Leon Pearson and Cornelia Otis Skinner. After listening attentively to the hour recording, Ernest said, "It sounds like Irving Stone's true fictionalization of The Life and Times of the Very Ernest Hemingway with footnotes by Frank Yerby." Then he went for his siesta.

At dusk we sat on the terrace as the first pale fireworks irritated the sky. As the dusk fell to night the fusiliers launched their more spectacular pyrotechnics and we watched the brilliant tracings dart among the low-hanging stars.

"I thought it would be pleasant to get away from the *finca*," Ernest said, his eyes fixed on the sky. "They've ruined it for me and I thought it would be pleasant to come here to a place I once loved and to reach into the past for a little peace and solitude. But I find I'm Black-Assed in this house because Pauline is dead now and this house is full of memories of the good times and of the kids when they were young and a real part of my life and of the times I worked good in the bedroom here.

"This is where I wrote 'The Snows of Kilimanjaro,' upstairs here, and that's as good as I've any right to be. Pauline and I had just come back from Africa and when we hit New York the newsboys asked me what my next project was and I said to work hard and earn enough money to get back to Africa. It ran in the papers that way and a woman who read it got in touch with me and asked me to have a drink with her. Very classy society woman, extremely wealthy, damn attractive. We had good martini conversation and she said if I wanted to return to Africa so badly, why put it off just for money when she would be very happy to go with me and my wife and foot the bill. I liked her very much and appreciated the offer but refused it.

"By the time we got down here to Key West, I had given a lot of thought to her and the offer and how it might be if I

accepted an offer like that. What it would do to a character
like me whose failings I know and have taken many soundings
on. Never wrote so directly about myself as in that story. The
man is dying, and I got that pretty good, complete with han-
dles, because I had been breathed upon by the Grim Reaper
more than once and could write about that from the inside out."

"But did the situation in 'Kilimanjaro' draw anything specific from your safari with Pauline?" I asked.

"Everything and nothing. What might interest you was Operation Amoebic Dysentery. You ever had unfriendly amoeba?"

"In the army."

"Then you know. Probably picked up mine going to Africa
on the putrefied French ship we took—long trip through the
Red Sea and Indian Ocean. Amoeba assault began soon after
safari started, but I managed to avert permanent latrine duty
on every hunting day but two. Then amoeba stepped up attack,
all-out, and I was really knocked down solid. We were in camp
on the Serengeti Plain at the time, and my condition, which I
had neglected, had suddenly turned so bad I had to fight pretty
good to hang on until we could get word back to Nairobi. Was
finally flown out in a two-seater plane that came to get me. It
was four hundred miles to Nairobi and we went by way of the
Ngorongoro Crater to the Rift Escarpment with a stop at
Arusha. It was coming out of Arusha that we had to climb fast
and wheel off the sudden-looming peak of Mount Kilimanjaro—
so there were those specifics in the story. But there was a hell
of a lot more; by the time I finished 'The Snows of Kilimanjaro,' I had put into it the material for four novels, distilled
and compressed, nothing held back because I had declared to
win with it. It took me a long time to write another short story
after that because I knew I could never write another as good as
'Kilimanjaro.' Don't think I ever did."

"Did you write any others here?"

"Sure—'A Way You'll Never Be,' for one. I had tried to write
it back in the Twenties, but had failed several times. I had
given up on it but one day here, fifteen years after those things
happened to me in a trench dugout outside Fornaci, it sud-

denly came out focused and complete. Here in Key West, of all places. Old as I am, I continue to be amazed at the sudden emergence of daffodils and stories."

The theater project which I had come down to discuss involved dramatizations of several of Ernest's stories. Over the following days he read the ones I had already done—*Hills Like White Elephants, The Sea Change, Today Is Friday, Cat in the Rain, The Battler*—and discussed them, but we spent most of our time on the stories I had not yet started work on.

"The problem for the dramatist," I explained to Ernest, "is that the very thing that gives sinew to your short story, challenges the dramatization of it. You long ago explained to me that your stories gain strength in direct ratio to what you can leave out of them, but this can be a fatal handicap to the adapter, who must guess at what was in the mind of the short-story writer."

Ernest pointed out that if what is left out is left out because the short-story writer doesn't know it, then it is a worthless story. It's only the important things you know about and omit that strengthen the story, he said. But he realized what a problem such a story creates for the dramatizer, who, he acknowledged, must achieve a different effect. He then proceeded to reveal that the real thing in back of "The Killers" was that the Swede was supposed to throw the fight but didn't. In the gym all afternoon he had rehearsed taking a dive, but during the real fight he had instinctively thrown a punch he didn't mean to and knocked his opponent out. That's why the boys were sent to kill him.

"Mr. Gene Tunney, the Shakespearean pugilist, once asked me if the Swede of the story wasn't actually Carl Andreson," Ernest said. "I told him yes, and the town wasn't Summit, New Jersey, but Summit, Illinois. But that's all I told him because the Chicago mob that sent the killers was and, as far as I know, is still very much in business. 'The Killers' was another story I tried several times before I invented it right, and that one didn't straighten itself out until I tackled it on an afternoon in

Madrid when a freak snowstorm canceled out the bullfights. I guess I left as much out of 'The Killers' as any story I ever wrote. Left out the whole city of Chicago.

"But come to think of it, I guess the story that tops them all for leave-out was 'A Clean, Well-Lighted Place.' I left everything out of that one. But you're not planning to use that, although I wish you would. May be my favorite story. That and 'The Light of the World,' which no one but me ever seemed to like. But that story has in it the only constructive thing I ever learned about women—that no matter what happened to them and how they turned, you should try to disregard all that and remember them only as they were on the best day they ever had."

Ernest went down the list of stories, giving me background and telling me in detail about the real-life bitch who was the prototype of Margot Macomber, a woman whose sole virtue was an overeagerness to get laid, "if that's a virtue in your book"; the races at San Siro, the track near the hospital in Milan where Ernest was a patient, which was the true background of "My Old Man"; and the jockey who became a good pal and about whom the story was written. He went over a manuscript of "The Snows of Kilimanjaro" and changed some of the fictional names to real ones. In this paragraph: "The rich were dull and they drank too much, or they played too much backgammon. They were dull and they were repetitious. He remembered poor Julian and his romantic awe of them and how he had started a story once that began, 'The very rich are different from you and me.' And how someone had said to Julian, Yes, they have more money. But that was not humorous to Julian. He thought they were a special glamorous race and when he found out they weren't it wrecked him just as much as any other thing that wrecked him," Ernest scratched out "Julian" and wrote "Scott Fitzgerald." Ernest said, "I called the character 'Scott' in the first printing and only changed it to 'Julian' when Scott complained to Max Perkins. Time has come to put it back."

By the end of the third day I could see that the oppressive

Key West heat was certainly doing Ernest no good. His body was covered with prickly heat, and a lymph gland under one arm became swollen. "If this balloons up, we clear out of here fast," he told Mary. "I'd rather eat monkey manure than die in Key West." But the gland eventually subsided and he conceded that survival was a distinct possibility.

Before returning to New York, I managed to have a private talk with Mary, who had been looking after Ernest marvelously, not reacting when he snapped and fulminated, and underscoring his moments of well-being. Ernest depended upon her heavily during those days and made constant demands to which she responded with good humor, but he also was very solicitous about her well-being and how she felt and if she was taking her various medicines, and he was highly complimentary about her cooking and housecare (there was no help). In the morning, to permit her to sleep late, he defended silence as he would have defended the *finca* if it had been attacked by a band of saber-toothed autograph-seekers. Mary and Ernest had become very close and loving and interdependent.

I realized that both Mary and I were relying upon Ernest's huge powers of recuperation. Of course the heat was very bad for him, and Havana was bad for him, and not to have any fun the worst of all. He had always kept tab on his blood pressure and his weight and swallowed a few pills every day with his tequila, but it was a ritual that no one, including Ernest, really took seriously. Now it was different. It had all suddenly become very serious. And the drinking was different too. The Prize, coming as it did on the heels of the crash, had had the impact of another beating.

It was apparent to me that it was essential for him to get away from Cuba and back to familiar and pleasurable haunts in Spain and France. It was bad for him to keep driving himself on the book he was writing. He was like a race horse who had won his race and passed the finish line but couldn't slow down and cool out before the next race. He was still running at full speed, but there was nothing to race against. He needed the quiet, unbuttoned freedom that he had always wisely used as his

antidote against stress. For some reason he was now resisting it.
Eventually, he would pack up and go, and it would restore him.
But for the time being, he was hard to move. I was finding out
that when he said he never left any place but with reluctance, he
really meant it.

Part Three

For luck you carried a horse chestnut
and a rabbit's foot in your right pocket.
The fur had been worn off the rabbit's foot
long ago and the bones and the sinews
were polished by wear. The claws scratched in
the lining of your pocket and you knew your
luck was still there.

A MOVEABLE FEAST

Chapter Ten

Zaragoza ✦ 1956

It took several months to achieve Ernest's exodus from Cuba, but what induced him to go was more a medical occurrence than Mary's and my gentle prods. Mary developed a recurrence of anemia, and when the doctor recommended a more temperate climate, Ernest issued emergency marching orders. "She is down to 3,200,000," Ernest informed me, "which isn't funny. Eisenhower has 5,000,000. Black Dog 5,200,000."

I had gone to live in Rome and it was there that I heard from Ernest when he arrived in Paris. His plans were to drive to Madrid in a Lancia, larger than his last one, which was being driven over from Italy. He wanted to know if I would like to join him for the *feria* of Zaragoza, where the young matador Antonio Ordoñez, with whom he had been so impressed in 1954, was performing.

We met at the Gran Hotel in Zaragoza the afternoon before the *feria* was to start. Zaragoza is in northern Spain, 323 kilometers northeast of Madrid. It is an unattractive, crowded industrial city, with what must surely be the homeliest cathedral in Christendom—a cavernous, square, fortlike structure which at night glows with neon trim that runs all around it, and the inside resembles the waiting room of a suburban-Chicago railroad station. The Gran Hotel, the city's best, had possibly been wrought by the same architectural hand.

I was in the lobby when Ernest came in; he seemed to have

regained some of his old vigor in the few months since I had seen him, although his face was pinched and heavily lined. He was smiling, and as he came toward me I noticed he had resumed his old style of walking forward on the balls of his feet. We went into the bar to have a drink, and he told me about his trip down from Paris.

"We stopped in Logroño, where we saw two fights. Antonio was wonderful, Giron very good and a Mexican named Joselito Huerta did the damnedest *faena* for exposure and variety and sheer *cojones* I've ever seen. He and Giron both dedicated bulls to us and laid it on the line like one Indian to another. Huerta cut both ears, tail and a foot in a tough plaza where they know bullfighting. Antonio wants to dedicate the best one he draws here in Zaragoza and will really put out. We have been hanging around together and he is a loving, unspoiled kid. Christ, how he can fight bulls! He has the three basics for being a great matador—courage, enormous skill, and grace in the presence of death."

It was good to hear enthusiasm in his voice again—the dullness of Key West gone—and to see him looking forward to the coming *feria* as he had looked forward to things all his life. "Awful glad you got here—it shapes up as a beauty *feria*. Antonio fights three, Huerta and Giron two each, two new kids, one a friend of ours, Jaime Ostos, and Litri, who for me is a bum in spite of Kenneth Tynan, who wrote a book called *Bull Fever* after seeing fourteen fights." It was also good to see him using his left jab.

He ordered another Scotch and half a lime, which he squeezed himself. "Didn't see any press in Paris, or on the way, or here. Been going good. Wrote six short stories when I quit fishing for the *Old Man and Sea* movie, and want to write some more here. Shooting season starts October fourteenth, so maybe we can make them feel the sting of a couple of hot guns from the American West. Georges is already at work on the Auteuil form and I made a preliminary recce before I left, so if you can spare the time we can actuate the old firm around the end of October." I had forgotten how he distrusted chance and how he planned fun as seriously as work, for he considered them of equal importance to Well-Being. He slid his drink closer to me and spoke intently. "Look, Hotch, my head is quite sharp now and not banged to hell like on our last trip to Spain when I was all beat up. So maybe I can make some sense about the bulls and the others things we like to talk about."

A bellboy informed Ernest that the call he had placed to New York City was ready, and he left the bar, which was rapidly filling with pre-*feria* celebrants. While he was gone, a pretty young girl who had been sitting at the end of the bar-room, eating grapes and drinking Tío Pepe, came over and offered me some grapes. "They taste better when you steal them," she said in American. I sampled one and agreed. "That's Ernest Hemingway, isn't it?"

A tall, bony young man who had been hunched over the bar, drinking rum on ice and staring at himself in the mirror, cocked his head at us. "That right? Hemingway? Where?" He had a twang straight out of the Corn Belt. The girl quietly disappeared as the young man introduced himself: said his name was Chuck and explained that he was bumming his way around the world to get atmosphere.

"Atmosphere for what?"

"To write."

"What have you written?"

"Nothing. How could I till I get the atmosphere?"

"How long you been in orbit?"

"Three years."

"You must have seen just about everything."

"Nope. Just Europe."

"Russia and Poland?"

"No. That's Iron Country. I just seen Europe; now I'm headed Far East."

Ernest returned, looking flushed and pleased. "That was Toots. Bad connection but we screamed it out and I got the bet down. Four hundred bucks on the Dodgers to take the Series."

"They ain't got a prayer," Chuck said.

Ernest turned a narrowed eye on him. "Who's the Horsehide Expert?"

I introduced him and explained his mission. "Made up my mind back in Chillicothe I was gonna write like you," Chuck said, unselfconsciously, "so I figgered I better go take a squint at the places you been writin' about."

"Good reasoning," Ernest said.

"Could I see you later on to discuss it?" Chuck asked.

"Well, have some people lined up, but why don't you show up for dinner?"

"Gee, really? You mean it? I mean, I didn't seriously think . . . gosh, I gotta run out and buy a shirt. I had this one on since Antwerp." He left hurriedly.

"Probably hasn't eaten solid since Antwerp either," Ernest said. No matter how they shaped up, Ernest always offered hospitality and encouragement to any young person who was a self-avowed writer. Chuck was a monument to this catholicism.

A plump, pretty girl, who had been sitting with a group of mantilla-decked women, came over and said in solemn Spanish, "Your books have given me so much pleasure I wish to kiss your lips." She did, and returned solemnly to her table.

The American grape-girl had returned, carrying a book which she asked Ernest to autograph. While he was writing in it, she said, "Mother said I'm not old enough to read *For Whom the Bell Tolls*."

"How old are you?"

"Nineteen."

After she had left, Ernest said, "You know what frail volume she had for me to sign? *To Have and Have Not*, a teen-age work devoted to adultery, sodomy, masturbation, rape, mayhem, mass murder, frigidity, alcoholism, prostitution, impotency, anarchy, rum-running, Chink-smuggling, nymphomania and abortion."

When you attend an entire *feria* you usually form up what Ernest called "a good *feria* mob," for the rigors of five or six or more days of continual bullfights, *apartados*, drinking, dancing, eating, and partying were such that a lone *aficionado* hardly stood a chance of survival.

The mob for the Zaragoza *feria* consisted of Ernest's old English pal Rupert Belville and his lovely English companion, Polly Peabody; a Scottish couple, Rafe and Baby Henderson; the American writer-photographer Peter Buckley; and the Maharajah of Cooch Behar, an independent Indian principality, and his maharanee.

At dinner that evening I was seated within earshot of clean-shirted Chuck, who proved conclusively that not one day of his three-year semi-worldwide investment had paid off. When he discovered that the handsome, dark-visaged gentleman to my left was a maharajah, he called over in nice clear Chillicothese, "Say, Maharajah, I'm headin' Far East. You know any one I can look up in India?"

The maharajah, an Etonian, did not flicker an eyelid but said that he did and that he would give Chuck a letter to the head of the Indian Department of State. Chuck was delighted. "Gee, Maharajah," he exclaimed, "that's awfully white of you!"

Mary immediately announced that coffee and cognac would be served in the bar.

I had hoped that when Ernest overstayed the closing of the bar that first night, it would prove to be an exception, but it wasn't. He drank heavily every night, Scotch or red wine, and he was invariably in bad shape when finally induced to go to his room. He passed up the things that used to attract him— young couples, gay girls, rough cafés, the bullfight people, the fireworks display, the street carnival—preferring to sit for hours in a rooted position, with one or more listeners, not really caring who they were, sipping his drinks and talking, first coherently, then as the alcohol dissolved all continuity, his talk becoming repetitive, his speech slurred and disheveled.

Ernest's mornings, unassailably vibrant all his life, were now silent newspaper-and-tea convalescences. Ernest would joke it off when I came into his room. "Am a little pooped," he'd say. "Went five rounds with the Demon Rum last night and knocked him on his ass in one fifty-five of the sixth." The morning drinks of tequila or vodka would partially restore him in time for his mob lunches, which he enjoyed, and he was back in full form by the time the bull-ring hour rolled around. Good or bad, he

enjoyed the bullfights very much. "I once told Scott," he said,
"that my idea of heaven was a big bull ring where I had two
permanent *barrera* seats, with a rushing trout stream outside
that could be fished by me and my pals. It's still my idea of
heaven."

But, in truth, the bullfights were a disappointment. On the
opening card Antonio, Litri and Ostos all fought without dis-
tinction, and one of Litri's *banderilleros* was hooked against the
planchón of a *barrera* and brutally gored in the groin. The
other programs were equally undistinguished.

On the day that Ostos brindied a bull to Ernest, Ernest rose
in response to Ostos' outstretched hat and the bull ring gave
him a spontaneous standing ovation, roaring his name; it was
an awesome and moving sight to see those thousands of Spanish
people, who do not express approval easily, on their feet, ap-
plauding an American.* Unfortunately, this highly emotional
brindying lacked a climax, for after fighting the bull rather well,
Ostos couldn't kill him; he hacked him about the neck a dozen
times until, weak from the blood-letting, the animal dropped to
his knees.

On another afternoon Antonio also brindied a bull to Ernest,
but this was an even sadder event, for Antonio's entire *faena*
was a failure. But by now Ernest had seen Antonio's brilliance
too often to rate him out for an occasional bad performance.
He had dinner with Antonio the last night of the *feria* and proposed that he and his wife, Carmen, go on safari in Kenya with
Mary and him. Antonio, a handsome, bright, fun-loving man,
assented immediately. That night after dinner Ernest talked
effusively about the safari plans, drank very little and turned
in early.

We got a fairly early start for Madrid the following day, with
a new driver, Mario, at the Lancia's controls. We had a lunch
rendezvous at Fornos with Rafe Henderson, who was driving

---

* I think there were two reasons for this reaction: Ernest, as a non-
Spaniard, had written about bullfighting, in *Death in the Afternoon*, as
well as any Spaniard ever had; and *For Whom the Bell Tolls*, banned by
Generalissimo Franco and never published in Spain, so eloquently bespoke
deep feelings long suppressed.

the others (*sans* Chuck) in his Mercedes. Ernest was in splendid spirits, and he talked and sang and told stories all the way. He sang in a tuneless husky voice, his repertoire ranging from "Hello, Frisco, Hello" and "My Sugar Daddy's in No Man's Land" (solo), to "La Cucaracha" and "Que Será" (duets with Mary).

"Well, Hotch," he said between selections, "it was a half-ass *feria*, but it had its educational aspects. On the first day we learned that contrary to published reports, blood does mix with sand. And, finally, by observing the retinue in the wake of Antonio, Litri and Ostos as they went through the hotel lobby, we learned another lasting truth: undeclared fairies follow bull-fighters."

At one point we stopped at a grated crossing and watched a coal-burning train chug by. Ernest began to laugh softly.

"What's funny, lamb?" Mary asked.

"That train. Took that train with Hadley. We'd been to Zaragoza to see Antonio's father, Cayetano, fight a *mano a mano*. What a beauty fighter he was! Hadley was in love with Cayetano and she wanted to go wherever he fought. Or didn't fight. Anyway, we used our last money for the tickets and we got on this train third-class to Madrid. Cayetano had thrown an ear to Hadley and she clutched it, wrapped in one of my handkerchiefs, next to her bosom all the way. The train was over-crowded. We squeezed into a compartment where there were two Guardia Civil with their guns slung across their backs, a boy taking three wicker-bound sample casks of his father's wine to a wholesaler in Madrid, two members of the clergy, and under the slatted wooden seats, three young ticketless bull-fighters in hiding from the conductor.

"The boy, who like all Spanish boys dreamed of the day he would be a matador, opened a spigot in one of the casks and let some wine run down into the mouths of the bullfighters, who were hot and cramped under the seat. He also passed wine in a cup to the Guardia Civil and to us, and although they declined the first offer, he finally converted the two clergy. As the conductor approached our third-class vineyard, I discovered I had lost our tickets, so Hadley and I got under the seat occupied by the two clergy, who spread their robes to hide us. By the time we reached Madrid the wine casks were empty and everyone was drunk. But we had a final problem—how to pass the station controller, who demands a surrendered ticket from everyone on exit. The two Guardia Civil put their guns at the ready and, one before and one aft, marched the five of us past the controller, pretending we were under arrest. The two clergy brought up the rear, reading their Bibles like we were marching the last mile."

Listening to the story, I began to think about Hadley and Cayetano. She was in love with him, Ernest had said, and carried the treasured ear in her hand. Ernest had identified Cayetano as the prototype for Pedro Romero in *The Sun Also Rises*. But Lady Brett's passion for him—was it derived from Hadley's infatuation with the lithe and romantic Cayetano? Brett, Ernest had said, had her genesis in Lady Duff Twysden, but Hemingway people, as he had demonstrated with Catherine Barkley, were compounded of many parts and I concluded that that part of Lady Brett that pursued Romero was as much Hadley as Duff. In *The Sun Also Rises* the ear of a bull is "cut by popular acclamation and given to Pedro Romero, who, in turn, gave it to Brett, who wrapped it in a handkerchief belonging to myself . . ."

Identifying Hemingway heroines has been a persistent literary preoccupation and one of the most curious of these identifications centered around Renata, the beautiful young Venetian countessa of *Across the River and into the Trees*. Ernest had withheld publication of the novel in Italy because, he once told me, "too many of the characters in the book are still alive"; but finally, in 1965, fifteen years after its publication in the United States, the book was brought out by Mondadori, Ernest's publisher in Italy. Shortly afterward an article in the weekly magazine *Epoca*, also a Mondadori publication, boldly pronounced over Adriana's prominent by-line, "I am Hemingway's Renata."

In the introduction to the article, written by the Mondadori editors, an elaborate attempt was made to prove Adriana's fictional identity by comparing her to passages about Renata quoted from the book. The article itself told about the first meeting between Adriana and Ernest, and then went on to relate how they saw each other day after day. "At first I was a bit bored with this man," Adriana confessed, "so much older and more experienced than I, who spoke slowly and whom I did not always understand. But I felt that he liked having me near him and liked to talk and talk." Adriana then recounted how their relationship grew, but that she didn't suspect that Mary was worried about her until Mary told her so one day. However, after their talk, Adriana said, Mary understood that her affection would never be transformed into love and that not only was she not a danger but was in fact a help.

Her helpfulness was, Adriana said, in restoring Ernest's writing vigor. "Hemingway told me that he had fallen ill while writing *Across the River and into the Trees* and had had to put it aside because he could no longer write, but after having met me he felt a new energy travel from me into him. 'You have given me back the possibility of writing again, and I shall be grateful to you for it always. I have been able to finish my book and I have given your face to the protagonist. Now I will write another book for you, and it will be my most beautiful book. It will be about an old man and the sea.'"

The curious part of this recitative is that Adriana confesses that when she read the novel she told Ernest that she did not find the dialogue very interesting and that, "as for Renata, no, a girl with that grace and family tradition, and so young as well, does not sneak out of the house to have amorous rendezvous and gulp one martini after another, as if they were cherries. No, she was full of contradictions. She was not real." Adriana says Ernest then told her, "You are too different to understand but I assure you that girls like that do exist. What is more, in Renata there is not one woman only, but four different women whom I have actually met."

This would seem to negate the title and entire theme of the article—as an amalgamated heroine, Renata would be following in the footsteps of her predecessors. Adriana concludes by quoting from a letter she received from Ernest in 1951, in which he told her that if he succeeded in writing well enough, people would speak of the two of them for several centuries because they had worked hard and well together. Ernest mused that perhaps it would have been better for her if he had never met her that day in the rain at Latisana, but he is thankful that he saw her before she was too wet. Then he tells her that it would have been the same if he had never written a book on Venice, that people would have noticed that they stayed together and that they were happy together and that they never spoke of serious things. People are always jealous of others who are happy, he said. And he told her to remember that the best weapon against lies is the truth; that there are no weapons against gossip, that it is like the fog, and the clear wind blows it away and the sun dissolves it.

It is my own belief that Adriana Ivancich is a fourth part of Renata, precisely as Ernest said.

Ernest began talking about the impending safari. "It will be fun showing Africa to Antonio and Carmen. Do you think it would discourage Antonio to learn that on our last trip I had a tick on my prick for four days? All local remedies, such as burning the tick's ass and rubbing lion dung on him, failed. Even tried a pair of tweezers. Finally Philip Percival, our White Hunter, suggested suffocating him in candle wax. We dripped a mound of candle wax on him and, sure enough, it worked. That's one remedy you won't find in *Black's Medical Dictionary.*"

As we drove along, Ernest pointed to the exact places where Civil War battles had been fought; he recalled the number of troops involved, nature of weapons used, strategy employed and result of action. I never ceased to marvel at his powers of retention. "This is where we turned them back . . ." and he described the scene as if he were painting it. "We were slaughtered here—we had Russki tanks with rubber treads but the dame with the signal didn't show at seven-thirty, so air went over and we waited until one-thirty, when the sun was in our eyes, and we were destroyed."

A partridge wheeled up in front of the car from a roadside ditch and Ernest took careful aim with his extended arm and

fired, his arm leading the bird in a perfect pattern of its flight.
He constantly practiced this way.

"Did you get him, lamb? Mary asked.

Ernest nodded. "Best training I got for shooting birds was
from my father. He used to give me only three shells for a
whole day's hunting, and he was very strict about shooting only
on the wing. He had his spies around, so I never tried to cheat.

"You know the professors in their thin, erudite volumes describe my unhappy childhood which supposedly motivated all
my literary drives. Christ, I never had an unhappy day I can
remember! I was no good at football, but does that make an
unhappy boyhood? Zuppke put me at center but I never knew
what a digit was—I skipped third grade so never found out
about digits—so I couldn't figure out the plays. I used to look
at my teammates' faces and guess who looked like they expected
the ball. I was called Drag-Ass when they put me at guard.
I wanted to play backfield but they knew better. There was one
guy on the team beat me up in the locker room every day for
two years, but then I grew up to him and I beat the be-Jesus
out of him and that was the end of that.

"In Chicago, where you only used fists, there was this guy
pulled a shiv—"

"A what, honey?"

"—a knife and cut me up. We caught him and broke both
his arms at the wrists by twisting till they snapped. That was
Chicago. Then, gentlemen, we have Kansas City. Contrary
to the professors' published reports, my first job on the Kansas
City *Star* was to find the labor reporter in one of several drinking haunts, get him sobered in a Turkish bath, and get him
to a typewriter. So if the professors really want to know what
I learned on the *Star*, that's what I learned. How to sober up
rummies.

"But the professional pundits don't want to settle for that.
Professor Carlos Back-up and Professor Charles Fender and
Professor Philip Youngerdunger, wearing the serious silks of
Princeton and Yale and N.Y.U., feed my collected works into
their Symbol Searcher, which is a cross between a Geiger

counter and a pinball machine, or maybe they use their econo-
my-sized death-wish indicators, which can also turn up com-
plexes, both certified and uncertified, at the flick of the dial;
then they ask me serious symbol-oriented, death-wish-oriented
questions for their serious works which they afterwards read
aloud to their classes in Serious Lit IV, three credits; but because I answer them in baseball terminology, which is a much
more exact science than literature, they feel I do not take
them Seriously. Mr. Hemingway, please expostulate on your
sublimated death-wish as expressed in *The Sun Also Rises*.
Answer: As sublimated as Whitey Ford's death-wish when he
throws to Ted Williams. Mr. Hemingway, do you give credence
to the theory of a recurring hero in all of your works? Answer:
Does Yogi Berra have a grooved swing? Mr. Hemingway, what
is the symbolism of Harry Morgan's maimed arm and Colonel
Cantwell's maimed hand and Jake Barnes' maimed genitals?
Answer: Put 'em in with Mickey Mantle's maimed legs, stir
well, and if they don't bat four hundred send 'em all to the
Decatur Minotaurs."

Mario stopped in a little town to get gasoline and we went
into the café next to the filling station to get something to
drink. A *boule* game was in progress outside, but inside it was
crowded with black-bereted men, some of whom were playing
dominoes, others watching. The café had a packed-dirt floor,
and an army of flies had pierced its beaded curtain.

Back on the road again, Ernest told us more shooting stories.
He recalled the time, coming back on the boat from Europe,
when, pretty broke, he entered a skeet-shooting contest and
won it by hitting forty consecutive birds and then all the birds
in the shoot-off. "But all through the shoot all I could see was
a blur, and since I know clay pigeons can't travel *that* fast,
when I hit New York I went to see an eye doctor. That's
when I got my first glasses. I went out of the office with them
on and I saw things so clearly for the first time in my life,
I began to get nauseated. I was only a block from Bob Benchley's so I went up to his place and we both got cockeyed
drunk and that got me over the nausea."

"My God!" Mary interrupted. "I forgot my purse. Turn back! My God, Mario, turn around!"

Mario turned back as Mary explained, between gasps, that while we were in the café, which by now was thirty minutes away, she had placed her handbag on a sidewalk table in front of the place. It contained both Hemingway passports and their total floating capital of two thousand dollars in traveler's checks and fifteen hundred dollars in cash, plus a few choice jewels. "Oh, God, but I'm sorry, Papa!" Mary said. "How stupid! Hotch took that picture and I put down the bag and . . . what a place to leave it! Roughest-looking men I ever saw."

"Well," Ernest said, in a too quiet voice, "let's all just sit back and offer up prayers to whatever saints we have an account with."

For the rest of the return trip no one spoke a word. When we pulled into the village, we could see a small group accumulated on the sidewalk in front of the café. Standing beside a table, virtually at attention, was a Guardia Civil who had been summoned to stand watch over Mary's bag, which was on the table exactly where she had left it.

As we pulled up, Ernest said, "Well, Senator McCarthy, now you know why we fought in the Lincoln brigade."

The Hotel Felipe II is located on the heights of the Escorial, in command of a golden panorama that extends clear to Madrid: the golden wheat fields and the golden autumn trees and the weathered roofs gilded by the Spanish sun. For Ernest, the Felipe II was his castle where he was "forted-up good." Goya was the architect, Velásquez the landscape gardener. You stand on the balcony of your room and breathe in the mountain air, which is as clear and sharply cold as the rushing water of the streams; the valley fans out below; from the distance you hear the musical sounds of workmen shaping the mountain stones for houses they are building; the Escorial eagles, the hawks, the inquisitive storks wheel patterns above and below, their widespread wings buoyed by the steady slip stream of air current. There is an old Spanish saying, "The wind off the

Escorial couldn't blow out a candle but it can kill a man."

Ernest joined me on the balcony and listened to the echoing tones of the rock-tapping. Far below us, in the little town of Escorial, school was dismissed and the children's cries spiraled up to us light as wood smoke. "You could have a house built here for the price of your electric bill in Westport," he said. Then he extended his arm into a shotgun and dropped a close-circling hawk in its tracks.

"I always feel wonderful here. Like I've gone to heaven under the best auspices. Very hard to worry under these conditions. Also feel very secure because of local motto, 'A man with a beard will never starve.' "

The first few days at the Felipe II, Ernest was busy and lively, although he still drank too much at night. Most of his activities centered around setting up the safari with Antonio, which necessitated a stream of cables to Abercrombie's and to Kenya.

One day he had the hotel fix us a picnic lunch and we drove high up into the Escorial mountains to the area that was the locale for *For Whom the Bell Tolls*. Ernest showed me the cold mountain stream where Pilar washed her feet, the cave where Pablo's band lived, the bridge, since rebuilt, that was the target of the book. The bridge was much higher and thicker and more impregnable-looking than I had imagined. We walked across it and Ernest pointed to where the real events fictionalized in the book had taken place. At one end of the bridge there was a small stone house that had been destroyed by Loyalist fire, and it remained in the state of ruin in which it had been left in 1933.

We ate our picnic lunch beside Pilar's stream, surrounded by pine beauty, and afterward we drove to the nearby ancient town of Segovia, which also figures prominently in *For Whom the Bell Tolls*. Its distinguishing feature is an awesome Roman aqueduct, in perfect repair, that towers magnificently over the ancient cobblestoned town. Ernest bought four partridges from an old hunter he knew and lottery tickets from a blind man, intending to distribute the tickets to various employees at the Felipe II. Ernest was always very considerate of hotel people who served him. There was a bellboy at the Felipe II who aspired to be a matador, and Ernest had already bought him a pair of two-year-old bulls to fight.

The food in the Felipe was ordinary, so we often dined in Madrid, which was thirty-two minutes away. Without exception, we ate at El Callejón, a windowless Pullman-shaped crowded restaurant that was low on atmosphere but very high on cuisine. Ernest took generous tastings from our plates, but in ordering for himself he always kept strictly to his diet of no beer, starches or meat; fish, salads, vegetables, and calves' liver were permissible; so was Scotch, without limit. I could never determine whether this diet was self-prescribed or doctor-prescribed.

Those first few days Ernest took events in stride. Ava Gardner came out from her home in Madrid, bringing Peter Viertel's shooting script for *The Sun Also Rises*. "You have to read it," she told Ernest. "I know you weren't paid, since they could remake the original for nothing, but for your own pride you have to read it and change things. Everyone in the script runs around saying, *'C'est la guerre,'* and peachy things like that."

Ava stayed all evening; we drank an impressive amount of champagne, and Ava was lively and funny and beat both of us in an impromptu olive-pit-flipping contest at the bar; Ernest enjoyed himself and said that Ava was one of the good ones.

The following day Ernest read the movie script and cabled Peter Viertel to come to Madrid immediately. I had never seen him so truculent. All these signs pointed to a revived Ernest, but the morning of the fifth day I was there, his revivification was shot down in flames. First, I received a cable from a magazine requesting me to return to Vienna to write a follow-up on a piece I had done on the Budapest uprising (this canceled out the races); then Antonio cabled to say that events had arisen to preclude going to Africa (safari canceled). As if this wasn't bad enough, Polly Peabody came out in the afternoon, frantic because Rupert, nine years in the bosom of Alcoholics Anonymous, had suddenly embraced *vino tinto*, plunged himself into a wild state of intoxication, and disappeared.

That night Ernest got very drunk. He was argumentative with Mary during dinner, which featured the partridges he had

bought in Segovia; he did not touch his. Mary left the table as
soon as she could, leaving Ernest and me in the deserted dining
room (it was off-season and we were the only diners that night).
Ernest talked endlessly and not too coherently about the war,
while drinking several bottles of wine. His plans had been destroyed and he was taking solace in the past.

When I finally got him up to his room, he stopped in the
hallway a few feet from his door and glowered at an electric
wall-fixture. He suddenly went into a boxer's crouch, feinted
with his left a few times, then hit the light with a neat right
hook that broke the bulb and knocked the fixture onto the hall
carpet. The metal tore a gash in his knuckle, which started to
bleed, but he paid no attention to it. He put his other hand on
my shoulder and looked at me intently. "Hotch, I been drunk
one-thousand five hundred and forty-seven times in my life, but
never in the morning." He opened the door of his room and
disappeared.

Ernest came into my room the following morning, accompanied
by the hotel barber, and asked if he could have his hair cut
there so as not to wake Mary. His face and eyes were parch-
ment. "Invented a new double *dicho* last night," he said.
"Thought is the enemy of sleep." He suggested that since this
was getaway day for me I should see some Prado pictures and
eat a last meal at the Callejón.

We planned to leave at ten o'clock, but it was eleven-thirty
by the time Ernest went through his usual predeparture check
list of his flask, his various car vests and caps, cleaning tissue
for his eyeglasses, his comb, his Swiss officer's escape knife, his
capital, his lucky chestnut, a spare coat, and, on this occasion,
urine specimens he planned to take to the doctor that afternoon.

As we walked through the lobby on our way to the car,
two men intercepted Ernest. They identified themselves as a
reporter and a photographer for a German magazine.

"I thought I told you guys when you phoned from Madrid,
no interviews," Ernest said.

The reporter said he had been instructed to go out anyway
and begged Ernest for just ten minutes so he wouldn't lose

his job. Ernest said we were trying to make the Prado to see pictures before they closed for the afternoon, but that he would give them ten minutes if they could stick to it and take absolutely no pictures. We all went out on the terrace outside the bar and Ernest sent for a Scotch to ease him through the ordeal.

From the beginning it was obvious that the reporter had never read anything Ernest had written. In a thick, sausage accent he asked, Is this your first trip to Spain? Have you seen any bullfights before? Do you speak Spanish? Do you write your novels or dictate them? Ernest was tolerant at first, but when the reporter asked, How many women have you been in love with? Ernest opened up.

"Black or white?"

"Well, how many of each?"

"Seventeen black, fourteen white." The reporter was getting it all down in his notebook.

"Which do you prefer?"

"White girls in the winter, black girls in the summer."

Ernest then made several efforts to ease off the questioning and leave, but the young German was wound up and insistent. Without warning, Ernest suddenly wheeled around and threw his whiskey in the face of the photographer.

"I told you no pictures, you son-of-a-bitch!"

The photographer put his camera down and wiped it off with his handkerchief and then wiped his face, explaining that he was taking a picture of the hotel and not of Herr Hemingway, meanwhile clicking his heels and apologizing; being an old Leica man myself, I found it strange to take a picture of a hotel by pointing the camera at a man's face.

"All I heard was the click," Ernest said. "To me the click of a camera is like the rattle of a snake."

Ernest helped the photographer mop up and suggested they complete the interview while riding with us into Madrid.

Mario, who had been waiting all this time in the Lancia and who had a previously expressed hatred for Germans as a result of certain Nazi brutalities visited upon his family, was obviously pleased when Ernest said, as the Germans got into the back with me, "We have to make the Prado before closing, Mario, so don't spare the horses." This meant that for the first time Mario could take the wraps off the Lancia and show us why he placed so well in the fast Mille Miglia.

The road to Madrid is narrow, twisting, high in the middle with trenches at the sides, in need of repair, and busy with horses and ox-drawn carts and motorbikes. Mario put the needle at one hundred fifteen kilometers and kept it there, carts, bikes or high water. I had a newspaper, which I pretended to read with what I hoped was nonchalance, and Ernest kept saying to the reporters, "Well, no other questions? . . . That all you want to know?" Out of the corner of my eye I watched their green, petrified faces as Mario darted between and around and virtually over the steady stream of slow-moving objects that cluttered the road. He double-shifted screaming tires around hairpin curves, and we pulled up in front of the Prado in nineteen minutes instead of the usual thirty-two. The two Germans had to be virtually helped from the car. They mumbled their thanks through frozen lips and wobbled off. Ernest shook Mario's hand and would have presented him with a trophy if he had one. "Mark it down," Ernest said to me as we mounted the Prado steps, "as The Day Honest Ernie Struck Back."

Ernest loved the Prado. He entered it as he entered cathedrals. Great art had always been an enormous force in his life (he said he learned everything he knew about describing landscapes, for example, from studying Cézanne and Monet and Gauguin in the Luxembourg Museum). The Prado contained the paintings which Ernest admired beyond all others.

When Ernest went to a museum, it was never to look at the pictures in general but only at particular canvases. Sometimes he would go to look at one picture, and then leave. He would walk across an entire room of Titians, not looking at any except the one he wanted to see, and then he would stand in front of that one picture, absorbed in it, looking at it for as long as his emotions demanded. On one occasion I was with him in the Accadèmia di Belle Arti when he stood in front of Veronese's "The Feast in the House of Levi" for

twenty minutes. Another time, we went to the impressionist
museum in Paris, to look at a Cézanne. Ernest said it had
been his life's ambition to write as good as that picture. "Haven't
made it yet," he said, "but getting closer all the time."

His knowledge of the artists he respected and of their works
came from his prodigious reading, his natural eye for form
and color, his familiarity with the people and the places
painted, and, in the case of artists like Miró, Picasso, Matisse,
Braque, Gris, Masson and Monet, who had been his contem-
poraries and acquaintances, his insight into their personalities,
their drives and their philosophy of living. Ernest always tried
to locate the heart of a painting, what he called "the pure
emotion," the real thing the artist set out to achieve; and
he identified with the difficulty of the artist's task, for he felt
that as a writer he had the same struggle to achieve the same
pure emotion, with the difference, however, that "artists have
all those great colors, while I have to do it on the typewriter
or with my pencil in black and white."

That day in the Prado he took me to see certain paintings
by Bosch, Botticelli, Velásquez, El Greco, and Goya, with
particular emphasis on Goya's huge portrait of the royal family
of Charles IV. "Is it not a masterpiece of loathing?" Ernest
asked. "Look how he has painted his spittle into every face.
Can you imagine that he had such genius that he could fulfill
this commission and please the King, who, because of his fat-
uousness, could not see how Goya had stamped him for all
the world to see. Goya believed in movement, in his own
cojones, and in everything he ever experienced and *felt*. You
don't look at Goya ▮▮▮▮▮ want neutrality."

As we ▮▮ leav▮ ▮▮▮▮▮▮▮▮▮ the
girl v▮

that a Prado guard had to tap him on the arm and tell him twice that the museum was closing.

Mary and I stayed in the bar of the Palace Hotel while Ernest kept his appointment with Dr. Madinoveitia. I had never seen her so concerned about Ernest. She felt that drink had become something for him that it had never been before and she did not know how to cope with it.

"I try to hold him down, but no matter how tactful I am, Papa resents it as nagging and, as you know, he can't stand policing up. So, if anything, that aggravates the drinking and we wind up quarreling, which I hate, but what can I do? Not say anything? How can you stand by silently while someone you love is destroying himself? The things that used to sustain him—working, reading, planning, writing and receiving letters— they are fading away. He doesn't even have people around to lean on him and bring him their problems—Papa always liked that. Now there's just *his* problems and *his* hurts and a day-after-day Black-Ass."

On my way to the airport we picked up Ernest at the doctor's. As usual, he had saved work discussion for the last moment; he asked about two of his stories, "The Undefeated," which I was in the process of dramatizing, and "The Battler," which had just been performed on NBC's "Playwrights '56." He listened with interest as I told him about *The Battler*. It is a ten-page short story which I had converted into an hour play, and James Dean was to have played the lead—a pathetic, punch-drunk ex-champion. A relatively unknown young actor named Paul Newman had been ca____ ___ __e secondary role of Nic_____eek_____ears_____re sched-
_____we were

feated when it was finished, and he said no, he'd rather continue trusting me until I made a serious mistake.

At the airport he came to the ticket counter with me, and while we waited for the check-in clerk he said, "Just had some pretty tough news. Besides liver situation, which we know about, tests showed inflamed heart vein, so Madinoveitia has lowered what's left of the boom; I flunked all the tests and he's put me on a strict food diet with no more than one glass of wine per meal and five ounces of whiskey per day, and no, repeat, no screwing. Would you say that's a bulletin designed to resurrect a former cheerful?"

The following year, 1957, was a dismal time for Ernest. In March he cut off all drinking except for two glasses of wine with his evening meal. By disciplining himself severely, he was able to get his weight down to two hundred, reduce his cholesterol count from a deadly four twenty-eight to a normal two hundred four, and improve his blood pressure considerably.

But it was certainly not the kind of life he enjoyed. Also, his children were having some problems and he was very concerned about them; he was trying to bury himself in work but having very little fun in the process and not traveling at all and not even getting out on his boat much. But it was a year of convalescence that he owed himself, and it made much more of a contribution to his well-being than he realized at the time. What made it particularly difficult was that all his life Ernest had relied on taking a drink to cheer himself up no matter how bad things were, but now one of the very things that was bedevilling him was a physical condition that precluded drinking.

Chapter Eleven

Ketchum ◆ 1958

In the fall of 1958, Ernest decided to go back to the American Far West, where he had not been for over a decade. The place he chose was Ketchum, Idaho, a tiny hamlet of 746 residents, located in the foothills of the Sawtooth Mountains, one mile from the Sun Valley ski resort.

Ernest once skied at Sun Valley, but he had given it up years back when his aluminum kneecap could not take it any more; now he had rented a furnished cabin from a family named Geiss, intending to tramp the lovely, familiar mountain-sides in quest of local game. Since local game consisted of doves, Hungarian partridges, pheasant, mallards, wild geese, hare, deer and bear, he knew there would be plenty to keep him occupied. And he had friends in Ketchum he had known for thirty years.

By November of that year I was at work on the teleplay of *For Whom the Bell Tolls* and Ernest suggested that I come out to case his new country and discuss certain aspects of the dramatization about which I had queried him. Also, he said he had an important new project that he didn't want to discuss on the phone.

It was easier to go to Hong Kong than Ketchum. You flew to Chicago, where you waited for the Portland Rose, the one and only decent train that went, once a day, in the direction of Ketchum. The oddity about Sun Valley is that although it was created out of whole mountain cloth by the Missouri-Pacific Railroad, it is situated ninety miles away from the nearest railroad station, which is in the town of Shoshone. And the way you traveled those ninety miles was either by Sun Valley limousine, which only operated during the skiing season, December to March, or by taxi (thirty-six dollars), of which there was only one and that one was not readily available during the hunting season because its owner preferred being behind a gun to being behind the wheel.

Luckily the taxi and its owner were just returning from a turkey shoot when I arrived. It was a cold ride through snow-capped country to Ketchum, which is a picture town cradled in a Sawtooth crease. I checked into a room Ernest had reserved for me at the Edelweiss Motel, a few minutes' walk from the Geiss cabin, which was a pleasant-looking chalet with split-log facing; the attached garage contained a bower of close-hanging ducks and pheasants.

Ernest saw me coming up the path and came out to greet me. He was wearing knee-high laced leather boots, Western pants, a sleeveless goatskin jacket over a plaid Viyella shirt, and he looked wonderful. Inside, there were flaming birch logs in a six-foot fireplace, a corner packed with guns, ammo, gun cases and game bags, hunting clothes on wall pegs, bearskin floor throws, elk heads, a rack of wine, magazine and book mounds, the smell of game stew slowly bubbling, and two kittens roughhousing on the sofa; three days anywhere, and Ernest made it look as if he had lived there for years.

I couldn't believe his metamorphosis. He had become taut, the slack was gone, the smile back, his eyes were clear, the old timbre was in his voice, and ten years had left his face. He was alive with enthusiasm and plans. He took me out to the garage to inspect his feathered trophies; he told me about the hunting he had arranged for us; he bestowed high praise on Mary for the splendid way she had been shooting, then cooking that which they shot; he was anxious for me to meet his friends; he took me into his bedroom to read a "beauty chapter" he had written that morning. It was indeed a beauty chapter, a poetic account of his early Paris days with Hadley.

On his last trip to Paris, Ernest had discovered an old trunk in the cellar of the Ritz. It contained notebooks in which he had written about those Paris days of the Twenties, and he asked me what I thought of a book of sketches like the one I had just read. I was strongly enthusiastic. He said Mary was too.

In the days that followed, Ernest worked every morning and hunted almost every afternoon. I had shot target and skeet but never open-field game, and Ernest, as always, delighted in teaching me his techniques and secrets.

Sometimes we went out alone, but usually Mary and some friends such as Bud Purdy, the rancher, Chuck Atkinson, the owner of the Ketchum market, a young Sun Valley doctor, whom I shall call Vernon Lord, and whose specialty, of course, was fractures, and old Taylor Williams, once one of the West's greatest hunters, would come along. When we shot on Bud Purdy's vast ranch, he would go up in his plane beforehand and scout the canals, noting those where the ducks were, and on those days we knew we'd come back with mallards' heads flopping out of our bulging game bags.

When we went to Picabo country for pheasant, Ernest studied the terrain and deployed us, using hand signals to communicate as if we were a patrol behind enemy lines. Outside of Hailey one day he spotted the dry remnants of a corn field, which he staked out with infinite care, for we had no dogs, stationing us at the corners and sending us in a few minutes apart. The maneuver forced any unseen ground-hugging pheasants toward the center, and when our forces finally converged, not aware of the hidden birds, they suddenly burst upward, a rising curtain of pheasants; we all shot doubles, and Ernest reloaded and dropped a second pair that had circled around and passed over.

Ernest had a few strict rules: guns in the car must never be loaded; guns being carried through or over fences must be broken at the breech; a bird, when spotted, must never be pointed at or the bird will be spooked and never bagged.

One afternoon Ernest spotted a big snowy owl sitting high

in a tree and he shot it in the wing. He picked it up and inspected the damage. "Have to be careful holding owl," he
said. "Once held an owl the wrong way and it grabbed my
stomach with both talons and wouldn't let go. Very mean
characters."

In his garage Ernest established headquarters for the owl.
He set up a box for him, which he lined and covered with his
hunting clothes, and fitted a cane into the box for a perch.
From that moment on, Owl became the autocrat of the house.
At the outset there was deep concern about his eating; Ernest
trapped mice every night so he'd have a fresh breakfast, and at
noon he was given duck heads and rabbit heads because Ernest
said he needed feathers and fur for roughage. When Owl began
to polish off his morning mouse and thus establish himself as
a captive eater, Ernest then shifted his concern to whether Owl
would eliminate satisfactorily. "Eating's one thing, crapping's
another," Ernest observed. It was only after there were significant droppings for proof, and a slight flurry of doubt was dispelled over whether Owl was drinking water, that Ernest began to relax about him. Mary wanted to give him a name,
Hammerstein I think it was, but everyone just called him Owl.

I asked Ernest why he had shot him. "Plan to train him.
Maybe make him think he's a falcon," he said.

Owl, because of his noted wisdom, became the household
arbiter. There was, for instance, the beginning of a quarrel
one evening between Mary and Ernest over whether a piece
of elk's liver she was about to cook was fresh. Everyone smelled
it but the vote was inconclusive, with Mary vigorously affirmative and Ernest vehemently negative. Ernest pulled out his
Swiss officer's escape knife, cut off a piece of the liver and
carried it out and offered it to Owl. Owl wouldn't touch it.
"Owl knows better than us what's fresh," Ernest said, and the
liver was given to the cats.

Owl and Ernest became great pals. Ernest talked him into
sitting on his hand, and only once in a while did Owl get
crabby and try to take a chunk out of a finger. Whenever we
returned to the cabin from anywhere, Ernest went in to see

Owl before he went into the house. Of course, all the game
that had been hanging in the garage had to be taken out
once Owl's wing started to heal and he could move around.

Ernest seemed content with the eating and drinking routines
he had imposed on himself. He drank a glass of wine at lunch,
a moderate amount for dinner, and kept his evening Scotch
down to two drinks. His favorite lunch was a glass of red wine
and a sandwich of peanut butter and raw onion. For the first
time since I had known him he went out freely to other people's
houses for dinner, for they were all good friends who let him
make his own drinks and whose simple Ketchum food he could
trust. He always brought the wine, which he selected from
his stock of good but relatively inexpensive bottles. "I gave up
expensive wines for Lent of 1947," Ernest once explained, "and
never took it up again. Also gave up smoking long before
that because cigarette smoke is the nose's worst enemy and
how can you enjoy a good wine that you cannot truly smell?"

Evenings that he didn't go out, Mary, who was an imagina-
tive and light-fingered cook, would prepare ducks or partridge
or venison in a variety of ways; afterward Ernest would read
for a few hours or, if he felt like it, he'd sit in front of the big
fire and talk about the old days out West. "There was this
Easterner who came to me one day and asked me to help
him shoot a grizzly. 'It's all my wife wants; night and day she's
after me, and since we were just married I'd like to please her.'
Hell, I say, the grizzly is the hardest of all bears to shoot,
the toughest and the smartest. I haven't shot a grizzly in eight
years.

"Well, I am out with this husband and wife one day, and
we are stalking a moose for food when there's a sound in the
brush and three grizzlies uncover. They are gargantuan sons-of-
bitches. I tell the wife to get behind me because we have no
time to try to get to cover. The husband, who is some distance
away, has already covered and is out of the action. Now, a
grizzly will drop when hit right but he will usually recover and
charge and won't drop again until he's dead. That's what makes
them so damn dangerous. The nearest grizzly, an eight-hundred-

pounder, takes one look at us and charges straight on. I drop him with a neck shot and then, as he starts the get-up, I drill him in the shoulder for keeps.

"The second grizzly charges as I am reloading and I empty both shells into him practically point-blank. He is dead on arrival. Now the third grizzly, who has cased the fate of his buddies and wants no part of it, turns and starts up the hill and I have to peg him four times before I put him away for good. The new wife emerges from the shadow of my behind and she says to me, 'My mouth is dry. Please cover me while I go to the stream to get a drink.' That's all she ever says about the whole episode. And they want to know if Margot Macomber was drawn from real life!"

On Sunday afternoons Ernest and I watched pro football on television and shot skeet in back of the house during half time. Friday nights, Ernest played host to a half dozen of his male friends who would arrive to watch the fights. Ernest was the bookmaker, quoting odds, covering all bets, marking them down carefully in a small ruled notebook. During the fight he would discuss the punches, or lack of them, being displayed, and he was particularly discerning about in-fighting. On the occasion when Gene Fullmer fought Spider Webb, Ernest was caustic about Webb's performance and at one point exclaimed, "There! He finally threw his one-punch combination." He was very solicitous about keeping his guests' glasses filled, and after the fight, food was served and the talk was good—the same convivial atmosphere Ernest created with the group that regularly convened in his *finca* in Cuba.

In the midst of all our Ketchum pleasures, however, there was an ominous event that Ernest was brooding about when I arrived, and he continued to brood about it every day. There was a Catholic church in Hailey, twelve miles distant, presided over by one Father O'Connor, a man of persuasive charm. He had called upon Ernest soon after his arrival, and as a result of that visit Ernest had contributed the cost of a badly needed new church roof. Ernest felt, reasonably enough, that that should have discharged his eleemosynary obligations for the year, but Father O'Connor had returned a month later

with a request that Ernest regarded as an infinitely bigger do-
nation: would Ernest come to the parish house and talk to the
forty high school teen-agers who met there every other week.
Ernest was stunned, in fact horrified, and tried to resist, but
Father O'Connor finally induced him to come on the basis of
no speech, only answer questions.

Ernest fumed about it every day. "Why does a man who
gives a roof have to make a speech?"

"You don't have to make a speech, lamb," Mary would remind him, "just answer questions."

"When you stand up in front of people and talk, that's a
speech."

The only occasion I knew about when Ernest had appeared
before an audience and made a speech occurred in 1937 when
he spoke to the Second American Writers' Congress in Carnegie
Hall on his return from the Spanish Civil War. Of course,
reporters on ships occasionally got to him en masse, but he
understood them and he could talk rough to them and, somehow, that was different. But this was a formal occasion, compounded by being in a parish house under the aegis of a
priest, and Ernest fretted about it every day. He fretted about
his throat, which he was sure was conking out, fretted about
not being able to talk at the kids' level, and fretted that they
probably knew more about his stuff than he did "since I have
not read my collected works since they got collected—and don't
intend to."

When D-Day loomed, there was an ice storm raging and
the roads were difficult. As I drove slowly over the ice-slick
road, Ernest sat quietly, staring ahead, saying nothing. When
we got to Hailey, we passed The Snug Bar, Ernest's favorite
drinking place, and I asked him if he'd like a drink before
he faced the parochial music, but he said no, he'd go it cold
turkey.

There was about an equal number of boys and girls, average
age sixteen; they sat stiffly on folding chairs and looked as
frightened and uncomfortable as Ernest did when he walked in.
Father O'Connor suggested that Ernest sit and urged everyone

to be informal; after a few minutes it was evident that Ernest and the kids were going to get along fine. Mary had asked me to take notes because she had a cold and had not been able to go with us. Ernest checked the notes the following day and made some additions and corrections; this is substantially how the evening with the teen-agers went.

Q: Mr. Hemingway, how did you get started writing books?
A: I always wanted to write. I worked on the school paper, and my first jobs were writing. After I finished high school I went to Kansas City and worked on the *Star*. It was regular newspaper work: Who shot whom? Who broke into what? Where? When? How? But never Why. Not really Why.

Q: About that book *For Whom the Bell Tolls*—I know that you were in Spain, but what were you doing there?
A: I had gone over to cover the Spanish Civil War for the North American Newspaper Alliance. I took some ambulances over for the republican side.

Q: Why the republican side?
A. I had seen the republic start. I was there when King Alfonso left and I watched the people write their constitution. That was the last republic that had started in Europe and I believed in it. I believe the republican side could have won the war and there would have been an okay republic in Spain today. Everybody mixed into that war, but knowing Spaniards, I believe the republic would have gotten rid of all non-Spaniards when the war was over. They don't want any other people trying to run them.

Q: How much formal education did you have?
A: I finished Oak Park High School—that's in Illinois. I went to war instead of college. When I came back from the war it was too late to go to college. In those days there was no G.I. Bill.

Q: When you start a book like *The Old Man and the Sea*, how do you get the idea?

A: I knew about a man in that situation with a fish. I knew
    what happened in a boat, in a sea, fighting a fish. So I
    took a man I knew for twenty years and imagined him
    under those circumstances.

Q: How did you develop your style of writing—did you do
    it to be commercial, to create a public demand?

A: In stating as fully as I could how things really were,
    it was often very difficult and I wrote awkwardly and
    the awkwardness is what they called my style. All mis-
    takes and awkwardnesses are easy to see, and they called
    it style.

Q: How long does it take you to write a book?

A: That depends on the book and how it goes. A good
    book takes maybe a year and a half.

Q: How many hours a day do you work?

A: I get up at six and try not to work past twelve.

Q: Twelve midnight?

A: Twelve noon.

Q: Have you ever had a failure?

A: You fail every day if you're not going good. When you
    first start writing you never fail. You think it's wonder-
    ful and you have a fine time. You think it's easy to write
    and you enjoy it very much, but you are thinking of
    yourself, not the reader. He does not enjoy it very much.
    Later, when you have learned to write for the reader, it
    is no longer easy to write. In fact, what you ultimately
    remember about anything you've written is how difficult
    it was to write it.

Q: When you were young and first writing, were you fright-
    ened of criticism?

A: There was nothing to be afraid of. In the beginning I
    was not making any money at it and I just wrote as well
    as I could. I believed in what I wrote—if they didn't
    like it, it was their fault; they would learn to like it
    later. But I was really not concerned with criticism and
    not in close touch with it. When you first start writing
    you are not noticed—that is the blessing of starting.

Q: Do you ever anticipate failure?

A: If you anticipate failure you'll have it. Of course, you are aware of what will happen if you fail, and you plan your escape routes—you would be unintelligent if you didn't—but you don't anticipate failure in the thing you do. Now I don't want you to think I've never been spooked, but if you don't take command of your fears, no attack will ever go.

Q: Do you outline a book before you write it, or make a lot of notes?

A: No, I just start it. Fiction is inventing out of what knowledge you have. If you invent successfully, it is more true than if you try to remember it. A big lie is more plausible than truth. People who write fiction, if they had not taken it up, might have become very successful liars.

Q: How many books have you written?

A: I think thirteen. That's not very many, but I take a long time to write a book and I like to have fun in between. Also there have been too many wars and I was out of the writing business a long time.

Q: In your novels are you writing about yourself?

A: Does a writer know anyone better?

Q. That book *A Farewell to Arms*, how many years or months did it take you to write it?

A: I started it in Paris in the winter and wrote on it in Cuba, and Key West, Florida, in the early spring, then in Piggott, Arkansas, where my wife's parents were; then came up to Kansas City, where one of my sons was born, and finished it in Big Horn, Wyoming, in the fall. The first draft took eight months, and another five months to rewrite, thirteen months in all.

Q: Do you ever get discouraged—did you ever quit on a book?

A: Been discouraged but can't quit—there's no place to go. Mr. Joe Louis said it very well—you can run but you can't hide.

Q: Do you ever get your characters in a spot from which they can't escape?

A: Well, you try to avoid that or else you'll put yourself out of business.

Q: All these stories you write about Africa—why do you like Africa so much?

A: Some countries you love, some you can't stand. I love that one. There are some places here in Idaho that are like Africa and Spain. That's why so many Basques came here.

Q: Do you read a good deal?

A: Yes, all the time. After I quit writing for the day, I don't want to keep thinking about it, so I read.

Q: Do you study actual people for your books?

A: I don't go where I go for that purpose; I just go where my life takes me. There are things you do because you like to do them, other things because you have to do them. In doing these things you find the people you write about.

Q: We write essays and stories all the time in school. It doesn't seem like a very difficult thing to do. Is it?

A: Not at all. All you need is a perfect ear, absolute pitch, the devotion to your work that a priest of God has for his, the guts of a burglar, no conscience except to writing, and you're in. It's easy. Never give it a thought. Many people have a compulsion to write. There is no law against it and doing it makes them happy while they do it and presumably relieves them. But the compulsory writer should be advised not to. Should he make the attempt, he might well suffer the fate of the compulsive architect, which is as lonely an end as that of the compulsive bassoon player.

Q: How did you learn so many languages?

A: By living in those countries. The Latin I had in school made language-learning easier, especially Italian. I was in Italy for quite a while during the First World War, and I picked up the language quickly and thought I spoke it rather well. But after I'd been wounded, I had to spend some time on therapy machines, exercising my wounded leg, and I became friends with an Italian major

who was also getting therapy on the machines. I told
him I thought Italian was an easy language. He complimented me on how well I spoke. I said I hardly deserved
compliments since it was so easy.

"In that case," he said, "you might take up some
grammar." So I began to study Italian grammar and I
stopped talking for several months. I found that learning
all the Romance languages was made easier by reading
the newspapers—an English-language paper in the morning and then the foreign-language paper in the afternoon
—it was the same news and the familiarity with the
news events helped me understand the afternoon papers.

Q: After you finish a book, do you reread it?

A: Yes. Today I reread and rewrote four chapters. You
put down the words in hot blood, like an argument, and
correct them when your temper has cooled.

Q: How long do you usually write?

A: No more than six hours. After that you're too pooped
and the quality goes. When I'm working on a book I
try to write every day except Sunday. I don't work on
Sunday. It's very bad luck to work on a Sunday. Sometimes I do but it's bad luck just the same.

Gary Cooper and Ernest had been good friends from the
time they first met in Idaho in the early Thirties. They respected
each other's hunting skills and knowledge of the outdoors,
and they were always completely honest with one another.
Cooper was an unaffected, compassionate man; and neither of
them played the role of author or actor, which also had a lot
to do with it. They shared rough jokes, swapped philandering
secrets and enjoyed their mutual disdain for the encroaching
years.

In the field Cooper was not quite as fast as Ernest in getting
a duck in the gun sight, but he had just as pretty a move
and was almost as accurate. We went out every day, regardless of weather, until a really fierce blizzard socked us in, and
on that day Cooper came over in the afternoon with a whole
smoked goose, Ernest brought in a half-gallon of Chablis that

had been chilling in a snowbank, and we sat around the table in front of the fire all afternoon cutting off slices of the delicately smoked goose and drinking the Chablis.

"Ain't this Mormon country wonderful!" Cooper said. "They know how to live."

"I'm practically one myself," Ernest said. "Had four wives, didn't I?" He took a sip of wine. "To tell the truth, if I were reborn and I had a choice, I'd be a Mormon."

A bit self-consciously, Cooper confided to Ernest that after all these years he had finally converted to Catholicism to please his wife, Rocky, and his daughter, Maria. But he said he felt uncomfortable about it and wondered whether he had done the right thing. Ernest said that since he himself was only a miserable, failed Catholic, he couldn't give him a reading on it but he thought it would work out all right.

The talk then shifted to work projects, with Cooper wondering whether there was anything of Ernest's that might be good for him. "When you get my age," he said, "you get to scratching pretty hard for lead parts."

Ernest asked me what I thought might suit Cooper and I suggested *Across the River and into the Trees*. "Good idea," Ernest said to Cooper. "You'd just be playing Robert Jordan ten years older." Cooper hadn't read the book but said he'd get a copy as soon as he got back to Hollywood the following day.

In March of 1959, after completing the taping of the three-hour telecast of *For Whom the Bell Tolls* with Jason Robards, Maria Schell, Maureen Stapleton and Eli Wallach heading the cast, I returned to Ketchum for a motor trek Ernest intended to make to Key West. I planned to drive him as far as New Orleans, where I had to catch a plane to Hollywood.

During my absence Ernest had bought from Dan Topping a Ketchum house of his own—a modern concrete abode that Topping had built into the side of the mountain rise, with the clear trout waters of the Wood River bowing around it. The view from any of its windows took your breath away.

Before we left Ketchum for Key West, Ernest released Owl,

which was quite sad. We took him back to the very tree where Ernest had shot him and placed him on a bough, but when we returned to the car Owl returned too. "Maybe we've softened him up too much," Ernest said worriedly, "and he'll sit around here, waiting for someone to bring him his morning mouse, and starve to death."

"You can't take him back, Papa," I said, sensing what was in his mind. "He's a one-man owl and I don't think any of your friends, all of whom he has nipped occasionally, will offer him room and board."

"Well, what am I supposed to do? Tie him in the tree?"

Once more Ernest tried to talk Owl into staying in the tree but Owl got back to the car before he did. So we all went back to Ernest's house, and later in the day, without Ernest, Duke MacMullen and I took Duke's car and drove Owl to the tree, and this time Owl stayed.

The route Ernest had charted took us due south through Nevada and Texas to the Mexican border, following the Rio Grande from El Paso to the Gulf of Mexico. Ernest's Ketchum car was too beat up for such a voyage so he rented the one and only Hertz vehicle in town, a four-door Chevrolet Impala. Mary cooked a quantity of game birds, which we packed in an insulated carry-bag, and Ernest laid a reserve supply of Sancerre in the trunk; the active supply was kept in the car in a waterproof leather bag that was filled with ice.

The highway through Utah and Nevada had been drawn with a ruler; there were very few cars in March and we traveled eighty miles an hour through gray sage and desert, mountains to right and left, range upon range—you could have put the wheel on automatic pilot. Ernest enjoyed every foot of the way. He remembered early motoring trips, gambling exploits in surrounding towns, hunting expeditions over distant terrain, and trail rides along the faintly glimpsed mountains; at every town we hit he recalled how things were in the good days before neon.

Lunches were roadside, Mary's partridges or teals with the

crackling cold Sancerre, and afterward, as I gave the Chevy the whip and she settled into her eighty-mile-per-hour gallop, Ernest would siesta, his chin resting against his chest.

The automobile was Ernest's favorite mode of travel because, he said, it was the best way to see the countryside, the most mobile, and it kept him safe from contact with his fellow travelers. The inside of the chosen auto—Lancia, Packard or Chevrolet—was always a morass of rain gear, vest gear, footgear, food, maps, binoculars, wine bottles, liquor bottles, medicine bottles, cameras, caps, magazines, newspapers, books, brief cases (containing work-in-progress), ice sacks, drinking glasses, limes, knives and spare socks.

The first night, we stayed at the Stockman's Hotel in Elko, Nevada, a small, neat wide-open gambling town. Ernest had a cheerful reunion with two old pals he hadn't seen since Ketchum gambling days, Frosty the Dealer and Pot-Right Purvis, who were working the wheel at the Stockman's.

The next day's routing took us to Las Vegas, where Ernest had never been before. Jack Entratter, owner of the Sands, had invited Ernest and was expecting him, but when we pulled up and Ernest saw the flow of mink revolving in and out of the hallowed portal, he would have gone on if Entratter had not come out at that moment and taken him to his rooms, which were in a building far removed from the main citadel.

We spent two days in Vegas and Ernest had a fine time playing a little roulette, seeing the entertainment and holding court in the Sands cocktail lounge, where he talked gambling with Entratter and some of his boys, talked prize fighting with a couple of fight managers, discussed the Battle of the Bulge with a waiter who had been in his outfit, and conversed about literature with a beautiful Sands chorus girl who had an English Master's from Texas University and had read all his books.

Our journey across Texas from Eagle Pass to Laredo and over to Corpus Christi took us through countryside covered with a profusive variety of spring flowers. In Corpus Christi we checked into an attractive modern motel, the Sun and Sand, which is right on the Gulf. After the clerk had registered us, he asked whether Ernest would give him his autograph for his son, who was a great admirer of his books. Ernest said sure, just to leave a book in his box and he'd write a personal greeting in it. "What's your boy's name?" Ernest asked.

"Nick Adams," the desk clerk said.

Ernest gave him a look but didn't say anything. On the way up in the elevator, Ernest said, "John Gunther would have still been explaining."

The fourth day out, we left Corpus Christi very early in the morning to see the marsh birds, for which this area is famous, and Ernest identified the herons, king rails, slate-colored sandhill cranes and olive-brown courlans, coots and avocets with incisive knowledge and joy. After the marsh birds, we passed another freshet of brilliant wild-flower countryside and it was Mary's turn to effuse over the variety and beauty. By the time we reached Château Charles, Louisiana, for the night, we were surfeited with good things.

On the night before we were due into New Orleans, Ernest began to talk about future plans, especially about the following summer. An American friend of his, Bill Davis, who lived in Spain and whom he had not seen in twenty years, had invited them to stay in his house in Málaga; Ernest was considering that invitation and the idea of touring the bullfight circuit with Antonio. He would then write an addendum to *Death in the Afternoon* to bring it up to date; if he undertook such a summer, he invited me to join up. "Would be a beauty summer," he said. "Would do Pamplona, which I visited briefly in '53 but haven't done properly since *Sun Also Rises*, and all *ferias* where Antonio and Luis Miguel will fight *mano a mano*. Might be the most important bullfight summer in the history of Spain."

While he was briefly away from the dinner table, Mary said, "Well, I'd say he was becoming the old Papa again, wouldn't you?"

"You mean the young Papa."

"As he often tells me, 'Never lose confidence in the firm.'"

"I never have—have you?"

"No," Mary said, softly, "but on occasion I've wavered a little."

Chapter Twelve

Spain ◆ 1959

Old wine in its cask sometimes reacts to seasons, and the summer of 1959 was, by Ernest's own avowal, one of the best seasons of his life. That aura of keen enjoyment I had found so overwhelming when we had first met in Cuba eleven years before, and which since then had been steadily blunted, now had a splendid renascence.

Ernest and Mary went to Spain in May aboard the *Constitution*, and in June I began receiving bulletins from Málaga, Madrid, Seville and Aranjuez on the "wizard ops in prospect." What made the ops wizard was that Ernest's plan to tour the bullfight circuit with Antonio had worked out: Zaragoza on the twenty-seventh, Alicante the twenty-eighth, Barcelona the twenty-ninth, Burgos on the thirtieth, and so on. Ernest informed me that Zaragoza would be the first fight after the Big Wound (Antonio had been severely gored in the left buttock in Aranjuez on May 30th) and that I should meet up with Bill Davis and him at the Hotel Suecia in Madrid on the twenty-sixth; he described the Suecia as a new air-conditioned hotel that was "an okay joint that gave maximum protection."

In his final bulletin Ernest said that it shaped up as the best summer of his life and I had to make it at all costs. All Antonio wants, Ernest said, except to be the greatest matador that ever lived, is to be part of our mob. For transport Ernest said he had a salmon-pink English Ford (color officially called Pembrook Coral) which he had rented in Gibraltar.

This attention to detail was characteristic of Ernest's good-times planning; and the itinerary was an indication of the schedule madness of a bullfighter's life. There is no such thing as reasonable geographical routing. The matador fights in Burgos in the far north, then drives all night to Málaga in the extreme south to fight the next day, then again drives all night to Barcelona in the north for that afternoon's *corrida*, and so on, all through the long months from May to October, zigzagging huge distances across the face of Spain. No one ever questions the procedure, for bullfighting is a monument to a tradition that is very old and very deep.

As it turned out, I arrived in Madrid the afternoon of June 27th, seven hours past Ernest's deadline, but as promised, there was an envelope at the desk of the Suecia. I was to hire a Madrid taxi first thing in the morning and proceed to Alicante on the southeast coast in time for Antonio's *corrida* that afternoon. Ernest's estimated transport time: six hours.

Maybe in the Pembrook Coral Ford, but not in a Madrid taxi, which is an amorphous vehicle, scavenged from the entrails of departed brothers, a product of its owner's alchemy; I rejected three taxis before settling on the one I considered choice because it had a windshield wiper and a spare tire. Our first mishap was that the driver took the road to Valencia instead of Alicante and had to retrace an hour's driving; the second was that we began to steam outside of Valdemoro and finally ground to a halt inside our own cloud bank just beyond Ocaña in the brutal midday sun. Alicante is four hundred sixteen kilometers from Madrid; we had gone sixty-two.

When you break down in Spain it is unheard of to call for help. The proper procedure is that the driver gets out his tool kit and starts taking the engine apart; when it is completely apart, he wipes off each of the long line of parts he has lined up beside the road, then carefully reassembles them while beseeching God to assist in the automotive miracle he is attempting.

Sitting in the springless back seat of my marooned taxi while my driver counted his spark plugs and his beads, I began to read various printed accounts Ernest had sent me, and as I read, the importance of the bullfighting aspect of this particular summer became clear to me. The country's two great matadors —proud men, the one married to the other's beautiful sister, a certain animosity between them—were about to engage in a series of deadly combats known as *mano a manos*. True *mano a manos* are rare, for only once in a generation, if that, are there two great matadors concurrently fighting. Ironically, the last *mano a mano* of such significance had occurred when this same Luis Miguel Dominguin, then a young and rising matador, had first electrified the crowds with his fresh and vibrant skills. He was considered a fit adversary for Spain's *El Número Uno*, the most revered matador in her history, Manolete. In that punishing duel the veteran Manolete, no longer as quick as he once was, was pushed by the young, reckless Dominguin beyond where he should have gone, and in one such moment he was severely gored and eventually died from it.

Now this same Dominguin, who had ascended Manolete's throne and ruled the bullfight domain until he retired in 1953, was returning to the wars to accept the challenge of a young matador of such supreme talent that many were saying he could well become the greatest bullfighter of all time. The difference in procedure between a *mano a mano* and a regular bullfight is that ordinarily there are three matadors on a card, fighting two bulls each, while in the hand-to-hand combat two matadors split six brother bulls by lot, and the one who cuts the most ears and tails plainly triumphs. In this case, the victor would be crowned *El Número Uno*, the champion of the world.

Ernest also explained to me in his letters that although every bullfight involved some rivalry, when two great matadors squared off, that rivalry became deadly. This is so, he said, because when one of them does something that is not a trick, but classic and exquisitely dangerous, compounded of perfect nerves, judgment, courage and art, then the other is forced to equal it or surpass it, and if in so doing he has any temporary failure of nerves or judgment, he will be seriously wounded or killed.

In addition to the exciting rarity of a truly great *mano a mano*, there was for Ernest the added factor that both Luis Miguel and Antonio were his good friends and he greatly admired both of them as men and as matadors. But it was Ernest's judgment that Antonio was the greater matador, for Ernest felt he had achieved perfection in all three categories: the cape, the *muleta* and the kill, whereas Dominguin, in Ernest's opinion, was weak with the cape and unnecessarily cheapened his performance with Manolete-inspired tricks. Paramount to those considerations, however, was the element of emotion— Ernest felt that Dominguin's performances were cold and unemotional, whereas Antonio on occasion moved him very deeply.

So Ernest had thrown in his lot with the young black-haired half-gypsy from Andalusia, whose matador father had also been his friend thirty years earlier. In the closeness of his relation with Antonio and his devotion to this summer-long roundelay of bullfights, I felt that Ernest was in effect transporting himself back to that happy time when he had roamed Spain with the true-life counterparts of Lady Brett, Bill, Mike and Robert Cohn, attending the bullfights, drinking the rough Spanish wine from goatskin *botas* and dancing the *riau-riau* on the streets of Pamplona.

My driver had finished reassembling the motor. Now he took from the trunk the largest collection of dirty rags I have ever seen in an automobile (or anywhere else, for that matter) and carried these to a nearby cattle watering trough where he soaked them and packed them solidly all around the engine. We then proceeded toward our destination, stopping every half hour to resoak the rags. We steamed into Alicante, and I mean steamed, twenty minutes before bull time, having clocked ten hours for the journey.

Ernest was waiting for me on the steps of the Carlton Hotel; we threw my bags into the lobby and started immediately for the ring. On the way he introduced me to Bill Davis, a pleasant, middle-aged ex-San Franciscan who had a misleadingly jolly Pickwickian face. He had used his ten expatriate years in Spain schooling himself on Iberian architecture, history, art, music, food, aristocracy, sports, wine, government, topography, customs, laws, regions, religion, literature and philosophy. He was a splendid listener, talked sparingly but pithily, and never intruded his knowledge unless asked. His attitude toward Ernest was openly reverential. All that summer and fall Ernest's predilections were Bill's commands. "Never had a true aide-de-camp," Ernest told me, referring to Bill. "Might make a new man out of me. God knows it's time we got rid of the old one."

Antonio was splendid that first afternoon in Alicante and earned the tumultuous approval of his deeply stirred audience. Afterward, Ernest took us up to Antonio's hotel room to congratulate him and arrange a dinner rendezvous, at La Pepica, a restaurant on the beach at Valencia, 182 kilometers away; from there we were all to drive through the night to Barcelona, 534 kilometers due north.

Thus the pattern for the summer circuit was established. Bill staunchly at the wheel; an insulated canvas ice bag containing several bottles of the light *rosado* of Las Campañas resting between Ernest's feet; the rear seat crammed with wearing apparel, overflow luggage and a wicker hamper that contained cheese, bread sticks and a varying supply of other comestibles; a brief serious visit to Antonio's room before the fight; a protracted joyful visit to Antonio's room after the fight; dinner at eleven or midnight en route with Antonio and his *cuadrilla*.

On our way to Valencia, Ernest told me about the fight at Zaragoza which I had missed. Miguel had turned in the best performance that afternoon with a substitute bull he had purchased for forty thousand pesetas after his last bull had gone lame. "Luis Miguel claims to be Number One, so he must substantiate that claim every time he appears now," Ernest explained, "but he has the handicap of having become rich. The daylight between a matador's groin and the bull's passing horns increases as his wealth increases. But I will say for Luis Miguel that he truly loves to fight when his stuff is going for him, and on those days he seems to forget he is rich. But Antonio does not forget it, ever—Miguel's wealth, that is—and that's where the gimlets get sharpened. Miguel has demanded more money than Antonio for these *mano a manos*, and he is getting it, but this has rancored Antonio, who is out to prove that Miguel does not deserve it. No one has a fiercer pride than Antonio and that's the deadliness of this combat. Antonio considers it an insult that Miguel does not treat him as an equal, and I can tell you that before this summer is over, Antonio will impale Miguel on the horns of his pride and destroy him. It is tragic but like all tragedy, preordained."

From June 29th to July 6th, Barcelona then Burgos then down to Madrid, then back up to Burgos and then Vitoria, along the way Ernest delighting in the sounds, sights, tastes and smells: great, succulent asparagus with white draft wine; Pamplona *riau-riau* songs to the whine of the Pembrook Coral's tires; country bread covered with huge crumbly slabs of Manchego cheese cut from the hamper's wheel, washed down with *rosado* poured from the ice sack; storks in their sloppily strawed chimney tops; hawks working low over heather-hued brambles for sage hen and rabbits; olive trees casting crooked shadows on the red earth; cork oaks as bare as sheared lambs; the heat and excitement of standing in the *callejón* with the quick-moving sword handlers, sweating managers, fence-vaulting panting *banderilleros* and gray-faced, dry-mouthed matadors watching Antonio and waiting their turn. And then, suddenly, Pamplona, *La Feria de San Fermin*, seven days and seven nights melted into one 168-hour day.

We arrived in Pamplona a day before the start of the *feria* (Annie Davis and Mary Hemingway had come up from Málaga to join us) because Ernest said we had to be "forted-up and the joints all scouted before the Eruption." Ernest's old friend Juanito Quintana—who had been impresario of the Pamplona ring and owned a hotel there before the Civil War—received a regular monthly retainer from Ernest for the express purpose of procuring bullfight tickets and lodgings when Ernest came to Spain. Ernest had given Juanito the Pamplona assignment in May, but when we met him at the Café Choko he was very nervous and tried to explain, but the fact was that he had promises instead of tickets and no hotel rooms. San Fermin is Spain's most overcrowded *feria* and Pamplona has fewer hotels than any other *feria* city, with a bull ring that is relatively small and limited in seats, but Ernest could not have been kinder and gentler with his old friend. Ernest knew very well what a miserable spot we were in, but he explained to Mary that the world had let Juanito Quintana down, not he us. Ernest then put a scalper to work on the tickets, and we found quarters in private houses.

"It really doesn't matter a damn except for the tickets," he explained, "because nobody sleeps or changes his clothes."

At noon the following day two rocket-bombs exploded in the hot bright sky and the town erupted. It happened before your eyes but you didn't see it. One minute the deserted square, the next minute a compact mass of revelers, pipes and fifes and drums playing the *riau-riau* music, men and boys all red and white, arms high, dancing and singing to the music, then crouching down, then up again, arms around, bobbing to the pounding rhythm. For seven days and nights, the streets never empty.

The cafés were jammed but the Choko maintained for Ernest the table he had staked out. It was easy to tell the tourists by their costumes, which were as distinctive as the white duck pants, white shirts, red scarves and berets of the Navarre men. The twenty-five thousand tourists were mainly American college kids and their costumes consisted of tight chino pants and T-shirts. Almost to a student they had been attracted to Pamplona by *The Sun Also Rises*, a book that had been published over thirty years ago, and when they discovered that the author himself was there, they descended upon the Choko in great adulatory waves, bearing everything from books to T-shirts for autographing.

By evening, with time out for the afternoon's *corrida* which featured worthless bulls and matching matadors, Ernest had filled his table at the Choko with the characters he had selected as his mob for the *feria*. Two of them had been anticipated, Dr. Vernon Lord from Ketchum and his wife, Lee, but the rest were impromptu. A young Glasgow girl I'll call Honor

Johns, red rounds on her cheeks and hair that shocked up like
a black wool tiara, supposedly a reporter for a Glasgow weekly
(we had our doubts); a tall, gaunt guitarist y-clept Hugh
Millet, who sang calypso verses he had composed and was accompanied by the sweet, soft voice of his pretty French wife,
Suzie; a pert canary-blonde named Beverly Bentley (now Mrs.
Norman Mailer), the star of a Smell-o-Vision motion picture,
A Scent of Mystery, then being shot in Spain; a young man
from Hawaii, Mervyn Harrison, who had interviewed Ernest
in Ketchum the previous winter for an English thesis he was
allegedly writing and had ended the interview by putting the
bite on Ernest for money to finance six months in Paris to learn
French at the Sorbonne. The six-month period had just ended.

Antonio, who was not on the card for the *feria*, showed up
that evening with his manager, Pepe Dominguin, who was Luis
Miguel's brother; Ernest, Bill and I joined them in an all-
night revel of dancing in the streets and singing and drinking
in the cafés. Everywhere Ernest went he ran into men he had
known years before, and these chance meetings always called
for an acceleration of drink and song.

Around four in the morning, as we were marching down
a narrow Pamplona street five abreast, arms linked, singing, we
were approached by a small white Renault that had a beautiful
young face peering from behind the right windshield.

"They shall not pass!" Antonio shouted.

"Capture the girl!" Ernest commanded.

Antonio jumped up on the hood of the Renault as Pepe
opened the door on the driver's side and extracted a short, perspiring Frenchman who wore a pork-pie hat and gloves and
was on the verge of incoherency. From the other side there
emerged a stunning young lady who first looked at Antonio and
said, in Midwest Americanese, "Aren't you Antonio Ordoñez?"
And then, as if it weren't enough to be captured by the ruling
matador, she turned and saw Ernest and said, "Aren't you
Ernest Hemingway?" and I thought she was going to faint.

By now the Frenchman had stammered out the message that
the car belonged to the lady, whom he scarcely knew, and he
was just driving her because she couldn't find her apartment,

and while we were loudly arguing over whether we should lock him up in the trunk he escaped into the night. Ernest solemnly informed the girl, who identified herself as Teddy Jo Paulson of Williston, North Dakota, that she was an official prisoner; she was absolutely delighted and asked whether we would please go to her apartment and take her traveling companion prisoner too.

Bill knew all the little streets in Pamplona the way he knew most Spanish towns, and in no time we had roused Teddy Jo's roommate, Mary Schoonmaker, from her sleep. "True beauty," Ernest said to me, "is to wake up looking like that."

Antonio took us to a club where there was a loud orchestra with everybody singing as they danced, and we had such a hell of a time we almost missed the first running of the bulls.

Each day of the *feria*, in the early morning, the bulls for that day's *corrida* are released from the pens at one end of town and they run along a street that leads to the bull ring. It is traditional to join the group of men and boys who race down the street in front of the onrushing bulls: front runners get a big head start, middle runners keep a modest distance ahead, and then the brave ones or crazies, depending on your point of view, try to stay as close to the bull pack as possible without getting gored.

Ernest ran with the bulls in the old days but now his legs were too unreliable. Antonio, of course, ran just in front of the bulls—with the crazies. I ran at the rear of the middle runners where, glancing over my shoulder, I had a good view of the bulls and the crazies. We were about halfway to the ring when the crowd, which solidly crammed the fences and windows and balconies, suddenly cried out, and I looked back to see that one of the crazies had slipped and a big black bull with huge antlers had splintered off to get him. That's when I noticed Antonio. He had been carrying a rolled-up newspaper and now he was running over toward the fallen man, unfurling the newspaper and yelling, "*Toro! Huh! Toro!*" at the bull.

The bull hooked once for the fallen man but his horn went over him and then Antonio swept the newspaper in front of his eyes and he went for that. The fallen man scrambled to his

feet and ran as Antonio again passed the bull with the newspaper, but this time the paper recurled itself and uncovered
Antonio's leg and the horn got him. At that moment Ernest,
who had rushed to the fence, pulled off his jacket and flapped
it against the fence and the bull charged that, banging his
horns into the wood planks, which he splintered. Antonio limped
to the opposite barricade, which a policeman opened to let him
escape.

I had stopped running to watch Antonio but now I realized
I was being swept up by the vanguard of the crazies, who were
coming on fast with the phalanx of horns on their tail, so I got
the hell out of there with a burst of speed that only wild bulls
can inspire.

Antonio's horn wound was in his right calf, but because of
the ignominious manner in which it had been inflicted he refused to pay any attention to it. He danced all day and night
and then again ran with the crazies the following morning just
to prove whatever he wanted to prove. Only then he finally
listened to Ernest and let Vernon Lord give him an anti-
tetanus shot and clean and dress the nasty gash.

Ernest was absolutely correct about sleep and the lack of it.
I went to my rented room only once; it was dark and smelled
of urine from the flat's one toilet which was next to it, so I
never went there again. Instead, whenever I felt like sleeping
for an hour or so I curled up in the back of the Pembrook
Coral. Sometimes Ernest would join me and sleep sitting up
in the front seat. He had recognized several pickpockets of
superior talent who were working the *feria*, so when we slept
in the car we put our money inside our pants. Before going
to the bullfights, we all gave our valuables to Ernest, who stowed
them in his pickpocket-proof Hong Kong jacket.

Teddy Jo and Mary Dos (Mary Hemingway, naturally, was
Mary Uno) became inseparable members of the basic *cuadrilla*;
when Ernest discovered that they both taught mathematics he
was delighted because, he said, it wasn't often a *cuadrilla* got
beauty and intellect in one handy package. But on the second
day we lost one of the mob—Mervyn Harrison of Hawaii. Quite
simply, he overslept and failed to show for that afternoon's bull-

fight, letting the hard-to-get and much-sought-after ticket go to waste. Then, that evening, when Ernest asked him if they had taught him how to oversleep at the Sorbonne, he confessed that he had not gone to the Sorbonne with Ernest's borrowed money but had discovered a superior way to learn French. "I met this Paris girl," Mervyn said, "who could not speak a word of English, so when we started to sleep together I *had* to learn. I tell you, Papa, that's the place to learn a foreign language— in bed!"

"Yes, but what you learn there," Ernest said, "is sometimes difficult to work into an ordinary, everyday conversation."

I don't know precisely how Ernest handled it, but we never saw Mervyn again. When he did not reappear Ernest simply said, "Well, our boy, Mervyn, has just become a complete stranger. Never discuss your casualties, gentlemen."

Just to the northeast of Pamplona are the Irati River and its forests, which were such an integral part of *The Sun Also Rises;* Ernest was afraid that they had been completely ruined, but his fears proved unfounded. For four afternoons we picnicked at various places along the river, going higher and higher up the mountain, leaving at noon, getting back just in time for the bullfight. We traveled in three cars, each car responsible for part of the picnic, which flourished with squabs, cheeses and cold smoked trout, Navarre black grapes and brown-speckled pears, egg plant and pimientos in a succulent juice, unshelled shrimps and fresh anchovies. The wine was kept cold in the clear Irati water, and each day we swam up the river, which flowed through a gorge between the high-rising walls of the beech-covered mountain. It was miraculous to leave the wild tumult of the *feria* and a half hour later to be in the midst of this primitive, quiet beauty.

One day after lunch Ernest and I sat on the pebbly bank, contemplating the view, which consisted of circling hawks, rising mountains, and the seven women of our *cuadrilla* who were napping at various levels on warm rock ledges above the opposite bank. "Nymphs on shelves in nature's store," Ernest said. "What a hell of a happy time." He watched a hawk plummet earthward and disappear, then re-emerge beating skyward with a small prey struggling in his talons. "You know, Hotch," he said, his eyes on the hawk, "it's all better than *The Sun Also Rises.*"

Ernest sat with his back against a beech trunk, his lips pleasurably parted, his old eyeglasses in his lap, patting an itinerant hound dog who had sought him out, and as I studied him I thought, This is different for Ernest than anything we have ever done, for this is not the enjoyment of memory, but the enjoyment of experiencing. This summer we are not revisiting the windswept slopes of the Escorial to see the vestiges of *For Whom the Bell Tolls*, or driving slowly along the road he once cycled with Scott Fitzgerald or walking along the circuitous Left Bank route he used to take from his unheated room to the Jardin Luxembourg to avoid the tantalizing restaurant smells; this summer, unlike the others, is young.

When we got back to Pamplona that afternoon, having missed the bullfights, there were two cables waiting for Ernest. One was from Toots Shor: ERNIE, WHERE SHALL I SEND THE FOUR THOUSAND BUCKS, YOU BUM? Ernest laughed. "Toots is burned up because I phoned him from Málaga, just before we met you, and asked him the odds on Johansson against Patterson. When he said the boys were laying four to one on Patterson I told him to put down a G for me on the Swede, but he tried every which way to talk me out of it. I don't bet much on fights any more. Have a new rule: never bet on any animal that can talk—except yourself."

The other telegram was from David O. Selznick, who had just completed a remake of *A Farewell to Arms* with his wife, Jennifer Jones, starred as the novel's heroine, Catherine Barkley. He had not paid Ernest anything for this version because back in the Twenties the book had been sold outright with no provision for remakes. This telegram said that Selznick had just informed the world press that although not legally obligated to, he was hereby pledging himself to pay Mr. Hemingway fifty thousand dollars from the profits of the picture, if and when it earned any profits.

Ernest, who had never kept secret his lack of affection for Mr. Selznick, dictated a telegram in reply saying that if by

some miracle, Selznick's movie, which starred 41-year-old Mrs.
Selznick portraying 24-year-old Catherine Barkley, did earn
$50,000, Selznick should have all $50,000 changed into nickels
at his local bank and shove them up his ass until they came
out of his ears.

After Pamplona we rested for a few days in Madrid before
going down to Málaga for a birthday party that Mary Uno had
been working on for nearly two months. July 21st was Ernest's
sixtieth birthday and also the birthday of Carmen, Antonio's
wife; the Bill Davis house, La Consula, in Churriana on the
southern coast of Spain, was to be the locale. Set in the midst
of a huge, elegantly gardened estate, La Consula is a colon-
naded mansion of delicate mien that looks like the palace of
a junior Doge. It is protected by outer and inner gates, both
manned, and its furnishings, mostly handmade by Spanish arti-
sans working from Bill Davis's designs, and its art complement
its exterior. Floors and balustrades, stairs and table tops, bath-
rooms and porticoes are all marble, and marble envelops the
swimming pool. There is no telephone.

Mary really knows how to give a party and she pulled out
all the stops on this one. She felt that Ernest's birthdays, because of his lack of co-operation, had always been observed
with a pause rather than a celebration, and she was determined
to make up for all the lost birthday parties this time. She
succeeded.

She had ordered champagne from Paris, Chinese foods from
London, and from Madrid, *bacalao*, which is a dried codfish
that is the basic ingredient for the highly seasoned Bacalao
Vizcayina, one of her specialties. She had hired a shooting
booth from a traveling carnival, a fireworks expert from Valencia, which is the citadel of fireworks, flamenco dancers from
Málaga, musicians from Torremolinos, and waiters, barmen
and cooks from all over.

The Davis house sleeps only twenty-five, so Mary had taken
over a couple of floors of a new skyscraper hotel, the Pez
Espada, on the beach in nearby Torremolinos. The invitees
came from all over, and they began arriving on the twentieth.

In addition to the members of the regular Pamplona *cuadrilla*, Ernest had invited a large number of other Pamplona people and some from Madrid. There also arrived the Maharajah of Jaipur with his maharanee and son, the Maharajah of Cooch Behar with his maharanee, General C. T. "Buck" Lanham from Washington, D.C., Ambassador and Mrs. David Bruce, who flew down from Bonn, various Madrid notables, several of Ernest's old Paris pals, thirty friends of Antonio's, and Gianfranco Ivancich, Adriana's brother, who arrived from Venice with his wife driving Ernest's new Barrata Lancia which had been bought out of his Italian royalties.

The prisoners, Mary Dos and Teddy Jo, had torn up their AAA motor itinerary, which would have taken them to ninety-two cities in sixty-two days, and Honor Johns had permanently forsaken her allegiance to her Glasgow weekly.

The party started at noon, July 21st, and ended at noon, July 22nd, and Ernest said it was the best party that ever was. He danced and popped champagne, proposing marvelously funny toasts to his guests, and shot cigarettes from the lips of Antonio and the Maharajah of Cooch Behar. When the orchestra, which played on the upper veranda, struck up the fiesta music of Pamplona, Antonio and Ernest led all the guests in a *riau-riau* that snaked all over the grounds. The one sober moment of the evening occurred at the end of the dinner when David Bruce, with whom Ernest had fought in the war, proposed a simple and affectionate toast; Ernest bowed his head against his chest and was visibly touched.

The firecracker wizard from Valencia put on a lavish and noisy display, but one of a salvo of giant rockets unfortunately lodged in the top of a royal palm tree near the house and set the treetop on fire. Attempts by some of the guests to climb a sixty-foot ladder and attack the blaze with a garden hose were perilously abortive, so the fire department was eventually summoned from Málaga.

The hook and ladder that arrived was straight out of Mack Sennett—and so were the firemen. But they fought the blaze courageously and the tree and the house and the night were saved. The firemen were immediately assimilated by the party, and so were their uniforms and their fire engine, which Antonio, wearing the fire chief's helmet and raincoat, raced around the grounds with the siren wide open.

After breakfast the guests started to depart but it was not until noon that the last of them had retired. The Churriana sun was up hot by now and Ernest and I had a swim before going to bed.

"What I enjoyed most about the party," Ernest said as we were going to our rooms, "is that these old friends still care enough to come so far. The thing about old friends now is that there are so few of them."

The very first *mano a mano* was scheduled for the fourth day of the *feria* in Valencia. On the afternoon of the third day of that *feria* Antonio's friend Juan Luis, whose estate was on the water just outside Valencia, invited Ernest and all his *cuadrilla* mob for lunch and swimming. The sea had polite little whitecaps and looked civilized, but we discovered when we went in that there was a strong current running away from the beach. I don't recall which girl it was who came swimming in and called to us from the surf; all we heard was "Papa . . ." over the breaking waves, but that was enough.

Juan Luis got to him first and Ernest put his hand on Juan Luis' shoulder and they came into shore that way with three of us swimming alongside. We stayed in the surf for a few minutes, not getting out before Ernest got to his feet. He sat with his back to the shore, looking out to sea. I could not help but think of the time at Varadero Beach, ten years before, when he had swum through much rougher waters with his pants held high over his head.

Ernest got to his feet rather shakily and started across the beach to where the main body of the group was camped. I don't think they were aware of what had happened. I looked at Ernest as he approached them. His color was gone and the smile on his face wasn't a smile.

The following afternoon's *mano a mano* was brief. A gust of wind caught Dominguin's *muleta* during a pass, and the bull drove his horn deep into Luis Miguel's groin, cutting through the abdominal muscles and into the peritoneum. It had been a good *feria* until then, with Antonio giving several brilliant performances, but his rivalry with his brother-in-law was over for the time being. Ernest felt bad that Miguel had been hurt by wind, which Ernest had always said was the bullfighter's worst enemy.

Then, a few days after Dominguin's *cornada*, Antonio was gored in the right thigh in a fight at Palma de Mallorca; that really put the quietus on our bullfight plans, and the intricately worked-out itinerary had to be discarded. Ernest's *cuadrilla* had all gone by now, and he, Bill and I went back to the Churriana house. Ernest spent his mornings making notes for the article which he had contracted to write for *Life* and working on his Paris sketches.

On days that we did not feel like working (I was writing television dramatizations of four of Ernest's stories which I was scheduled to produce for CBS during the coming season) we traveled to Córdoba or Gibraltar or the Alhambra in Granada.

Ernest was not being social now, since he was working, and Bill had cut off all guests; but Mary returned from Málaga one afternoon and said that she had run into a distinguished television commentator who was on a honeymoon with a new wife and that he had asked to meet Ernest, so she had invited them for lunch. Ernest was dismayed at having to face a television pundit, but Mary assured him this commentator understood that the visit would be strictly social.

For half the lunch it was, but then the commentator, who has a truly noble and honorable profile, began to ask Ernest direct questions about the fights between Antonio and Dominguin. Although Ernest explained that he didn't like to discuss anything he was going to write about because he didn't enjoy seeing it in print under somebody else's name before he got to it, the nobly-profiled commentator insisted that he knew nothing about bullfighting and was only asking in order to learn and would *never* violate his host's hospitality. (A few months later the commentator's verbatim account of this luncheon interrogation appeared in an American magazine.)

The *mano a manos* were scheduled to resume on August 14th

in Málaga, but it seemed impossible that either of the matadors
could recover that soon. They did, although their wounds were
far from healed. Antonio got out of the hospital on the eleventh,
with his wound still discharging, and came down to Churriana
on the twelfth to get into shape. Bill's son, Teo, had a baseball
bat and Ernest suggested that we teach Antonio, who had never
had a bat in his hands, how to hit. I pitched to him with a
tennis ball and it was astonishing to see how quickly, with his
great co-ordination and reflexes, Antonio was able to smack
even my best pitches over the tops of the royal palms.

That night at dinner Ernest and Antonio decided that in
repayment for having made a baseball player of Antonio, Antonio would make a matador out of me (he called me "El
Pecas," The Freckled One). "Does El Pecas have the necessary
reflexes?" he asked Ernest.

Ernest answered with the "impromptu" throwing-and-catching
act (forks, plates, wine glasses, etc.) which was part of our
"loosening up" repertoire. That convinced Antonio that my
reflexes were all right and he solemnly announced that I would
be the *sobresaliente* at the next scheduled *mano a mano* in
Ciudad Real. We drank down our wine to that and again to
Ernest's announcement that he would be my manager.

Ernest called the following day's *mano a mano* "one of the
very greatest bullfights I have ever seen; maybe the greatest."
Antonio was awarded six ears, two tails and two hoofs for his
three bulls, and Dominguin garnered four ears, two tails and a
hoof for his; it was an afternoon of such competitive artistry,
such fierce display of courage that Ernest called it unreal.

I had thought that all the talk about my going into the bullring
in Ciudad Real was a bibulous joke, but when we arrived in
Antonio's room before the *corrida* on August 17th, there were
two sword handlers and one of them was for me. Antonio had
set out two of his matador suits and my sword handler was
standing beside the ivory and black one, ready to fit me into it.

I would go into the ring as the *sobresaliente*, the substitute
matador in a *mano a mano* who has to kill the bulls if the two

contending bullfighters are injured. Of course I would just be
masquerading as the *sobresaliente*, but Spanish officials take
such infractions very seriously and I had been told—whether
true or not—that a few years back a pal of the bullfighter Litri
had been unmasked and spent a year in a rather depressing
dungeon for having impersonated a bullfighter. "The only one
we know who got away with it," Ernest told me, "was Luis
Miguel. He took his friend Count Teba, nephew of the Duke
of Alba, into the ring as a member of his *cuadrilla*. But that
was in France."

Everyone had a fine time dressing me, particularly my manager, Ernest. Instead of the usual pre-bullfight air of heavy
solemnity that hangs in the matador's room, there was the light-
hearted atmosphere of a fraternity initiation. You cannot have
an idea of how complicated the matador's costume is—and how
tight. Everything fits like new skin and is tied down so that
when you finally stand there, mummified, no part of your costume can possibly flap in the wind, and thus attract the bull's
eye during a charge. Frankly, I thought that when the moment
came to depart for the ring I would be released from this
grandiose joke; so for the time being I happily went along
with it.

"Remember, you must not make the matadors look bad in
your first appearance, Pecas," Ernest said. "It would be unfriendly."

Antonio said, "Only think about how great you will be and
our pride and confidence in you."

When it came time to leave for the ring, everyone left us
alone in the room; Antonio went over to a small table where
all his religious objects were spread out for him as always,
and as he prayed he kissed each one. I stood in a corner, wish-
ing like hell that I had something I could pray over.

The door opened and Antonio's entire *cuadrilla* was waiting
there in the hall in their costumes. Antonio put on his hat and
picked up his ceremonial cape, as I did mine; and I followed
him out of the room with difficulty because my pants were so
tight I couldn't bend my legs at the knees.

My memory of getting to the ring that day is pretty fuzzy, although I do remember almost falling down the stairs going down to the lobby (try walking stiff-legged down steep old stairs sometime in new shoes). But Ernest noted this historic event in his account of it:

"When they came downstairs Antonio had his same dark, reserved, concentrated before the bullfight face with the eyes hooded against all outsiders. Hotch's freckled face and second baseman's profile was that of a seasoned *novillero* facing his first great chance. He nodded at me somberly. No one could tell he was not a bullfighter and Antonio's suit fitted him perfectly."

We passed through a crowd that had been waiting in the lobby and through a denser crowd that waited outside around Antonio's *cuadrilla* wagon. It was a big custom-made Chevrolet with a panel-truck chassis to withstand the beating from the bad Spanish roads. My manager got in with me and sat beside me.

"Papa," I said, "what the devil do I do? I've got to walk in the *paseo*, don't I? Is this a big ring?"

"Holds eight thousand. One of the biggest outside Madrid." A vision of walking clear across a big ring before eight thousand people alongside the world's two greatest matadors, followed by our *cuadrilla* and picadors on their horses, passed before my eyes and I dizzied a little. "There are just three things the matador must do," Ernest said. "Remember them and you'll be all right. First, always look tragic, like you're on the verge of tears."

"Have you taken a good look at me?"

"Fine. Now, second, when you get to the ring, never lean on anything; it doesn't look good for the suit. And third, when the photographers come around to take your picture, put your right leg forward—it's sexier."

I gave him the look he deserved. He patted my unbent knee. "This is my first time as a matador manager, and I'm a little nervous," he said. "Are you?"

My nerves got their biggest jolt when I saw the huge posters on the outside of the bull ring. Under ORDOÑEZ Y DOMINGUIN, it said SOBRESALIENTE: EL PECAS.

When we were all assembled under the stands, and I looked over the top of the big wooden gates that would soon swing open to start the *paseo*, and saw the thousands of Spaniards who jammed the arena, I was suddenly overcome by a frantic desire to escape. But the photographers were now descending on us, so I braced myself and tried to follow Ernest's instructions. Then as we stood there being photographed, a terrible truth dawned on me. I got Ernest to one side.

"Look at Antonio and Dominguin," I said. "Their pants. Then look at me." Ernest looked. "I am a positive disgrace to the United States of America," I said.

"Well, how many handkerchiefs did you use?" Ernest asked.

"What handkerchiefs?"

"They're using two, I'd say. That's the customary number although I hear Chicuelo II uses four."

"You mean handkerchiefs in their pants?"

"Don't tell me you didn't use handkerchiefs?"

"How the hell would I know about handkerchiefs? I was relying on my manager."

"But you've been to enough bullfights . . . how did you think they got bulges like that?"

"The subject never interested me until now."

The band struck up, the wooden gates swung open, the picadors moved close in on their high, skinny horses, and somebody pointed me in the right direction as the two grooms on their horses started into the ring, followed by Antonio and Dominguin, walking side by side, with El Pecas the customary three steps behind them. All the other men fanned out in back with the mule teams bringing up the rear. We got a big hand. I still couldn't bend my knees, but I watched Antonio and tried to swing my right arm stiffly the way he did. The distance across the ring was easily four miles.

We stopped in front of the President's box, saluted and bowed our heads, and I followed Antonio into the *callejón* where Ernest was awaiting me.

"How did it look?"

"You had just the right amount of modesty and quiet confidence."

"I felt like a bull's behind."

The trumpets sounded and Luis Miguel's first bull came charging in, a great black swirl of hump muscle and horn. Miguelillo, the sword handler, gave me a cape.

"What do I do now?" I asked Ernest.

"Hold it at the ready and look intelligent but not too eager."

"Do I know you?"

"Not too well. I've seen you fight. You're no pal. I want you to have fun but don't get caught. They don't have habeas corpus in Spanish jails."

Luis Miguel's cape work was pretty good.

"Study the bull," Ernest said.

"He looks all right to me."

"What's wrong with him?"

"He's got awfully big horns."

"They all look bigger down here."

"Aren't they *pic*-ing him an awful lot?"

"Yes."

"Too much?"

"They're cutting him down for Miguel because he hurt his leg in Málaga."

"I thought he was limping a little."

"How are your legs?"

"Awful but under control."

Dominguin cut one ear for his performance, but Antonio was fabulous with a splendid bull with whom he danced exuberantly; "dance" is the only word for the ballet-*faena* he performed with his mesmerized beast who responded to his every lead as if this were a *pas de deux* they had rehearsed all morning; Antonio was awarded both ears and the tail and he demanded a tour of the ring for the courageous bull.

As Antonio passed by us during his own triumphant circuit of the ring he shouted to Ernest, "Tell Pecas he's looking great. Have you told him how to kill yet?"

"Not yet."

"Tell him."

"Don't look at the horn," Ernest told me. "Sight for where the sword is going in. Keep the left hand low and swing it to your right as you go in."

"What do I do then?"

"You'll go up in the air and we'll all catch you when you land."

Luis Miguel did badly with his last bull, but Antonio really turned it on with his, and the President gave him the ears, tail and a hoof, which is the ultimate that can be awarded, but if the crowd had had its way they would have quartered the bull and given him the whole thing. He beckoned to me. "He wants you to take the tour with him," Ernest said, giving me a helpful nudge.

Antonio waited until I trotted over to him. An avalanche of flowers, sandwiches, cigars, candy, hats, wineskins, shoes, fans, cigarettes, handbags, sunglasses, mantillas, boots, fountain pens, money, pipes, belts, and tiaras was cascading down on us. "Keep handbags and slippers. Let my men pick up everything else," Antonio said.

So around we went, the crowd wildly showering us, and by the time we had completed our second tour of the ring I was pretty heavy with handbags and an assortment of ladies' shoes.

Suddenly Antonio was swept up on the shoulders of a large group of men who intended to parade him across the ring and through the town all the way back to his hotel.

I looked around. All the *cuadrilla* had left. I was alone in the center of the ring. I suddenly discovered how fast you could move in that tight-legged suit and I reached the Chevrolet just as they were pulling out.

When we were safely back in Antonio's room and getting peeled out of our suits, I found out about the handbags and shoes as a succession of beauties showed up to reclaim them. Wine and food came up from the kitchen and soon the room was packed with jubilant people. My only bad moment came when one of the more spectacular ladies, who had come for

her alligator bag, asked about my scars and I didn't have even
the remains of an appendectomy to show her.

Four days later, in Bilbao, the *mano a manos* ended abruptly
and for keeps when the mounting pressure from Antonio finally
caught up with Dominguin. It happened while Dominguin was
placing the bull for the picador. It is one of the most elementary moves in bullfighting and every matador does it thousands
of times. But Dominguin inexplicably moved into the bull instead of away and its horn caught him in the groin and slammed
him against the horse. The picador drove his lance into the bull
as Dominguin was tossed into the air, but the bull disregarded
the lance and caught Dominguin again as he came down and
chopped at him several times on the sand before they made
the *quite* and ran him to the infirmary.

Ernest went to see him in the hospital that evening. Dominguin was suffering very much from the penetration of the horn,
which had ripped up into his abdomen and very nearly taken
his life. Ernest talked to him for a short while in a low voice,
and Dominguin nodded and smiled a little.

Afterward, walking back to the hotel, Ernest said, "He's a
brave man and a beautiful matador. Why the hell do the good
and brave have to die before everyone else?" He did not mean
die as in death, for Dominguin was going to survive, but what
was important to his living had died. I remembered Ernest
once telling me, "The worst death for anyone is to lose the
center of his being, the thing he really is. Retirement is the
filthiest word in the language. Whether by choice or by fate,
to retire from what you do—and what you do makes you what
you are—is to back up into the grave."

A heavy mist was falling and the Bilbao streets glistened with
refracted light. I looked at Ernest, who was pulling up the
collar of his trench coat against the rain, and I felt the eerie
sensation of walking down a sidewalk in Lausanne alongside
Lieutenant Henry, who had just left his dead Catherine in the
hospital.

The following day we drove from Bilbao to Saint-Jean-de-Luz, a town on the Gulf of Vizcaya, a few miles beyond the Spanish border and close to Dax, where Antonio was to perform before Gallic *aficionados*. The new Lancia, which was the first Ernest had actually owned, took the bad Spanish roads in beautiful stride and Ernest was very proud of it.

We stayed outside of town in a gracious, flowered, commodious hotel, the Chantaco, where we ate wonderful Basque food, and afterward we went into Saint-Jean-de-Luz to the Bar Basque for coffee and cordials. (Mary and Annie had gone back to Málaga from Bilbao, so we were just Bill, Ernest, myself and Honor, who, for some time now, had been functioning as Ernest's secretary, filing the notes, clippings and photographs that Ernest needed for the *Life* article.) Ernest raised his glass.

"I have a *dicho*," he said. "The *cuadrilla* will miss El Pecas."

"El Pecas will miss the *cuadrilla*," I answered. "I certainly will."

After Antonio's *corrida* the following afternoon, a rather lackluster performance, Bill drove me to Biarritz, where I boarded the *rapide* for Paris. The following day, I received a cable from Madrid telling me to disregard the newspaper accounts, and that the Lancia was wrecked but they were okay. It was signed: Love Papa. I telephoned the Suecia, where I knew they would be. Ernest told me that after leaving Biarritz they had stopped for dinner, then set out on the road to Madrid. Bill had fallen asleep at the wheel; the Lancia had left the road at high speed, ripped up several cement roadmarkers, careened across a ditch and a field, but had not turned over; nor did any of them have so much as a scratch.

"Absolutely can't blame Bill," Ernest said. "He's done all the driving all summer, and damn fine, and I shouldn't have pushed him on this. I should have known it was too late to start out."

"I guess he feels pretty bad about it." I knew Bill prided himself on his driving.

"He does now but I'm working on him. He'll be all right. He feels awful about wrecking the Lancia."

Ernest returned to New York on the *Liberté* toward the end of October. I had had no news of how the rest of the summer had passed, other than this item which ran in *The New York Times:*

HEMINGWAY ASKS THIEF TO RETURN HIS WALLET

MADRID, Sept. 16 (UPI)—Ernest Hemingway appealed today to the pickpocket who robbed him at a bullfight in Murcia last week to return his wallet even if he keeps the $150 that was in it.

He said the wallet was a gift from his son Patrick, a professional hunter in the East African colony of Tanganyika.

"I beg of you to send back my billfold with the image of St. Christopher in it," Hemingway said in an ad published by the newspaper Pueblo. "As for the 9000 pesetas ($150) it contained, your skill deserves that prize as a reward."

When I met Ernest at the boat he seemed preoccupied and subdued; one of his preoccupations was with a diamond pin he had bought for Mary at Cartier's in Paris. It was a beautiful pin but he was worried because Mary had really wanted a pair of diamond earrings which he had refused to buy because they were too expensive; this pin was being brought as a peace offering.

"How did Mary seem to you?" Ernest asked. Mary had left a month earlier and I had seen her briefly in New York on her way to Cuba.

"Well, fine, but she was pretty upset about the summer."

He nodded his head slowly. "I know. Neglect. And she has a proper beef, you know. I was just having so damn much fun . . . well, it wasn't organized around her. There were us guys and the road and Antonio's fights and all that, and Miss Mary was mostly parked in various places. Pretty great places, but still and all . . . of course, I invited her on almost all of the trips but she said they were too tiring or too dull. She didn't want to go and she didn't want me to go."

"Well, summers fade away pretty fast."

"Yes, but I've invited Antonio and Carmen to Cuba and then to drive with us to Ketchum and stay there for a while, and Mary just sees it as a lot of work."

"Which it will be."

"But a lot of fun, too."

"Fill me in on what happened after I left," I said.

"Sorry to say, it wasn't the September and October we had planned on. Antonio wound up spending a month in jail for using picadors who had been suspended—so there were no bullfights. And just before that my Hong Kong security pocket was pierced for the first time—lost everything."

"I read about it."

"Those events certainly cooled off the summer, which had the ultimate chill put on it by a letter I received from my brother Leicester. It seems he has written a book about me that, among other things, contains some of my letters and he wanted permission to print them. I wrote him my general attitude toward books about people who are still alive, and especially one member of a family writing about that family, especially one as vulnerable as ours where my mother was a bitch and my father a suicide. It always seemed better to me to skip the whole thing and try for a better record, and I am damned if I will permit the Baron to write about it and dredge up all the trouble I've ever been in as well, just to make money. It might be better to buy the whole thing from him and get a release, but as I explained to him, no Hemingstein has ever yet paid for anything he could prevent with his own two hands." *

Ernest stayed in New York for a few days to conduct some business but the air of preoccupation clung to him. The summer was over. Not just another summer, but *the* summer, the last good time of a life of good times. Unfortunately, some of what had happened that summer in the disguise of levity was to come back to haunt Ernest. The tide that he had always easily swum against was destined to push him out to the open sea. But this had been the best summer of his life, he had said, and no one could take that away from him.

As I drove him out to the airport he continued to worry about Mary. "Do you think Miss Mary will like the pin?" he asked.

"Sure she will. It's a lovely pin."

* Leicester Hemingway did not publish this book, *My Brother Ernest Hemingway*, until shortly after Ernest's death.

"I hope so."

"Sure she will."

"I guess it wasn't much fun for her. I just wish she wouldn't take it out on poor Bill."

"She had some fun, quite a lot. She'll be all right."

"She hasn't written since she left. And I've got Antonio coming."

"Don't worry, Papa. Please don't worry. Everything will be all right."

"I just hope she likes the pin."

Part Four

Our nada who art in nada, nada be thy name
thy kingdom nada thy will be nada in nada as it
is in nada. Give us this nada our daily nada
and nada us our nada as we nada our nadas and
nada us not into nada but deliver us from nada;
pues nada. Hail nothing full of nothing,
nothing is with thee.

A CLEAN, WELL-LIGHTED PLACE

Chapter Thirteen

Havana ✦ 1960

All of San Francisco de Paula was at the airport with banners to greet Ernest. He was well loved by his little village whose residents treated him like a benign feudal lord. He was generous and inconspicuous in his charities and he enjoyed occasional evenings in the village bar, talking with the men whom he had known for more than two decades.

Ernest reported that Mary was not interested in the pin but was being friendly toward him and cordial and hospitable to Antonio and Carmen. Also, in view of the fact that on Ernest's desk there were ninety-two letters awaiting answers, she had agreed that he should import Honor to be his secretary. Until this time he had never had full-time secretarial help.

Ernest and I talked on the phone before he left for Ketchum. "Things at *finca* under control," he said. "Antonio and Carmen are having a grand time. I act cheerful as always but am not."

"Why? I thought you said things . . ."

"At the *finca*. But the Castro climate is something else. Not good. Not good at all. Can't tell what it will be when I come back to work in January, and what I want most is to get back to writing. I just hope to Christ the United States doesn't cut the sugar quota. That would really tear it. It will make Cuba a gift to the Russians. You'd be amazed at the changes. Good and bad. A hell of a lot of good. After Batista any change would almost *have* to be an improvement. But the anti-United States is building. All around. Spooks you. If they really turn it on, I'm sure they will put me out of business."

"Well, not really. You could always set up in Ketchum."

"Twelve months of the year? Summers without the boat?"

"You could summer in Key West."

"No, that belongs to the kids. And besides, there are too many ghosts. No, hell, I'll just get one of those 'Going Out of Business' signs and hang it around my neck: *After 25 Years at This Location Everything Must Be Sold at a Sacrifice.*" There was a pause at the other end of the wire. "A hell of a sacrifice."

From Ernest's account of it, the motor trip with Antonio and Carmen from Key West to Ketchum was not a success. Nor was the stay in Ketchum, where none of the 746 inhabitants spoke Spanish or, with the exception of the Lords, had ever seen a bullfight. Ernest tried valiantly to entertain him, but nevertheless Antonio returned to Spain much sooner than scheduled.

The other negative event of that Ketchum sojourn was that while shooting ducks one afternoon, Mary fell and shattered her left elbow. Vernon Lord had to piece the bone together like a jigsaw puzzle and his prognosis was for a long haul in a cast and a longer haul in therapy. Ernest rallied, as he always did in physical emergencies, and devoted all his time to caring for Mary and running the house. When I came to Ketchum in early December, Ernest was so concerned with his chores that he only got out hunting once.

By January, Ernest was back in Cuba hard at work on his *Life* account of the *mano a mano*, which he was calling *The Dangerous Summer*. From January until June we telephoned each other quite often about the television plays I was working on and about the summer in Spain he was writing about. In February he reported that he was over seventeen thousand words into the article.

On one occasion he called because he was worried that the commentator's piece, just published in *Esquire*, might have made the *Life* editors think he had given away what was rightfully theirs. He said that in giving him a ten-thousand-dollar advance they had a right to expect him to protect them, and he asked me to call Ed Thompson, the editor of *Life*, and explain that the commentator was just the usual character who comes to lunch and stuffs his pocket with your ideas instead of your silver.

In March, Ernest telephoned to say that the piece was running much longer than expected, that it would be about thirty thousand words, and that I should tell *Life* he was shooting for an April 7th deadline. He also told me that Gary Cooper had spoken to him about *Across the River* and was in the process of preparing contracts for its purchase.

The next time I heard from Ernest he sounded tired and his voice was tense. The article for *Life*, which now stood at 63,562 words, had missed its April deadline with the end not in sight.

"I wrote Ed Thompson today," Ernest said, "to explain why the piece is running so long, that what I'm attempting to do is to make a real story which would be valuable in itself and worth publishing after there had been no deaths or dramatic endings to the season. As you may remember, when I hired on to write the piece it looked like one or other of the men might be killed and *Life* wanted coverage of it. Instead, it turned out to be the gradual destruction of one person by another with all the things that led up to it and made it. I had to establish the personality and the art and the basic differences between the two great artists and then show what happened, and you can't do that in four thousand words.

"If I could have done it shorter I certainly would have, but it was necessary to make the people come alive and to show the extraordinary circumstances of what we both saw last summer and to make something which would have some unity and be worth publishing. Certainly the price that *Life* was paying was worth more than the simple account of the *mano a manos*, which were no longer news and had been picked over by various vultures and large-bellied crows. What I was writing was worth much more than thirty thousand dollars but I thought the hell with that since I only know how to write one way: the best that I can."

"But now that it's longer, don't you intend to up the price?"

"Well, actually what I did was to give them an out on both deadline and price. I told Thompson that I could jam through and finish by the April deadline as said I would, but thought that was unfair to *Life*, Literature and the Pursuit of Happiness. I explained it needs a month more solid work and then typing, correcting and retyping to be what I want it to be. So I gave them an out and offered to return the advance, but I said that if they still wanted it with a May deadline, then they would have to renegotiate the contract. I offered them forty thousand words for ten thousand dollars more than the five thousand words they contracted for. This is the minimum price I have been paid per word for any writing since before the Spanish Civil War. But offered to let them off the hook if they preferred."

"They'll take it. It's a bargain."

"I wrote young Scribner and told him to scratch the Paris book from the fall list due to this overextension on *The Dangerous Summer*."

"You sound tired."

"I'm dead-house. Try to slow it down but can't. Has been building up too long. Do you think I am charging *Life* enough? It should divide into three parts."

"I'd say it should be at least three times the original price."

"And a limit of forty thousand words."

"When do you think you'll be finished?"

"By the end of May, if my eyes hold. I haven't wanted to worry you, but old eyes started getting bad in February and the doctors here say it's a rap called *keratitis sicca*. Cornea is drying up. Tear ducts dried up already. Only book in the joint with type big enough for me to read is *Tom Sawyer*."

"But what are they doing for you?"

"Medication, but doctors say if it doesn't arrest I'll be blind in a year."

"What! Oh, I can't believe—"

"So haven't been running as a cheerful these days."

"But that's Cuban medicine. When you come to New York I'll get you to the best man—"

"So I'm down to one glass of booze, two glasses of wine and

Tom Sawyer, which is a great book but begins to pale on the ninth reading."

On the fourth of May I was awakened in the early hours of the morning by the overseas operator. Ernest had just heard on the radio that Cooper had had a prostate operation in a Boston hospital and there was speculation that it was malignant. I assured him that from what I had heard it was not malignant and that Cooper was scheduled to make a picture in Naples that summer. Ernest asked question after question about Cooper, most of which I couldn't answer. He was very upset; Cooper was one of his oldest friends, and although they did not see each other very often, their bond was strong.

Ernest was also perturbed over *The Dangerous Summer*. It had reached 92,453 words and he figured it would finish out around 110,000. What bothered him was how it could be brought down to 40,000 for *Life*. I advised him not to think about cutting until he had completely finished it, but he said he had nightmares over its emasculation of 70,000 words.

I clearly recall my reaction to that phone call: For the first time since I've known him, I thought, Ernest is unsure of himself. He had always been completely the master of what he wrote and how he wrote and where and when it would be published. But on the phone that morning that sense of control was missing. Perhaps the news about Cooper had undone him for the moment, or the worry over his eyes. Actually, I did not doubt that by the time *The Dangerous Summer* was finished he would be in command again.

Ernest finished *The Dangerous Summer* on May 28th and it came to 108,746 words. He said he had to go back to Spain to get what he needed for a coda that would bring it up to date, and to check certain things nobody would risk putting in a letter. The main thing he had to find out about was whether the practice of shaving the bull's horns, which he alleged was being done to bulls fought by Dominguin, was still going on. He also wanted to search out additional pictures.

But his immediate problem was excising seventy thousand words. Between June 1st and June 25th he telephoned me twelve times, with mounting anxiety at his inability to cut the

manuscript. *Life* had offered to cut it for him, but he did not
trust their judgment. After twenty-one days, working from
early morning all through each day, Ernest had cut a total of
two hundred and seventy-eight words. When he phoned on the
twenty-fifth his voice was husky with fatigue. "I have been over
every page a dozen times," he said, "and all I have is five
hundred and thirty words to show for it. I can't see another
word I can cut. I can't cancel out on *Life* because they've
already advertised the piece. But I just can't go over it again,
Hotch; it all seems locked-in to me and I can't use my eyes
any more; I can't see the damn words—in the morning I can but
by ten o'clock I can't see the goddamn words any more. So I
was thinking this morning—I know it's a hell of an imposition—
but could you possibly come down and work on it with me?
You'll have your sharp head and your good eyes and it won't
take more than a few days and we'll get the piece off to *Life*
and then we can go out on *Pilar* and relax and catch some
fish and it will be like old times."

I flew down to Havana on the morning of June 27th. Ernest
was waiting at the airport and Juan drove us directly to the
finca. It was very hot and humid; as we drove through the
streets of Havana I noticed anti-United States slogans scrawled
everywhere on the walls, and there were CUBA SÍ! YANKEE NO!
banners stretched across the street tops. A big anti-Yankee
demonstration was in the works for July 4th, and for its climax
Castro was scheduled to harangue a giant rally in the heart of
the city.

Ernest sat in the front seat, as he always did, looking straight
ahead, keeping his eyes off the signs. "You can see," he said,
"this is the last summer."

The villagers waved to him as we passed through San Francisco de Paula and he smiled and waved back. We ate lunch
with Mary quietly and pleasantly in the high-ceilinged dining
room, with its horned beauties watching us from the walls, and
Ernest complimented Mary on the cold-fruit soup and the
bonito. But he ate very little and filled half his wine glass with
water. He closed his eyes frequently and often pressed his
fingers against them. His beard had not been trimmed for

months; the forward part of his head had become bald but he covered it successfully by combing forward the long hair at the back of his head, giving himself the mien of a Roman emperor.

After lunch he gave me the 688-page typed manuscript of *The Dangerous Summer* and I took it up to the study at the top of the tower and started to read. It was so hot I had to hold my handkerchief in my hand to keep the perspiration out of my eyes. (There were no fans or air conditioners in any part of the *finca*.) I read and made notes all that afternoon and evening. At night it seemed to get even hotter and it was difficult to sleep.

By the following afternoon I submitted to Ernest a list of eight suggested cuts in the first hundred pages; he went into his bedroom to look them over while I resumed working in the tower. The shimmering, unyielding heat gave me the sensation of operating in slow motion. It occurred to me that despite my many visits to Cuba, this was the first time I had been there in the summer.

Ernest and I conferred on cuts the following morning in his bedroom. He had in front of him seven different-colored pills, which he swallowed one by one with siphon water, and a lined pad of paper on which he had neatly written his reasons for rejecting each of the cuts. He handed me the list.

It was a startling document: in the first place, some of it didn't make any sense; for example, in rejecting one five-page cut, Ernest listed four reasons why those pages should be retained and then concluded by stating: "But has effect of making things happen no-where"; secondly, the whole thing had an uncharacteristically disorganized, badly phrased, petulant ring; and in the third place, I could not figure out why Ernest painstakingly wrote all this out and sat there watching me read it. We had many times in the past conferred about his manuscripts for *Across the River and into the Trees*, *The Old Man and the Sea*, the Paris sketches, and short stories, but this was the only time he had gone through the process of writing notes, and strangely incomprehensible notes at that.

But I accepted them without discussion, and for the next

three days I continued to work on the manuscript, suggesting cuts that Ernest would consider and then carefully reject with written notations on his pad. I explained my reasons for each suggested cut but did not press them, for I realized that Ernest was being severely harassed by conflicting desires to save every word of what he had written and to deliver a properly cut version to *Life*. "What I've written is Proustian in its cumulative effect," Ernest explained, "and if we eliminate detail we destroy that effect."

In the late afternoons we went down to the big, cloudy pool to swim. The water was as bracing as a hot bath. I watched Ernest slowly enter the pool. He looked thin. His chest and shoulders had lost their thrust and his upper arms were macilent and formless, as if his huge biceps had been pared down by an unskilled whittler.

One night when it was too hot to sleep, I found in my room an old volume that contained issues of a magazine called *This Quarter* which had been published in Paris in the Twenties. Thumbing through it, I came upon "Big Two-Hearted River" and "The Undefeated" in what was obviously their first publication. I also found an article by the poet Ernest Walsh, the magazine's editor, in which he prophesied: "Hemingway selected his audience. His rewards will be rich. But thank God he will never be satisfied. He is of the elect. He belongs. It will take time to wear him out. And before that he will be dead."

On the fourth day Ernest finally approved a cut of three pages, and from then on he slowly, grudgingly, painfully began to accept cuts until finally at the end of nine days he had a total of 54,916 excised words. The following day Ernest said he could not use his eyes any more. "I can see the words on the page for only ten or twelve minutes," he said, "before my eyes cut out, and then I can't use them again for an hour or two." We decided that I should bring the manuscript back to New York and give it to *Life* to make additional cuts from the 53,830 words it now contained. "I'll tell you, Hotch, although I move about as cheerfully as possible," Ernest said, "it is like living in a Kafka nightmare. I act cheerful like always but am not. I'm bone-tired and very beat up emotionally."

"What bothers you most—the Castro business?"

"That's part of it. He doesn't bother me personally. I'm good publicity for them, so maybe they'd never bother me and let me live on here as always, but I am an American above everything else and I cannot stay here when other Americans are being kicked out and my country is being villified. I guess I knew it was all over for me here the night they killed Black Dog. A Bastista search party, looking for guns, came barreling in here in the middle of the night and poor Black Dog, old and half blind, tried to stand guard at the door of the *finca*, but a soldier clubbed him to death with the butt of his rifle. Poor old Black Dog. I miss him. In the early morning when I work, he's not there on the kudu skin beside the typewriter; and in the afternoon when I swim, he's not hunting lizards beside the pool; and in the evenings when I sit in my chair to read, his chin isn't resting on my foot. I miss Black Dog as much as I miss any friend I ever lost. And now I lose the *finca*— there's no sense kidding myself—I know I must leave it all and go. But how can you measure that loss? Everything I have is here. My pictures, my books, my good work place and good memories."

"Can't you do something about the pictures?"

"I'd settle for the Miró and the two Juan Gris."

"Maybe I could get them out in my luggage if we took them out of their frames and rolled them."

"No, I wouldn't let you risk that."

"What about a request from The Museum of Modern Art to exhibit them? You told me Alfred Barr had asked you several times for a loan of the Miró."

"I guess it's worth a try. I'll write him."

"I read the new chapters of the Paris book last night—they're wonderful, Papa. They make me feel I was living there and that those times were mine, and the next time I go to Paris I will expect it to be just that way."

"Will I be boiled in Congressional oil for being kind to poor Ezra?"

"No, that's all over. I don't think this Congress knows who Ezra Pound is."

Ernest was in a quandary as to which book should be published first—*The Dangerous Summer* or the Paris book. He
even wondered whether *The Dangerous Summer* should be published as a book at all. After a long, vacillating discussion I
suggested we both think about it and discuss it again when he
came to New York. I asked him to give me advance notice
of his arrival date so I could try to arrange an appointment
with the eye specialist, a very difficult man to reach.

"Well, don't worry if you can't get the appointment," Ernest
said. "There isn't much anyone can do for *keratitus sicca* . . .
or for anything else, I guess."

We were going to go out on the boat with Mary and Honor
the following day, but Gregorio reported that the sea was
worthless and no one had taken anything for four days. Ernest
and I drove into Havana and had one daiquiri each at the
Floridita and then Ernest went to the bank to get a manuscript
out of the vault. It was a short novel called *The Sea Chase*,
which Mary thought could be made into a good motion picture, and Ernest wanted to know what I thought. Across the
top of the first page, and above the title, he had written in
longhand, "The Sea (Main Book Three)," which indicated that
this was the sea section of what he had always referred to as
his "big book," or "blockbuster," a work that was to have had
three parts to it: the land, the sea and the air.

I read it that evening. Mary was absolutely right; it was a
compact, exciting adventure, set in the Bahamas during World
War II, that involved hunting down the escaped Nazi crew of
a sunken U-boat. It was in fact a fictionalized account of what
might have happened to Ernest (Thomas Hudson in the book)
and his *Pilar* crew if they had picked up the trail of a U-boat
in 1943. It has not yet been published, but undoubtedly will be.

When I told Ernest my reaction, he said he guessed he had
better reread the manuscript. After Honor had read it to him,
he said, uncertainly, "Some things I ought to do to it. Maybe
after the Paris book, if I can still see enough to write."

I tried to discourage Ernest from going to the airport with
me; he was terribly debilitated from the heat and his own

pressures, but he insisted. "Transport out is heavy and tricky these days," he said, "and I want to be sure you're okay." We had been able to get a reservation only because one of Ernest's Cuban friends was an executive with the airline. Castro had cut down outgoing flights to two a day, and there were a lot more people than that who wanted out.

In the car Ernest turned to me and said, "Hotch, I've been up all night worrying. I wasn't going to say anything because a deal's a deal and you've already done so damn much for me, but it's something I couldn't live with."

"Well, if it's anything I can possibly do . . ."

"This deal with *Life*. I know it's all set and *legally* I'm bound to it, but Christ! How did I ever sign on like that? I'll sell out three issues for them for less than I got for the one issue that had *The Old Man and the Sea* in it. You see, it started to be one thing and then became another and then another and I boxed myself into a corner. But this will be a year of heavy taxes and I don't know where it's coming from. I don't want to borrow from Scribner's; I don't like borrowing there now that old Charlie is gone, but this forty thousand figures to be all I earn in 1960. And now I've got to go back to Spain to work on the piece some more so that I can cable them something to update it, and that will eat up a lot more dough."

He was so anguished that against my honest judgment, which was that Ernest had firmly committed himself to terms, I found myself saying, "Well, why don't I talk to Ed Thompson when I get back?"

"Promise him first look at the Paris book. With some good Paris pictures it might be a good entry for them."

"How much more do you want, Papa?"

"If I could get seventy-five, I could put forty in the tax account and have thirty-five to live on."

I happened to know that Ernest's annual income from royalties on his former books was around a hundred thousand dollars, that he had large holdings of stocks and bonds, most of which he had bought twenty or thirty years ago, and that his tax account was stocked beyond any possible demands his income could make on it, but I respected his pretense that he

had to live each year on what he earned that year. In the
precarious world of free lance, it is a highly desirable attitude,
albeit a rather unrealistic one when the writer has reached the
eminence that Ernest had attained. It was probably a holdover
from his hungry times.

The airport building was choked with people. The crowd in
front of the ticket counter was so thick I had to use my best
New York subway maneuvers to clear a path for us. At the
counter we found out the bad news: Castro had issued an
order that morning canceling all flights to the United States
until further notice. It was an act of reprisal for a new requirement that all Cuban aircraft refueling in the United States pay
cash on delivery.

We fought our way back out of the mob, and Ernest led
me to an office in the terminal building where one could charter
flights. The man there was an old friend who knew Ernest back
in the early Thirties when he ran contraband rum into Key
West. Ernest and he had a short discussion in low voices,
and then the man picked up my bag and said to meet him in
ten minutes on the airfield ramp on the other side of his
office.

While we were waiting out the ten minutes, Ernest gave me
the pad of lined paper on which he had been making his
Dangerous Summer notes. "I did some final work on the cutting," he said. "You can read it on the way back. You know
your way out of Key West, don't you?"

"Sure."

Ernest's pal flew me to Key West in a Cessna, without benefit
of Havana customs. I hired a car in Key West and drove along
the magnificent highway that stretches across the water and
the keys to Miami, where I eventually got a seat on a jet to
New York. I took out the pad Ernest had given me. It was
crammed with page numbers and directions, some of them
countermanding a few cuts he had previously approved and
suggesting cuts in their stead, but most of them simply detailing
cuts we had already made, with explanations about them. These
latter notations covered fifteen pages of the note pad and

seemed to have been written mainly as private explanations to himself.

Ernest and Mary arrived in New York on Friday, July 13th. In the intervening week I had had lunch with Ed Thompson and, after warning him to get fortified with a double Old Grand-dad, had told him the bad news. If ever a decoration is awarded for bravery under editorial fire, I recommend Ed Thompson as its first recipient. He drained the last of his Older Grand-dad, ordered another, expelled a short sigh and said, "Well, there is only one Ernest Hemingway and I guess there is some merit in what he says. Tell me gently."

I said a hundred thousand dollars and we agreed upon ninety thousand with rights to *Life*'s Spanish edition thrown in for an additional ten thousand.

Almost every day after I left Havana, Ernest had called me to discuss the dilemma of which book to publish first, and I finally suggested that it might be a good idea to get his publisher's opinion. I set up a meeting at Ernest's Sixty-second Street apartment on the afternoon he arrived, and I had also arranged an appointment for Ernest with the Chief of Opthalmology at New York's biggest hospital. He was reputedly the country's foremost specialist and he had a Park Avenue office where he saw a few private patients. He had told me on the phone that *keratitis sicca* was a rare and serious condition that not only caused blindness but was, in most cases, fatal.

Charles Scribner, Jr., arrived at the apartment with one of his editors, L. Harry Brague, Jr. They took the uncut manuscript of *The Dangerous Summer*, along with two copies of all the Paris sketches, and said they would be there Monday morning to discuss which should be published first.

We also heard from Alfred Barr that arrangements were being made for a representative from The Museum of Modern Art to go to the *finca* and crate Miró's "Farm" preparatory to flying it up to New York.

I had hoped that with the favorable resolution of the *Life* money and the Miró painting, and with the burden of the publishing dilemma temporarily shifted, Ernest would relax a bit and enjoy some of his New York places, but he said gloomily, "How can I go into Toots' without drinking, or the Old Seidelburg, or Sherm's joint or anywhere else?" Mary cooked for us and we ate most of our meals in the apartment; Ernest drank only Sancerre wine, in moderation.

He mostly discussed *The Dangerous Summer*, worrying about whether he had been completely fair to Luis Miguel, fearing that Miguel would be offended, worrying about how the Spaniards would react to his criticism of their great hero, Manolete, worrying about whether he would harm Antonio by describing his arrest and the *scandale* of his pics, worrying, worrying, worrying.

I did manage to get his mind off *The Dangerous Summer* for a short while with a new offer which had come from movie producer Jerry Wald at Twentieth Century-Fox: the studio wanted to buy the seven short stories that had been used in my teleplay *The World of Nick Adams*, add three more, and make a movie of it. They were offering a hundred thousand dollars for the stories. This infuriated Ernest. "Christ, that's what they paid for *one* story! 'Snows of Kilimanjaro,' they paid that, and for 'My Old Man.' "

I pointed out that the stories involved here were very fragmentary, that many of them had already been seen on television, and that they were getting the rights to do only one movie. "Once you set a price in Hollywood, you can't back down," Ernest said definitively. "They can have the ten stories for nine hundred thousand."

On Monday morning Charles Scribner, Jr., and Harry Brague, Jr., returned. Charles Scribner, Jr., said that both works were simply wonderful; he thought that *The Dangerous Summer* should be published first so as to capitalize on the *Life* publication. He also thought that not too much time should elapse between the summer it happened and the publication. Harry Brague, Jr., said he had not read all *The Dangerous Summer* but that on the basis of what he had read, he agreed with his boss. Ernest smiled and said that was fine, for he inclined

toward that decision himself. I was shocked to realize that it
was the first time I had seen Ernest smile since I went down
to Cuba.

After they departed he said, "Guess they like product. Maybe
won't have to close down machine for repairs after all. Let's go
over and have a dish at Toots' to remind ourselves how good
Mary's cooking really is."

Ernest enjoyed his lunch at Shor's. He had a couple of drinks,
cracked rough jokes with Toots, as always, and exchanged pleas-
antries with Leonard Lyons and sports columnist Jimmy Cannon, who was also a long-time friend. We walked back to the
apartment, Ernest stopping to inspect windows along the way.
"It's good to be back on the town," he said. I felt hugely relieved at his resurgence of spirit; unfortunately it was short-
lived.

We were barely in the door when the telephone rang.
It was easy to follow the conversation from Ernest's end of
it. Charles Scribner, Jr., had had another conference with Harry
Brague, Jr., who had finished *The Dangerous Summer* during
his lunch hour, and they now had decided to reverse themselves and recommend that the Paris sketches be published first.

"Well, I sent off a lot of cables for bullfight pictures and a
hell of a lot of other stuff," Ernest said testily. He listened and
then said: "I don't say it isn't good thinking, Charles, but it
isn't very constructive to mount one offensive in the morning
and then mount another in the afternoon with the same troops
in the opposite direction . . . No, hell, if you and Harry see it
that way, I'll go along with it."

Ernest ate no dinner that evening. He got into bed early with
all the New York papers and a pile of magazines he had bought
on our way home from Shor's. He also had a note pad and
pencil, and when I left he was writing in that.

The following morning we went to the eye specialist, and
Ernest was there for almost two hours. He had brought with
him a large manila file folder that contained reports, records
and test results from the Havana ophthalmologists who had
been treating him. Part of the two hours was spent sitting in

the waiting room while various drops that had been put into his eyes did their work. Ernest was very impressed with the doctor, who he said was wizard, and even more impressed with his equipment, which, he said, made the Cuban stuff look like it had been left behind by Louis Pasteur.

When we departed the nurse handed Ernest a prescription, but he did not say anything about the results of the examination until we were almost back at the apartment. "Turned out pretty good," he said matter-of-factly. "Haven't got the dire crud diagnosed by Cuban medicos. Just need stronger glasses."

Ernest never mentioned his eye trouble again; nor was I aware that after that he had any further trouble reading. And to my knowledge he never used the prescription for stronger glasses.

That afternoon while Mary was out shopping, the telephone rang, and when I picked it up, the voice sounded familiar—from out of the past—but it was so slurred and incoherent that it took me a few moments to place it. It was Jigee. She had been out of our lives a long time. Ernest got on the extension and we had a three-way conversation; Jigee had trouble forming her words and often didn't complete her sentences. She was calling long distance but was evasive about telling us just where she was. She wanted to know how long Ernest and I planned to be in New York, for she was thinking of coming there, she said, since she hadn't seen us for so long; Ernest told her he was sorry as hell not to be able to see her but that he was leaving in a day or two for Spain.

After we hung up, Ernest couldn't say anything. I had known about Jigee's drinking for a long time, but it had come as a shock to Ernest. Finally he said, "I'm the son-of-a-bitch who gave her her first drink. You remember that Scotch sour that day at the Ritz?"

"Now, Papa, if it hadn't been you it would have been someone else."

"Maybe, but I was the one and I could kick my brains out for that!"

"Papa, you can take the rap for a lot of things, but not for that. Whatever we are we are—does it matter who turns it on?"

"It matters to me! It goddamn well matters to me!" He walked over to the windows and for a long time watched the pigeons strutting along the rain spouts.

Charles Scribner, Jr., and Harry Brague, Jr., came to lunch at Ernest's place the following day and apologized for upsetting him with their change of mind. They then said that they had arrived at an absolutely final and irrevocable decision, which was that they were right in the first place and that *The Dangerous Summer* should be published just as soon as possible.

Ernest calmly said that he would take their third change of mind under advisement and that's how it was left.

Ernest had planned to leave the following day for Spain but it took him three more days to get organized. He wrote many lists: some lists detailed chores he had to perform before leaving, some he left with me as reminders of various things we had discussed, and I think he left still other lists for Mary. An item on one of my lists was "Re 20th offer, will settle for $750,000." I had never been aware, before my last trip to Havana, that he had ever before made lists like these. His highly organized and retentive mind was all the list he had ever needed; all I could think was that quite suddenly he didn't trust it any more.

I had not planned on going abroad that fall but after I midwifed the last of *The Dangerous Summer* installments Ernest, who was in Madrid, became unnaturally anxious to get to an immediate agreement with Twentieth Century-Fox on the Nick Adams stories. It was enigmatic that after assiduously discouraging movie projects all of his life Ernest should suddenly be so solicitous about them.

I arrived in Madrid the evening of October 2nd, looking forward to a happy reunion with Ernest's mob (now reduced to Bill, Annie, Honor and Antonio) and the kind of fun we had had the summer before. I checked into the Suecia and went to Ernest's suite. The door was open. Annie and Honor were seated side by side on a sofa, talking and drinking wine from a bottle of *rosado* that rested in a silver cooler on the table, and Bill, who saw me first, was packing photographs into a small suitcase. Worry hung in the room like black crepe.

As Bill came toward the door to greet me, Ernest emerged from the bedroom. He was wearing his old woolen bathrobe, secured by his GOTT MIT UNS belt, with a sweater underneath the robe, his elkskin slippers, and a white tennis visor that was pulled far down over his eyes. Annie had risen and I was crossing the room to give her a welcome hug, but Ernest stepped in front of her and said rather accusingly, "Been sweating you out since nine thirty-four this morning."

"I got routed into Barcelona and had to fight my way out of there."

"Barcelona? You had me plenty worried. Thought you had gone down in the drink. Couldn't get any gen from the goddamn Spanish airline. Figured they were covering up."

"We were really sort of in mourning," Annie said. "Ernest was so worried it was already reality for me. Now, of course," she said reproachfully, "I'll have to get drunk."

"My state of mourning got me half-drunk already," Honor said.

"I have some Scotch in our room," Bill said, and he started out.

"And what am I supposed to do while you all are having drinks?" Ernest asked in a cutting voice. "Hit myself over the head?"

No one said anything. There was an awkward silence. Then Bill went back to packing the photos. "How was Antonio?" I asked.

Ernest had gone to stand in the doorway, and I didn't think he was going to answer. "He was super in Ronda," he said, finally, coming back into the room. "The fights in Tarifa were blown out by a near hurricane, and they almost called off Jerez de la Frontera because of the high wind, but the civil governor said fight or jail so they fought. Antonio was wonderful with his final bull. Then Salamanca two days, bulls worthless, Antonio very good, and we saw the new boy, Camino, twice." He came very close to me and looked into my eyes piercingly. "Have

you seen the *Life*s? Did you see those pictures? I'll bet all hell
has broken loose."

"About what? As far as I could tell . . ."

"About *what?* The way *Life* crossed us up on the pictures in
the second issue. That's what!" (*Life* had run eight photographs
of Antonio and Luis Miguel in action to demonstrate the
various basic passes used in bullfighting.) "After me working
literally weeks for them to get wonderful pictures, fair to both
boys, showing things at their best and okayed by *Life*'s Paris
man, Will Lang, after arguments—after all that, they used the
most inferior of the okayed pictures and one of Miguel that
they took last year in Bayonne . . ."

"Which one?"

"The one labeled *pase ayudado*—hell, that's the kind of
picture photographers use to blackmail bullfighters. After all the
hours and days of checking and rechecking . . ."

"But wasn't that photo okayed by you?"

"No, of course not! I'm the laughingstock of anyone who
knows anything about bullfighting and has seen the piece. I'm
regarded as the crook and double-crosser of all time. Didn't
that photo knock you down when you saw it?"

"Frankly, Papa, no. But I don't have your knowledge about
. . ."

"Didn't Mary say something?"

"It seemed all right to her, too."

"Then you weren't looking. Neither of you. Just like Bill.
Why don't you use your goddamn eyes? Well, I can tell you
when I saw that page of pictures, it made me feel worse than
any kind of wound or disaster. I guaranteed the pictures would
be accurate and good and show both men at their best, and
instead that picture is malicious. To be made both an all-time
fool and a double-crosser! There is nothing to explain, as Antonio and Miguel know how carefully I went over the pictures,
and the hours put in. Nobody had a copy to show me at
Salamanca though the *Time-Life* people had seen it. If they had
only shown it to me, I could have made some explanation to
Antonio and tried to have him make Miguel understand. Never
felt so completely sunk. Head was getting in good shape and

I thought with the right pictures, the fatigue and overwork to point of destruction was justified because we would have the results. Does no good to explain that promises to me were not kept. Nobody would believe that. Would shoot myself if it would do any good. But would have to get things neatened up for any such luxury as that. When I got a letter from Mary saying that the second number was fine, I quit worrying and was figuring on starting to have the fatigue beat and that everything would work out fine. Now this."

"But why don't you send an explanation and apology to Antonio and Luis Miguel?"

"I guess I could send a cable to Antonio. He's in Arles. But what the hell good can I do with a cable when he's in France for only one day and probably dressing at some friend's house instead of at the hotel?"

"But it's worth a try. And maybe you'll find that he and Miguel aren't as sensitive about the pictures as you think."

"That's what Bill said—what difference do a few pictures make? But the work that went into getting those pictures right and my obligation to be straight and see things through makes me sick right through my bones. Would rather be smashed up like in Africa any number of times than have the feeling that page of pictures gave me."

He went into the bedroom. I turned to look at the others; from their attitude of complete resignation I could see that this was something they had been enduring for a long time.

I went into the bedroom and said, "Papa, no matter how bad the situation is, there's no sense beating yourself to death over it. You know you had nothing to do with it." He was sitting on the edge of the bed.

"I have been trying to convince myself that am not destroyed as an honest guy, but it is not easy. If I can only make the people involved believe it was not done by me in carelessness or malice. You mean to say nobody in the States picked me up on that picture?"

"Not to my knowledge."

"I ought to write Lennie Lyons and get the true gen. He'll level with me."

"Well, why don't we forget it all for now and go over to the Callejón and have a good dinner like old times?"

"I don't know. I haven't been going out much . . ."

"Come on. It will do you good."

"We were supposed to go to Nîmes but we canceled that because Luis Miguel was there and I couldn't face him after the *Life* picture."

"Why don't we have a drink at the bar here—your diet will permit one drink, won't it?—and I'll phone the Callejón and have them reserve your table?"

"I'm too beat to go, Hotch, but you take Honor and go with Bill and Annie. It hasn't been much fun for Honor. I haven't been going anywhere."

He went over and shut the door and took me by the arm and led me to the corner of the room farthest from the door. "You watch yourself," he said in a low, ominous voice. "Keep your eye on all of them. Especially Bill. He has been trying to crack up the car again. He missed killing me the first time and he's waiting for another opening. That's one of the reasons I've been staying put. Last time out he tried to run me off a cliff. There's no sense discussing it with Honor because she tries to make excuses for him."

"Oh, come on, Papa. What are you saying? You're joking, of course."

He tightened his hold on my arm and his face grew more tense. "Would I kid about a thing like that? I don't know what he's up to but if you go to the Callejón, don't take the car. Take a taxi. Maybe he'll be all right with you. But it's been hell the whole month of September. I've got to get out of here as soon as I can. I asked Bill to make a reservation but you better check on it. Don't want reservation in my name. You've got to keep me off the manifest until just before take-off."

Bill and I had a drink at the bar while Annie and Honor dressed for dinner. "Jesus," Bill said, the words tumbling out of him, "am I glad to see you! I don't think I could have lasted another week. Ernest came over here so nervous and fatigued and right away plunged into traveling and collecting hundreds of photographs from all over Spain, and then worked night and

day writing captions for *Life* and worrying about them, and
arguing with Will Lang, and down on everyone, and . . . Christ,
I don't know, Hotch. What's wrong with him? Is there something wrong with him? He talks about his kidneys, constantly
about his kidneys, or maybe it's one kidney, I don't know,
but that's all you hear all day long. Did the doctors give him
bad news about his kidney? What's he got that it would turn
him this way? He never smiles or even looks pleasant. You remember how he always talked when we traveled, always talking about the countryside or the cattle or the old days and the
places he fought? Now he doesn't say a word. Not one word.
Just sits there tense as hell and looks straight ahead. At first
I tried to do the talking, asking questions to get him to talk,
but he barely answered so I gave up. And no wine bag.
Can you imagine Ernest in the front seat without the wine
bag?"

It was a glum dinner; nobody ate much. Annie was convinced that Ernest had been told that he had a fatal kidney
ailment. I asked whether Ernest had also been complaining
about his eyes. Honor said he had not once mentioned them.
"But now he carries on about his kidneys the way he used to
carry on about his eyes," she said.

"We must help him to get back to the States," Bill said. "He
keeps making reservations—I make them in my name—but then
he changes his mind. You see, what I'm afraid of is that the
Spaniards will start to get on him for the Manolete stuff. Can
you imagine what that will do to him? That Dominguin picture doesn't mean anything, but in the *Life* piece he says that
Manolete used cheap tricks and all that, and a lot of Spaniards
are going to get on him for that. Manolete is their most revered hero and it's bad for a foreigner to spit on his grave.
Ernest *has* to be out of here before *that* hits him." *

"It's just fatigue," Annie explained. "He's so exhausted he
can't think straight or eat or sleep or be cheerful or *anything*.

* Bill was referring to Ernest's statement in *The Dangerous Summer*
that the public loved certain tricks introduced by Manolete because they
had been taught he was a great bullfighter. It will be years, Ernest had
said, before they know that Manolete was a great bullfighter with cheap
tricks. That he used the cheap tricks because the public wanted them.

Bill's right. We have to get him away from bullfights and Luis Miguel and all the rest. Maybe he'll listen to you. We can't seem to . . . well, *interest* him any more. Try to help him, Hotch."

"He has a thing about Bill and the car," Honor said.

"He sure has," Bill agreed.

"He talks to me about it all the time," Honor said.

"I guess it goes back to the accident," Bill said.

"It's best that we not use the car at all," Honor said.

"What's *happening* to Ernest?" Annie asked. "Sometimes the way he gets scares me. Really scares me. What in the world is *happening* to him?"

Ernest came into my room early the following morning and we had breakfast together. He said his kidney had kept him up most of the night and his hand was unsteady when he raised his teacup. He was very anxious to know about the movie offer and the projects with Cooper. He said it figured to be a very bad year and repeated the financial fears expressed on previous occasions. I told him that Twentieth had informed me that the most they would pay was a hundred twenty-five thousand. This infuriated him.

"Look, Papa, I told them I thought you'd call the whole thing off, so why don't we?"

"No! We can't!"

"But why?"

"Got to have the money. I want you to get the dough for the screenplay and I don't want to pass up a hundred twenty-five thousand dollars."

"But, Papa, I have other things to do. I certainly don't need the screenplay . . ."

"How much are they offering you?"

"Seventy-five thousand."

"We can't pass it up. Tell them I'll come down to five hundred thousand. They like to bargain. It's their way of life."

"They won't pay it. I've already said—"

"You try. You can't tell. But don't let the hundred twenty-five thousand get away."

We also discussed the *Across the River* project, for which Gary Cooper had been negotiating, and I put in a call to Cooper, who was then in London. Ernest asked me to check on the airline reservation and to be sure it was in Bill's name. While he talked he massaged his right kidney with the fingers of his right hand. The call to Cooper came through and Ernest enjoyed talking to him; his voice became animated and he laughed several times. By the time he hung up he was a little like his old self.

"Coops sounds fine. From what he says, don't think they tipped him the black spot on the prostate. Do you think he's too old to play Colonel Cantwell?"

"No, not if we got a certain Italian lady to play Renata."

"Who?"

"Sophia Loren."

"Who's she?"

"You've never seen her? Or heard of her?"

"I lead a very sheltered life."

"You've got a lot coming to you."

He snapped his eyes at me. "That's out of 'The Battler.' Did you realize that?" His voice was hard and threw me off balance. I hadn't been aware I had said anything out of anything, and I said so.

"I'm sorry," he said, meaning it. "I don't usually go around hearing dialogue from my published works. Why don't we all have an early lunch at the Callejón? A piece of broiled calves' liver might be good for kidney."

I had a copy of Ernest's volume of short stories in my luggage because it contained the Nick Adams stories that Twentieth wanted to buy. I looked up "The Battler," which is an account of Nick's meeting with a punch-drunk fighter and his Negro companion, Bugs, at a camp site next to a railroad embankment.

"Where you say you're from?"

"Chicago," Nick said.

"That's a fine town," the Negro said. "I didn't catch your name."

"Adams. Nick Adams."

"He says he's never been crazy, Bugs," Ad said.
"He's got a lot coming to him," the Negro said.

I closed the book and buried it deep in my luggage.

Lunch at the Callejón started out pleasantly. It was a lovely
fall day and we had walked to the restaurant through the
heart of Madrid along busy and interesting streets. The proprietor had Ernest's usual table ready when we arrived. We
all drank *vino tinto* and Ernest ate his broiled calves' liver approvingly and drank the *vino tinto* without watering it. He
talked to Honor, who was next to him, and to Annie, who
was across the table, and he seemed to be enjoying himself as
he always used to.

It was while the salad was being served that it happened. I
don't know what preceded it; I had been talking with Bill
and the first I knew, Ernest had a waiter by the sleeve and
was shouting at him, in English to begin with, and then in
Spanish. The waiter was terrified. He tried to balance the large
wooden salad bowl while attempting to free the sleeve that
Ernest had hold of. I do not to this day know what the waiter
had done. Probably the waiter himself did not know. At one
point Ernest demanded to know his name, which sounded like
"Pollock," and Ernest demanded to know whether he was
Spanish or Polish, and when the waiter said Polish he lit into
him about that.

The restaurant was crowded and everyone by now had
stopped eating and was watching Ernest. The owner, whom
Ernest had known since his first days in Madrid, came to make
peace, but Ernest turned on him too and accused him of having
turned Shylock that summer when Ernest and I had tracked
down Rupert Belville at the Callejón, drunken almost to the
point of expiration. In order to get him on an airplane that
would immediately take him back to London, where he
could be taken to a clinic, Ernest had asked the proprietor
to advance him the air fare until he returned that evening.
The proprietor had advanced the sum but apparently not in
the spirit that Ernest had approved of, and now, four years
later, Ernest gave him both barrels of this long-smoldering

grudge. The altercation with the waiter ended abruptly. Ernest rose suddenly, threw a large amount of pesetas on the table, and left. He never went back.

The afternoon he returned to the hotel from the Callejón, Ernest got undressed and went to bed and stayed there for four days. Every day he was scheduled to fly back to New York, but every day he postponed his departure. The morning after the Callejón incident, he called us—Bill, Annie and I were sorting photographs in the sitting room—and he said he had just had a terrible thought: What if Iberia had a rule against excess baggage and would not let him take the photographs with him?

I could not believe my ears. For as long as I had known him, Ernest had traveled with an amount of luggage which had exceeded in baggage fees the cost of his air ticket. He once came up to New York from Havana with thirty-six pieces of luggage. I pointed this out to him.

"Yes, but this midnight plane isn't a jet and maybe they don't allow excess baggage on prop planes. If the photos don't get on, neither do I."

Ernest had collected hundreds of bullfight pictures, and he was referring to the three small suitcases that held them. The more we said we were sure it was all right, the more Ernest stiffened, so I suggested we phone the airline and get the word direct.

"Okay," Ernest said, "but first we've got to weigh everything. They'll want to know total weight and we've got to be exact." Bill and I glanced at each other; then while Ernest held a heating pad against his ailing kidney, we started to pack his bags. It took us over an hour; when we had everything in valises, Bill called the desk and asked for two porters. They took all the things down to the luggage room and weighed each piece. Ernest tipped them lavishly and then added up the precise number of kilos.

Bill called Iberia on the bedroom telephone and after giving the number of the flight which Ernest was taking, he asked whether a passenger on that flight would be permitted that amount of excess luggage. The reply was in the affirmative. Annie and Honor, who had since joined us, began unpacking Ernest's things.

"Who were you talking to?" he asked.

"That was Iberia itself," Bill answered.

"That's just it," Ernest said. "Some nameless flunky who doesn't know his ass from his elbow and I'll show up and they'll turn me away."

No amount of discussion would dissuade Ernest from this new doubt, so that afternoon I went over to the Iberia ticket office and got a written statement, signed by the manager of the Madrid office, that a passenger bearing that amount of excess luggage would be permitted aboard. Ernest took the letter, folded it carefully, and placed it inside his passport.

The flight that Ernest was insisting upon taking was one of the few nonjet transatlantic flights from Madrid. It was an ancient Constellation that required fourteen airborne hours whereas the jets made it in seven. I tried to talk Ernest out of taking it, but he said it would give him "better security" since no one would be looking for him on that flight, and also he preferred a slower descent when going into the drink, a calamity he was anticipating.

Antonio unexpectedly came to see Ernest the evening before he left. Ernest was sitting up in bed reading when Antonio came in. He sat on the edge of the bed to talk to Ernest, and they were happy to see one another. Antonio, I thought, looked pale and drawn, and Ernest, in the harsh reading light, looked terribly old. Ernest told Antonio about his kidney ailment and Antonio described the liver trouble he was having, and each sympathized with the other. Then Antonio complimented Ernest on *The Dangerous Summer.*

"Did you look at the photos?" Ernest asked.

"Yes, they're wonderful."

"Has Luis Miguel seen them?"

"Yes, when we were in Nîmes."

"And he liked them? The ones in the second issue? Including the *pase ayudado?*"

"He thought it was all very nice. As did I."

After Antonio had left, Ernest came into the sitting room, where Bill and I had gone to give them privacy, and sat down heavily, his shoulders slumped forward. "Antonio is thinking of retiring," Ernest said. "He asked my advice."

"Did he say why?" Bill asked.

"The grind. He says it is now an effort to get himself 'up' for a fight. He is troubled by his liver and his energy is not what it should be. And he says that sometimes now he is spooked by a bull. That's what really bothers him."

"What did you tell him?" I asked.

"Said it had to be his decision. No one can advise you on something as delicate as your own machinery. But did tell him that when you're the champ, it's better to step down on the best day you've had than to wait until it's starting to leave you and everyone notices it."

Ernest's flight was scheduled to depart at eleven in the evening but did not get off until after midnight. Ernest waited in the automobile with Honor and Annie until the last moment, while Bill and I took care of various matters at the Iberia counter, including the switch of name and passport. Ernest wanted to take the suitcases that contained the photographs into the cabin with him and that presented certain complications which were eventually worked out.

When we returned to the car Ernest said to me, "I sure as hell hate to go back to New York after what my lawyer did to me."

"What did he do?"

"The last thing I told him before I left was to pay my Abercrombie bill, but yesterday in the mail that was forwarded to me from Ketchum there was this Abercrombie bill with an unpaid balance. Been a customer there for forty years and never had an unpaid balance. Now I can't show my face in there any more. Have to go to the gun department to check on my guns, and have to buy shoes and wool socks, but he's fixed it so I can't do any of it."

I pointed out that department-store bills are often slow in reflecting payments, and that, besides, an unpaid balance was

a very common billing condition and would in no way affect
his status there; but he was unconvinced. I asked whether I
could see the bill. "Papa, look at the date—this was billed
September first. It's now October. It's an old bill. I think you'll
find it's been taken care of."

"I'm not so sure. It's getting so I have to do everything myself."

Bill motioned to us that it was time to board the aircraft
and we started to walk toward the plane. "Papa," I said, "please
don't get down on everyone. Your friends are just as much
your friends as they ever were. You're tired and upset now,
but you'll be all right once you get to Ketchum and breathe
that good mountain air and get some rest; then everything
will start to look okay again."

"I don't know, Hotch."

"Oh, sure. The hunting season has already started."

"Yes, but . . . all the work I've got to do . . . listen, I left a
bottle of Scotch in my room. Be sure to get it when you go
back."

We were at the plane. "I'll wire you about Coops as soon as
I get to London," I said.

"And let me know about the five hundred G's."

"Good-bye, Papa. Good trip."

"You really think it's all right about Abercrombie's? I'd sure
as hell like to get my guns."

I assured him again.

When we got back to the hotel I went to his room to get
the bottle of Scotch. It was on the writing desk. There were
several pieces of Suecia stationery covered with handwritten
lists of things to do, and on a page of typewriter paper he
had written in neat diagonally ascending lines a paragraph
which ultimately appeared in *The Dangerous Summer*.

"Nothing is as much fun any more as it was when we first
drove up out of the grey mountains above Malaga onto the
high country on the road to Madrid we drove so many times
that year. Everything you read in the paper every morning
makes you feel too bad to write. Probably the moral is you
never should have got mixed up with bullfighters. I knew that
once very well and I should not have had to learn it twice."

Chapter Fourteen

Rochester • 1960

There was a telegram from Ernest waiting for me when I
returned to New York on October 22nd, 1960, from seeing Gary
Cooper in London. It contained two items: Ernest had been told
that Wald wanted the Nick Adams film badly; I was to inform
"our guests, if arrived," that they had "no financial problems, no
worries."

I could not understand the euphemism of "guests" in reference
to Honor, who was coming to live in New York but had not
yet arrived. As long ago as Cuba, Honor had discussed going
to New York and it was Mary who had suggested that since
Honor had been interested in the theater in Glasgow she might
like to study at a good drama school, and Ernest had offered
to pay her tuition.

I telephoned Ernest in Ketchum to tell him that everything
was fine with Cooper and that we would draw up contracts in
Hollywood. I started to say that Honor had not yet arrived,
but he cut me off and said it was best not to use names on
the telephone.

"I have just sent you a check for fifteen hundred dollars
to apply on our guest's tuition at the dramatic academy," he
said, "and for her living expenses in New York during her
studies this semester. I do not want her to arrive in New York
and not know that she has something to back her up in her

studies. New York is a murderously expensive place to live. Not only room but to eat properly."

He said all this in a rather stilted voice, as if it were a formal announcement. I asked him how the hunting was; he said he had not yet had a chance to get out but that he would catch up when I arrived. I said I would probably not be able to go hunting with him because I had been traveling so much and had a backlog of work. This disturbed him very much. He said he had been counting on my coming and if I didn't it would be the first fall we hadn't hunted; he was so insistent and disturbed that I said I would get there if I possibly could. I promised to call him the moment "our guest" arrived.

Honor flew in from Madrid a few days later, and in the course of my telephone conversation with Ernest, while informing him that our guest was established at the Barbizon and had already gone to see the people at the American Academy of Dramatic Arts, the long-distance musical tones danced in and we were disconnected. When I got Ernest back on the phone a few moments later he was very agitated. He said we should not talk any more but that I positively *had* to get out there, the sooner the better.

"Wire me your date of arrival," he said. "Don't use the phone any more."

I subsequently received a letter from him asking me to find out whether anyone had spoken to Honor about what she was doing in New York, or how her trip was financed or anything else of that nature. His handwriting had changed: the letters were broader and less carefully formed; straight lines, as in the letter *i*, were open loops, and most of the *t*'s were uncrossed.

The Portland Rose, scheduled to arrive at nine in the evening, arrived in Shoshone a few minutes early. I went into the bar across from the railroad station where we always had a drink before starting the long drive to Ketchum, knowing that Ernest would find me there.

He did. Duke MacMullen was with him. But instead of com-

ing over to the bar to have a drink as usual, he asked me to finish
mine as soon as I could and meet them outside. While he was
speaking to me he kept looking nervously at the men at the
bar and the people sitting at the tables. I left my drink and
paid up and followed them out to Duke's car. Duke is a cheerful,
outgoing man, but he was very subdued and had greeted me
the way you greet a friend you meet at a funeral.

During the first part of the drive, to break the heavy silence,
I started to tell Ernest about our project with Cooper (good
progress), and the Twentieth Century-Fox situation (no progress beyond the hundred twenty-five thousand dollars), when
Ernest interrupted me abruptly: "Vernon Lord wanted to come
but I wouldn't let him."

"Why?"

"The Feds."

"What?"

"Feds. They tailed us all the way. Ask Duke."

"Well . . . there was a car in back of us out of Hailey . . ."

"That's why I wanted to get you out of the bar. Was afraid
they'd make their move and pick us up there."

"But, Ernest, that car turned off at Picabo," Duke said.

"Probably took the back road. That would take them longer,
so I wanted to be out of Shoshone when they got there."

"But, Papa," I said, trying to collect myself, "why are federal
agents pursuing you?"

"It's the worst hell. The goddamnedest hell. They've bugged
everything. That's why we're using Duke's car. Mine's bugged.
Everything's bugged. Can't use the phone. Mail intercepted.
What put me on to it was that phone call with you. You remember we got disconnected? That tipped their hand."

"But long-distance calls are often cut off. How can that
mean . . . ?"

"I have a pal with the phone company in Hailey. He traced
the disconnect for me. It was here, at this end, not the New
York end."

"But what does that have to do with it?"

"For God's sake, Hotch, use your head—you placed the call,

didn't you? A legit disconnect would be at your end. But the
disconnect was *here*, in Hailey, where our phone calls are re-
layed. That means the Feds were monitoring the call *here* and
that caused it to cut out." He was very agitated. I settled back
into the rear darkness of the car. There were no other cars
in either direction and Duke was driving very fast. I wanted to
ask Ernest why he thought he was being tailed and bugged
and why Vernon couldn't come to the station, but I just sat in
the darkness, watching the white corridor of the headlights,
feeling dispirited.

We rode for miles in absolute silence; I thought Ernest had
fallen asleep, but suddenly he asked: "What did our guest say?
Anybody talk to her? Anybody come around asking questions?"

"No, no one."

"They call her in about her passport?"

"No."

"Nobody from Immigration called her in or talked to her?"

"Not a soul."

"I'll be a son-of-a-bitch if they haven't bought her off."

"What do you mean?"

"I mean she's lying. She's gone over to them."

"Oh, that's impossible. I'm sure no one has—"

"She's turned state's evidence. Let's write her off and forget
it. I don't want to hear any more about her."

We turned off the main highway into Ketchum. It was November 14th and there had not yet been any snow to attract
skiers, so the streets were empty. Ketchum only comes out of
hibernation when the lifts at Sun Valley start working after
the first good winter snow. There was one bar open and the
diner had a few customers, but the rest of the town was dark.

As Duke turned onto the street that would take me to the
Christiana Motor Lodge, Ernest said in a very quiet voice,
"Duke, pull over. Cut your lights."

Ernest rolled down his window and peered across the street
at the bank. It was lighted and you could plainly see two
men working in back of a counter. Ernest had his head partially
out of the window, fixedly watching them. Then he carefully

looked up and down the street and inspected the dark store fronts adjoining the bank. He rolled up his window and Duke turned on his lights and drove on.

"What is it?" I asked.

"Auditors. They've got them working over my account. When they want to get you, they really get you."

"But how do you know about those men? That it's your account?"

"Why would two auditors be working in the middle of the night? Of course it's my account."

"But what have you done? What will they find?"

"Hotch, when they want to get you, they get you."

We had pulled into the Christiana, which adjoins Chuck Atkinson's supermarket and is also owned by him. Duke helped me carry my bags to my room while Ernest waited in the car.

"Hotch, you've got to do something," Duke said desperately. "Nobody's doing anything and let me tell you, somebody has got to *do* something."

"But what can *I* do, Duke?"

"You see how he is. Everybody whispers about it, but . . . Jesus!"

When we got back to the car, Ernest asked me to come up to the house in the morning as soon as I could for breakfast.

"I'll be watching for you," he said.

"I'll come early," I said.

Those first few days in Ketchum, Ernest's close friends sought me out, one after the other, and confided their worries and fears about him. He had changed so. He seemed depressed. He refused to go hunting. He carped about old friends. He no longer invited a Friday night group to watch the fights. He looked bad.

In the beginning I naïvely tried to deal with Ernest in a straightforward and logical way, as a month before Bill and I had dealt with his anxiety over his excess baggage. But he refused to talk either in his house or in my room at the Christiana because both were bugged, so we put on our jackets and walked a little way up the hill beside his house, along the bank of the rushing Wood River, until we found a log to sit on. Ernest began by repeating most of the things he had said the night before. The Feds were after him because of Honor. The Feds were immigration agents and they were getting the goods on him. For what? Impairing the morals of a minor. I pointed out that Honor and he had never been together in the United States—only in Spain and Cuba—so United States Immigration could not possibly sustain any such charge against him, even if it were true, but he just got up and began walking around the log agitatedly, saying that she had just functioned as his secretary and there was absolutely no truth in the charge but they were out to get him and rather than go through any more of this he would turn himself in and get it over with. I led him back over the illogic of his surmisal, but the more I tried to dissuade him, the more irritated he became with me for challenging the danger that he was sure threatened him; I finally realized that he was using the phrase "impairing the morals of a minor," not for what it specifically meant, but for its menacing sound. The phrase could just as well have been "murder with intent to kill" or "with malice aforethought," almost any words that could be strung into the evil noose that the Feds were attempting to slip around his neck.

He wanted to know whether I had been questioned by the immigration agents about Honor and him, and when I said I had not he gave me a look, his face totally disbelieving, and my stomach was hit by the awful realization that in Ernest's eyes I too had now become part of the conspiracy.

Ernest sat down on the log again. He wanted to know whether, as he had asked me to, I had told his lawyer about declaring his four-thousand-dollar winnings on the Johansson fight. I said I had and that it was being included in his return. "Well, it's too late," he said gloomily. "You saw those auditors at the bank. They're on to it." I said that there could not possibly be an infraction, since this was the proper year in which to report the winnings, and since there was more than enough in his tax account to cover it, the men at the bank could not possibly be interested in that. Ernest said summarily that I was wrong—gambling winnings had to be reported the moment they were received and he was definitely in arrears and the evidence had been turned over to the Feds. Then he warned me that Vernon Lord was not to be told any of this because Vernon was a great guy and had taken very good care of him and he did not want to get him into any trouble. That was why, he said, he had not let Vernon come to the station to meet me.

"But, Papa," I said, "Vernon is your doctor. His communications with you are privileged. You don't have to worry about him." He said he *did* have to worry about him because a doctor is not privileged in a federal court. I decided to make my stand on this. Ernest knew that I had practiced law for a brief time, so I attempted to force him to see that at least in this one matter his anxiety was unfounded. The more I documented the fact that doctors are as privileged in federal courts as anywhere else, the more Ernest battled me, his arguments veering from allegations about the federal courts, as if they were Star Chambers, to attacks upon my knowledge of the law and, eventually, my fidelity to him. But I did not give ground. I did not try to mollify him. We were both off the log, pacing about. Finally he turned on me and said in deadly accusation, "Let's get it straight, Hotch. Either you make me out to be a liar, or a crazy—which is it?"

His head was thrust forward; his chin was unsteady and his face drained of color. "I'm sorry," I said. "Let's have a walk and forget it." We started back to the house.

I tried to get Ernest to go hunting, but every day he had some flimsy or imagined obligation that kept him from getting out; having to write a single letter to his lawyer or publisher was reason enough. I felt that if I could get him out of the house and away from his worries, doing one of the things he enjoyed the most, it might improve his entire temperament; that the beauty of the autumn fields and the excitement of stalking the big brilliant birds might loosen him up so we could get through the tenseness that was blocking everything out. Eventually I did get him to go on a pheasant shoot but its dismal conclusion convinced me that it should be my last effort.

I had assembled all his favorite hunting pals: Bud Purdy, Pappy Arnold, Don Anderson and Chuck Atkinson. You need at least that many guns to hunt pheasant in the open field properly. Pheasant was scarce that fall but we drove down to Picabo, where Bud Purdy had a farmer friend who had given him permission to hunt his fields. It was huge acreage, some of it containing dried corn stalks, which, as we knew from our previous experiences, often attract pheasant.

When we reached our destination and got all our gear ready and our guns loaded and started over the barbed wire that bordered the field, Ernest balked. Going into that field was trespassing, he said, and he didn't want to be shot. In addition to the fact that Bud knew the owner and had talked to him, it was also the custom in that wide-open country that fields could be hunted unless they were posted, and these were not posted. But Ernest said he could not afford to let the Feds get anything else on him. He wanted us to go ahead while he waited in the car. It took us a half hour to coax him onto the field, but even then he remained desultory.

Pappy Arnold took the first shots at a pair of cocks that broke a little out of range; Ernest insisted on waiting to see if anyone showed up to protest the shots, and again it took coaxing reassurances to get him moving. We were fanned out in an arc, about thirty yards apart, Ernest holding down the left wing, and had been combing the fields for almost an hour without results when three absolutely wonderful cock pheasant suddenly winged up not more than ten yards from Ernest's position. It was a hunter's dream and with Ernest's ability to reload quickly he had a good chance at a triple; he flicked off the safety and snapped shut the breech in one move as he snugged the knurled butt of the gun into his shoulder and cheek, now swinging with the birds, that graceful and effortless fluidity of his locking the gun into the flight of the cocks.

But he did not fire.

The birds rose fast and disappeared. "I'll be goddamned if

I'll get myself shot as a trespasser for a couple of lousy birds," he said, breaking the breech and removing the shells.

We all stood there for a few minutes, not able to say anything; then Bud suggested that we hike to the farmhouse, which was a tiny roof on the horizon, and recheck about the permission. Ernest was agreeable to that. Nothing flew up on the way there, but I don't think any of us would have shot if it had.

Bud knocked on the kitchen door and the wife of the farmer greeted Bud, who introduced Ernest and the rest of us. She said her husband had gone to the market in Twin Falls but that it was perfectly all right to hunt the fields. She suggested an old corn field not far from the house.

When we started again, spread across that corn field, a single bird broke out in front of Chuck and he put him down on the rise. Ernest went over to look at the dead pheasant. He said he was still spooked about hunting there because it was one thing to get permission from the farmer's wife but what if the farmer came driving in and saw them shooting up his field, mightn't he just take a shot at them as trespassers? Ernest said emphatically that he thought we shouldn't hunt any more but should wait at the farmhouse until the farmer got back.

I felt beaten by an accumulation of hopelessness. Not just this afternoon, but the days before, and the fall and summer before that; I had reached the moment of facing up to serious reality about Ernest. I did not want him to see my thoughts, so I turned my head down and looked at the desiccated soil; the others were also helplessly silent, except for Bud, a gentle man, who took over and said, "To tell you the truth, Ernest, there aren't enough birds in there to bother about. Let's drive over to my place and have some cider."

That was the evening that Ernest had agreed, out of consideration for Mary's long kitchen duty, to let me take them to the newly opened Christiana Restaurant for dinner. This was the first time Ernest had been out of the house in the evening since his return. It turned out much the same as our last restaurant venture at the Callejón.

Ernest had one cocktail and one glass of wine with his meal
(a regimen he was strictly adhering to); he seemed at ease as
he pleasurably recounted some amusing stories about his days
in the old Ketchum when there was gambling and it was as
wide open as a gold-rush town, when he suddenly stopped in
the middle of a sentence and said we had to pay up and go.
Poor Mary, who had been so enjoying her evening out, her
meal only half-eaten, asked what was wrong. Ernest gave his
head a little nod toward the bar. "Those two FBI men at the
bar," Ernest mumbled. "That's what's wrong." Mary asked how
he could possibly know they were FBI men and Ernest told
her to keep her voice down. "Don't you think I know an FBI
man when I see one?" he said. "We've got to get out of here,
Hotch."

I went to find the waiter and on the way passed a table
where Chuck Atkinson and his wife were having dinner. I
asked Chuck whether he knew the two men at the bar. "Sure,"
he said. "They're salesmen. Been coming through here once a
month for the last five years. Don't tell me Ernest is worried
about *them*." He shook his head sadly.

When I told Ernest they were salesmen, he scoffed, "Of
course they're salesmen. The FBI is noted for its clumsy dis-
guises. What do you think they'd pose as—concert violinists?
Come on, Mary. You can have coffee back at the house."

Mary had been anxious to speak with me from the time I
had arrived, but Ernest had made it very difficult. He had
become hypersensitive to the critical reactions around him, and
whenever he saw any of his friends talking to Mary he was
certain that they were discussing him—in reality, they probably were. Mary was understandably nervous and distraught;
she had been subjected to Ernest's accelerating anxieties since
his return from Spain and she was exanimated from inability
to cope with him. On our way out of the Christiana that
evening, she was able to tell me, without Ernest hearing, that
she would be shopping at the supermarket at eleven the next
morning.

We had our talk over a shopping cart in back of the cereals.
Mary said she was desperate. She showed me a letter she had

found on Ernest's desk the day before; it was addressed to his
bank, the Morgan Guaranty in New York. The salutation and
first sentence were in order but then the words became gibber-
ish, as if he had been experimenting with a new language.

Basically, Ernest's ability to work had deteriorated to a point
where he spent endless hours with the manuscript of *A Moveable Feast* but he was unable to really work on it. Besides his
inability to write, Ernest was terribly depressed over the loss of
the *finca*, and although Mary had suggested that they get an
apartment in Paris or Venice, or a new boat that could take them
on a long sea voyage, there was no way to get a reaction from
Ernest that could relieve the bleakness out of which the constant
delusions and hallucinations seemed to rise. His talk about destroying himself had become more frequent, and he would
sometimes stand at the gun rack, holding one of the guns, staring
out the window at the distant mountains.

I told Mary that I thought it was perfectly obvious that
Ernest needed immediate and thorough-going psychiatric help,
and even went so far as to suggest Menninger's, but she registered concern over what effect such publicity might have. I
then suggested that if she wanted me to take over, I would go
back to New York immediately and contact a very fine psychiatrist whom I knew; she urged me to act as soon as possible, and
reiterated her fear that Ernest's threats to destroy himself might
become a reality.

Before leaving, I arranged to see Vernon Lord, because if
Ernest was to receive treatment it had to be with his own
consent and approval and Vernon, I felt, was the key to achiev-
ing this. Vernon told me that Ernest had given him a note to
be opened after his arrest. Vernon said he had already read
the note, which contained instructions for taking care of Mary
and rabid disclaimers intended to protect Vernon from imagined
prosecution. Some of the note, Vernon said, was garbled and
made no sense; he was as fearful as Mary about Ernest's condition.

"I'm just a country doctor," he said, "and a pretty young one
at that. I have the responsibility of knowing that Ernest needs
immediate help that I can't provide. Oh, I have prescribed

various tranquilizers and even a few new drugs I've read about in the journals, but Ernest is in a serious condition that is so far out of my field I cannot even diagnose it; yet I can see almost daily deterioration in these past few weeks. If you could bring in a New York psychiatrist it would be vitally helpful."

I asked Vernon whether, when he next took Ernest's blood pressure, he could find that it had risen perceptibly.

"You mean, enough to alarm Ernest over it?"

"Well, enough so that you could convince him that he must go somewhere for tests and treatment. I'm just thinking of how we can lay the groundwork for getting him to go wherever the New York doctor recommends, if that's what he recommends."

"It might work," Vernon said. "His blood pressure is one of the things he really cares about. Keeps running statistics on the readings. We have an appointment this afternoon. I'll do what I can. The irony is that this psychogenetic deterioration has developed just when after all these years he's finally rounding into shape—following his diet, virtually not drinking. It's an ironic seesaw, isn't it?"

The New York psychiatrist, whom I shall call Dr. Renown, acted quickly. He described Ernest's general condition as depressive-persecutory, and in a telephone conversation with Vernon Lord he prescribed certain new drugs that he felt would be helpful, pending hospital treatment. Dr. Renown's first hospital choice was Menninger's, but Vernon felt that because of the stigma of the name, there was no possibility that Ernest would go. I pointed out that Mary would probably also resist Menninger's to avoid public awareness of Ernest's condition.

It was apparent, therefore, that the only acceptable hospital would be one that had both physical and psychiatric facilities so that Ernest could be admitted for some physical ailment, thereby masking his true malady. On that basis Dr. Renown suggested the Mayo Clinic. Vernon reported that Ernest had reacted to the increased-blood-pressure readings with the alarm we had anticipated, and Vernon said he thought he might be able to get Ernest to go to Mayo on the basis of blood pressure tests and special treatment. Subsequently, Dr. Renown made all arrangements for Ernest's hospitalization and discussed his general condition in telephone conversations with the Mayo doctors.

On November 30th Vernon accompanied Ernest to Rochester, Minnesota, in a small chartered plane, and Ernest was admitted to the Mayo Clinic that afternoon. He was admitted under the name of Vernon Lord and placed in a room in St. Mary's Hospital.

Ernest was not permitted to receive or make phone calls, and he wrote no letters, but during December, I occasionally spoke on the phone to Mary, who was staying at The Kahler Hotel and seeing Ernest every day. She was very lonely in the town. It was a hell of a place for her to spend Christmas, and my daughters sent her a boxful of little-girl presents to try to cheer her up.

During the month of December, Ernest was given eleven treatments with electric shock, technically referred to as ECT's. Mary told me about them, how terrible they were for Ernest and how he suffered, more psychologically than physically, from receiving them. But she said he seemed to be getting along well with his doctors, who reported that he was making good progress. She said, however, that they were at a disadvantage since they did not know him as well as she did.

The ECT's were abruptly stopped during the first week in January. Shortly thereafter Ernest asked the doctors whether he could speak to me on the phone, and they had agreed. It was Ernest's first outside contact since his admission and obviously very important to him. I asked whether there were instructions as to what I should and should not talk about, but there were none. The call was for a specific time on a specific day.

The operator said to hold on, Mr. Lord was coming to the phone; after he greeted me Ernest said, "Hell of a thing having a name like [Lord] in a Catholic hospital—and me a failed Catholic." He sounded vigorous and in control but there was a heartiness in his voice that didn't belong there. He told me that during the past few days he had been able to read for the first time since his arrival; what he had been reading were the galleys of a new book by our friend George Plimpton. It was called *Out of My League*, and Ernest said he was enjoying it very much. "But it's hard to enjoy anything," he said, "in a room where they frisk you and lock the door on you and don't have the decency to at least trust you with a blunt instrument."

Hearing this from him was startling, simply because I had not properly imagined his physical life there. I asked whether he thought his doctors would permit me to visit him. He said he would inquire and let me know but that Rochester was really too far out of the way to ask anyone to come. "But there's no denying," he said, "I'd be glad as hell to see you."

We talked for fifteen minutes and there was not one word about any of his old delusions. He spoke a good deal about the Paris sketches and getting back to work on them, for he had decided to publish them in the fall. The hospital operator cut in to say, "Mr. Lord, will you please conclude your call," and he quickly said good-bye.

The town of Rochester, Minnesota, is the Mayo Clinic, and vice-versa. It stands upon a flat plain, a needle ringed by thimbles. The needle is the skyscraper clinic and the thimbles are the hotels that house its patients. They come from all over the world and stay in the hotels, which have subterraneous passageways connecting with the clinic, which is an elongated honeycomb of examining cubicles. Stretchers and wheelchairs fill the hotels' elevators and are pushed back and forth through the passageways.

The Mayo Clinic itself has no hospital facilities. An affiliation has been arranged, however, with the town's St. Mary's Hospital, which is run by an energetic order of nuns, whereby doctors of the clinic can administer to patients whom they hospitalize there.

I was scheduled to fly to Rochester on January 13, 1961. On the tenth I received a telegram from Ernest telling me that Northwest Airlines was on strike, and I should take Capitol direct to Minneapolis, then Braniff or Ozark to Rochester, or a Jefferson Transportation limousine that took ninety minutes, left every four hours and cost eight bucks. He gave me his weight as one seventy-three and a quarter, and said all of it would be glad to see me.

This was a flash of his old self, I thought, this concern about his friends and attention to details for them. I bought a large tin of béluga caviar from Maison Glass and set out from Newark via Capitol. Unfortunately, the kitchen of the Capitol plane was taken off in Chicago, with my caviar in the refrigerator, never to be seen again. I had intended it for Mary as a lift from the Grande Cuisine de Rochester.

I checked into The Kahler, then went directly to the hospital. Ernest looked shockingly thin: 173 pounds on a frame that normally held 210 or 220. His face had lost its conformation and even his features seemed changed. He introduced me to his nurse, a large, pretty young woman who obviously relished her patient, and later on to his doctors, whom he had already invested with "pal status." He had been to their houses for meals, and one of the doctors told me they had shot skeet in back of his house the preceding Sunday, following a luncheon attended by many of the doctor's friends. We were sitting in Ernest's room, which was small but pleasantly furnished, and one barely noticed the bars on the windows. Ernest joked and laughed and remembered things for the doctors' enjoyment, like our triumph at Auteuil and my afternoon in the ring; despite his disappointing physical appearance, Ernest certainly seemed restored. But I got the uneasy feeling that the doctors were treating him like a celebrity as much as a patient.

When they left they said it was perfectly all right for Ernest to get dressed and go for a walk with me. The nurse brought him his clothes, and as he was dressing, Ernest pointed to a pile of letters on the dresser, saying that he had always been a good letter-answerer so he felt bad that he hadn't been able to answer all those. He said he wished he had Nita there so he could dictate them.* I suggested that he arrange for the public stenographer at The Kahler to come in every afternoon for an hour or two, and this possibility cheered him. "Would like to

* Juanita Jensen, who worked for the American Embassy in Havana and part-time for Ernest.

clean up all correspondence here," he said, "so when I get back to Ketchum I can go right to work on the book."

Then he asked the question I had been dreading to hear ever since I left New York. "How are things with Coops?"

Cooper had come to New York the early part of January to tape a television show about the American cowboy and had called me to have lunch. "I'm going to have to check out of my plans with Papa," he had said. "The medics have given me the word on that operation I had—it was cancer. They say I'm not gonna hang around too long. I hope to Christ they're right."

They had told him just after Christmas, when he had started to experience severe pain, and he had asked them point-blank. Now the pain was so bad that despite all the things he took for it he could only work in front of the cameras an hour at a time.

"How's Papa coming along at Mayo's?" The subterfuge of the Vernon Lord name had been pierced, and newspapers across the country were speculating about Ernest's illness.

"Fine."

"What's exactly wrong with him, Hotch?"

"High blood pressure. But they've got it under control now." I was damned if I would load Ernest's real trouble on top of his.

"You better tell him about me. We always have leveled with each other, absolutely, about everythin', all our lives, and I wouldn't like him to find out from someone else or in the papers. I tried to call him but they wouldn't put me through, and I don't like to write about something like that."

So now I told Ernest. He didn't say anything. Just looked at me as if I had betrayed him. Then he picked up his windbreaker and slowly put it on, fitted his hound's tooth cap on his head, and started out of his prison.

We walked away from the center of town, which quickly became outskirts. "Your doctors appear to be awfully good guys," I said.

"You mean because they trust me with a skeet gun?"

"Well, it is pretty nice of them to have you over . . ."

"What these shock doctors don't know is about writers and

such things as remorse and contrition and what they do to them. They should make all psychiatrists take a course in creative writing so they'd know about writers."

"Have they stopped the treatments?"

"Well, what is the sense of ruining my head and erasing my memory, which is my capital, and putting me out of business? It was a brilliant cure but we lost the patient. It's a bum turn, Hotch, terrible. I called the local authorities to turn myself in but they didn't know about the rap."

My heart stopped. I couldn't believe . . .

"I looked into this whole business about the federal court and you're wrong, or maybe you were trying to con me, but there is no privilege and they can nail Vernon, especially now that I've used his name for cover. That's why I wanted to turn myself in. Have you seen Honor?"

There then followed the same exhaustive, exhausting interrogation about Honor and the immigration agents and all that. The delusions had not changed or diminished. His room was bugged and so was the hospital phone and he suspected that one of the interns was a Fed in disguise. I made the walk as short as I could, but even at that it seemed interminable.

I had dinner with Mary that evening in the hotel dining room. She said that in the six weeks she had been in Rochester, this was the first time she hadn't eaten alone in her room after leaving the hospital. We discussed Ernest's duality, his behaving one way in the doctors' presence and another way around us. Mary said she had spoken to the doctors about this but felt it would help if I also discussed it with them.

The doctors told me they were aware that Ernest still clung to some of his delusions, but they indicated that his growing desire to return to work was, for them, the predominant element in his recovery. I expressed my concern over his weight and asked whether they could allow him to eat more and have a few drinks; I asked whether for a man like Ernest who had drunk heavily all his life the complete stoppage of alcohol could not be as harmful psychologically as it was beneficial physically. They said they thought he was pretty sound for the time being; they wanted his weight where it was and two

glasses of wine per day was sufficient. I said that I realized it
was presumptuous of me, but I just wanted to say that Ernest
was such an extraordinary man, that he so defied the "norm"
that he could in no sense be looked upon and treated as an
ordinary patient—that any accepted procedure, whether in relation to electric shock or anything else, should be re-examined
when applied to him. Again I apologized for my presumption,
but it was something I had to say.

I saw Ernest again the following day. Mary was there and
his mood fluctuated from being very deferential toward her
and appreciative of her loving attention and care, to being
brutally abusive. After one of these abusive outbursts, Mary
excused herself and went out into the hall; when she later re-
appeared her eyes were quite red. When two of his doctors
came by to see him, Ernest underwent the same abrupt
change I had witnessed the previous day.

Interest in and ability to work were definitely stirring in
Ernest; he had arranged all his letters in expectation of the
public stenographer who was due that afternoon, and he was
very eager to get to work answering them. He had also written
a coherent, effective puff for George Plimpton to use on the
jacket of his book:

"Beautifully observed and incredibly conceived, this
account of a self-imposed ordeal has the chilling quality
of a true nightmare. It is the dark side of the moon of
Walter Mitty."

Thus, bad and well-being in Ernest were now in cross-current
with no clear indication as to which would predominate.

A telegram had been delivered to Ernest that morning inviting Mary and him to be President-elect Kennedy's personal
guests at the inaugural. Ernest was pleased and moved by the
invitation, and we spent some time composing a proper reply
of declination.

When it came time for me to leave to catch my plane, Ernest
walked with me to the elevator; when it arrived he held the
doors, reluctant to let me go. "This coming spring we'll be

back at Auteuil," he said, "the Hemhotch colors striking terror
in the hearts of the touts." He chuckled. "Remember that tout
who saw me counting my winnings and said, 'One can see
Monsieur is of the *métier*?'" He patted my shoulder. "Good old
Hotch. Put you through a lot, haven't I, boy?"

"Put me through the best times I ever had."

"And this?"

"Hell, Papa, you're the one who once said when you go the
distance you've got to expect to get dumped on your ass once
in a while. You've been decked before."

"Sure have. But was always up at the count of three."

"Swinging."

"Sure. But we're up to six this time. Maybe seven."

"There's a mandatory eight now."

"Goddamn but I wish we were out at Bud's now, jump-shoot-
ing the canals. But Auteuil in the spring is a promise. I'll write
Georges to start working on the form. Save your money, Hotch,
for the ghost of Bataclan rides again." The elevator buzzed
insistently. I became aware that Ernest's nurse had been standing in back of him. I stepped into the elevator.

"Thank you very much for coming," he said.

Chapter Fifteen

Ketchum ◆ 1961

To my surprise, Ernest was released from the Mayo Clinic on January 22nd, nine days after I had seen him there. He called me in Hollywood to say how delighted he was to be home in Ketchum and back at work. He had gone hunting the day after his return, he said, and there were eight mallards and two teals now hanging over the woodpile outside the kitchen window. He sounded fine.

When I hung up, I felt relieved that he was out of his prison and back where he belonged; but when I recalled our conversation during that walk I felt an overriding uneasiness.

A few days later Ernest decided to accept the long-standing Twentieth Century offer on the Nick Adams stories; his letters during February, and his phone calls, were succinct and businesslike. We phoned each other every week; his only expressed worry was about his weight, which at one seventy was too low, he complained, to permit him to operate with his old steam. I urged him to put on a few pounds, but he refused to budge one calorie from the strict diet the doctors had given him. Ernest treated this diet like a military order, and I doubt if those doctors ever had a patient who so rigidly conformed to their commands.

On February 18th Ernest called me in New York to discuss disposition of his hundred twenty-five thousand dollars of movie money. His primary concern was about taxes. "I called my lawyer on the phone," he said, "to tell him to deposit seventy percent in the tax account and thirty percent in the checking account. He thought that was too high a percentage but I don't think he figured me having a book due in the fall and so forth. Plus how taxes may rise."

"But taxes are scheduled to be cut, Papa." I sympathized with the problem of trying to keep Ernest's top-heavy tax account from getting even heavier.

"One thing I do not count on in life is the diminishing tax. So with seventy percent in the tax account and ten off to the lawyer for agenting I am banking only $20,250, which is a rather slim take for getting hit for ten stories."

Toward the beginning of March the handwriting in Ernest's letters began to change again, and so did the content. The writing became severely cramped, the letters so small and tight it was difficult to read the words. The letters themselves began to be more complaining, with less reference to work.

It was about this time that Ernest suggested that instead of sending letters to him directly, I address them to Vernon Lord at the Sun Valley Hospital. I was to use a return address that had a name that began with an *O;* Vernon would thereby know that the letter was for Ernest. I was to tell Honor to write to him in the same manner.

During the last week in March, when I spoke to Ernest on the phone, he sounded listless and, I thought, rather discouraged. "I wish I could make some plans," he said, "but I can't until I finish the Paris book. Have to go day to day on this health business; the weight is awful low, so want to be sure on that end of it before planning further work and movements. Don't want to worry Mary on that nor anything else, nor worry myself. I'm learning to be strong at one sixty-nine but it is too low to fool with. I tell you this so you know the true gen." His voice sounded very old. The ends of sentences tailed off as if he didn't have the energy to finish them. "Am following doctors' orders exactly and pressure is good. But weight reaction's a little spooky."

"Can't you put on a little? What does Vernon say?"

"Don't mind being spooked if I could find a way to get my mind off it and have a little fun. Guess I'm spoiled. Always had such a damn good time."

By the beginning of April, Ernest had started to be wary of the telephone again, and he did not mention Honor either in his letters or in conversations. It had become difficult to talk to him on the phone. He was getting depressed about his work, although I could never clearly determine whether it was because he did not like what he wrote or because of difficulty he was experiencing in writing. I would mention friends and try to tell him about them, but he really wasn't interested. I tried to discuss the general form of the Nick Adams screenplay I was about to start on, but he wasn't interested in that either.

On April 18th I went to a cocktail party in New York which Harvey Breit had given to celebrate the publication of George Plimpton's book. It was a good party with good people and at one point Harvey suggested we call Ernest and all talk to him. I did not want to say that Ernest was in no condition to chat on the phone with the hubbub of a gay cocktail party in the background, so I tried to prevent the call by pretending I didn't have Ernest's unlisted phone number with me; unfortunately Harvey found it in his address book.

First Harvey spoke to him, then George, and they were merry and funny and George told him how well his book was going. When I came on, Ernest said, "Hotch, please try to hold off these calls." His voice was dead, the words coming at me like rocks falling down a well. "It's gotten pretty rough. I can't finish the bloody book. I've got it all and I know what I want it to be but I can't get it down." Harvey and George, looking happy, were watching me, so I curved my mouth up and tried to keep my eyes down on the phone.

I said some terrible inanity like, "Well, it's good that you're that far."

"Hotch, I can't finish the book. I *can't*. I've been at this goddamn worktable all day, standing here all day, all I've got to get is this one thing, maybe only a sentence, maybe more,

I don't know, and I can't get it. Not any of it. You understand, I *can't*. I've written Scribner's to scratch the book. It was all set for the fall but I had to scratch it."

"Then they'll do it in the spring."

"No, no they won't. Because I can't finish it. Not this fall or next spring or ten years from now. *I can't*. This wonderful damn book and I can't finish it. You understand?"

When I hung up, Harvey said, "He sounds fine, doesn't he?"

That was April 18th. At eleven o'clock Sunday morning, April 23rd, I received a call from Ketchum. Ernest was in the Sun Valley Hospital under heavy sedation, sodium amytal every three hours, nurses around the clock.

When Mary had come into the living room that morning, she had found Ernest standing in the vestibule, where the gun rack was; he was holding a shotgun in one hand, with the breech open; he had two shells in his other hand. There was a note propped up on top of the gun rack addressed to her. Mary knew that Vernon Lord was due to come by to take Ernest's blood pressure, so she just tried to hold Ernest's attention until he got there. She knew he had been terribly depressed about his inability to write, but she had had no inkling that his depression had driven him this far.

Ernest was calm and did not make a move to put the shells in the chamber, so Mary did not mention the gun at all but asked for the note. Ernest refused to give it to her but read her a few sentences here and there. There was a reference to his will and how he had provided for Mary and she wasn't to worry. Also, that he had transferred thirty thousand dollars to her checking account. Then he got off the letter and onto his latest worry, which concerned filing income taxes for the cleaning woman; talking on and on about how the Feds were sure to get him for the cleaning woman's taxes, and then Vernon arrived. When Vernon took hold of the gun Ernest let him have it without a protest.

Vernon had already put in a call to the Mayo Clinic and I was asked whether I would contact Dr. Renown and brief him on the situation.

Vernon phoned at four-thirty that afternoon. He reported that
the Mayo doctors were insisting that Ernest go to Rochester
voluntarily but that Ernest absolutely refused to go.

"I called Dr. Renown," I said, "and he was to call Mayo and
then call you."

"He has. He made all the Mayo arrangements and discussed
procedures, but I don't think he knows about this condition
they've imposed, that Ernest go of his own free will. Hell, he
doesn't have any *free* will! What are they talking about? I have
my associate, Dr. Ausley, helping me with Ernest, but we're
fighting the clock. We don't have proper facilities for this kind
of thing and, Hotch, honest to God, if we don't get him to
the proper place, and *fast*, he is going to kill himself for sure.
It's only a question of time if he stays here, and every hour it
grows more possible. He says he can't write any more—that's
all he's talked to me about for weeks and weeks. Says there's
nothing to live for. Hotch, he won't ever write again. He can't.
He's given up. That's the motivation for doing away with himself. At least, on the surface. And that's what I have to accept
because I'm not equipped to deal with anything beneath the
surface. But that's strong enough motivation as far as I'm concerned, and I can tell you I'm worried sick. We've got him shot
full of sodium amytal, but how long can we keep him in that
state? I can tell you it's a terrible responsibility for a country
doctor. It's not just that he's my friend, but he's *Ernest Hemingway*. We've *got* to get him to Mayo."

For the rest of that day we phoned back and forth between
New York, Ketchum, Hollywood and Rochester, but the Mayo
doctors could not be induced to come to Ketchum or vary in
any way from their adamant policy that patients must enter
the clinic voluntarily. Dr. Renown suggested to Vernon Lord
several procedures to be tried on Ernest to induce his co-operation. I wanted to go to Ketchum to help out, but Dr. Renown
thought I should wait and go as a second echelon if Vernon
failed.

The following day Mary phoned, terribly shaken. There had
been a nightmarish incident. Vernon had finally gotten Ernest
to consent to re-entering Mayo, and the charter plane had been

summoned from Hailey. Ernest said, however, that before he went there were some things he had to get from the house. Vernon said he would send Mary for them, but Ernest said they were things he had to get himself and he would not go to Mayo without them. So Vernon reluctantly consented, but first he called Don Anderson, who is six foot three and over two hundred pounds, to come along. Vernon took the nurse and Mary also.

They drove up to the house, the five of them, and Ernest started toward the door, followed by Don, then the nurse, then Mary and Vernon. Suddenly Ernest cut loose for the door, slammed it and bolted it before Don could get there. Don raced around to the other door, charged into the house and spotted Ernest at the gun rack, holding a gun and ramming a shell into the chamber. Don hurled himself at Ernest and knocked him down. There was a terrible struggle over the gun. Vernon had to help. Luckily, the safety had been on so it did not go off. Ernest was now back at the hospital, more heavily drugged.

He was now saying he would not return to Mayo's, but Vernon was keeping the plane at the Sun Valley airstrip in the hope that he could change Ernest's mind. In the meantime, discussions were being held with people at Menninger's.

The next morning Mary phoned to say that Ernest had suddenly consented to go and the plane had just taken off for Rochester. Vernon and Don Anderson had gone with him. Mary was just barely holding herself together. She promised to have Vernon call as soon as he got back.

It was after midnight when the call came through. Vernon said that he had given Ernest a heavy sedation before taking off but that shortly after they had become airborne, Ernest had made a strenuous effort to get the door open and jump out of the plane. It had taken all of Don's and Vernon's combined strength to get him away from the door. Vernon had then given Ernest a large injection of sodium amytal, and soon thereafter he had become drowsy.

Shortly afterward the small plane had begun to develop engine trouble and had had to be landed at Casper, Wyoming. On leaving the plane, Ernest had tried to walk into a moving

propeller, but Don had had him by the arm and pushed himself
between Ernest and the propeller, although in so doing Ernest
had almost inadvertently bumped Don into the whirling prop.

It had taken a couple of hours to repair the plane, but Ernest
had seemed quiet until they were on their way again; then
over South Dakota, having feigned sleep for an hour, he had
made a second attempt to jump out of the plane.

Mayo doctors were waiting for them when they landed in
Rochester, and Ernest, who was now docile and greeted the
doctors like old friends, was immediately taken to St. Mary's,
where he was placed in a special security section and put
under constant surveillance.

"You know the date?" I asked.

"The twenty-fifth, isn't it?"

"Yes, almost three months to the day since they discharged
him."

"Not a very long cure, was it?"

The first week in May, I went to see Cooper for the last time.
During February and March on his good days, he continued
to enjoy life the way he always had. One afternoon he had
invited me to his splendid modern house on Baroda Drive to
witness in the garden a spectacular demonstration by five
karate experts. And there were occasional dinner parties at the
Coopers', when old-time friends would carry on as if Cooper
were perfectly all right.

But by April the pain and ravages of the cancer had finally
knocked him down for keeps, and when I went to see him that
afternoon in May he was a wasted figure, lying immobile in
his darkened room. His hair was gray-streaked where the dye
had left it. His wife took me into the room, then left us alone.

"Papa phoned a couple weeks ago." He paused between
words, because it was very painful for him to speak. "Told me
he was sick, too. I bet him that I will beat him out to the
barn." He smiled and closed his eyes and seemed to doze off.
"Heard on the radio he was back at Mayo's." The eyes flickered
open. "That right?"

"Yes."

"Poor Papa." His eyes shut again but he seemed to be listening as I told him how the hunting had been the previous season in Ketchum and related little gossips about people he knew there.

He was hit by a big pain and his face contorted as he fought it off; sweat instantly covered his face. When the pain had passed, Cooper reached his hand over to the bed table and picked up a crucifix, which he put on the pillow beside his head.

"Please give Papa a message. It's important and you mustn't forget because I'll not be talking to him again. Tell him . . . that time I wondered if I made the right decision"—he moved the crucifix a little closer so that it touched his cheek—"tell him it was the best thing I ever did."

"I'll tell him."

"Don't forget."

"Don't worry, Coops, I'll tell him."

He died ten days later.

This time the Mayo doctors had advised Mary not to go to Rochester. They thought it would be better for Ernest if he were cut off from all contact with the outside world. So Mary stayed in Ketchum and kept in touch with the doctors by telephone.

Two weeks after Ernest had entered the hospital Mary telephoned me in New York. "I have a letter from Papa, the first I've received. Long letter, the handwriting pretty good, much more lucid than he's been for a long time. But still harping on our lack of finances—and presenting me with a new worry which, do forgive me, I have to share with you. Poor Hotch. Papa writes he has to buy clothes—of course I filled his Val-pack with everything he could possibly need—and then he says, 'Also I should start working and want to be out of here the soonest I can.' "

"Do you think the doctors read that letter before he sent it?"

"I don't know, but I wrote back telling him all the local news and all that, and then I said, 'Please don't con your friends there into letting you come home until they are absolutely sure your cure is complete because neither of us wants a repetition of the last three months of hell we spent in Ketchum.' But, Hotch, I worry that he'll do just that. And then I worry that that may not have been the proper thing to write him. You know how direct I am. But for all I know, by writing to Papa like that he may turn the persecution convictions against me. So far I've been spared that."

"I can see that the direct approach may not be the best, but we don't know what approach the doctors are taking."

"That's it. Well, what I wanted to ask you is if you could talk to Dr. Renown about this. I hate taking your time, also worrying you. But being totally ignorant of the whole subject, I have nothing to guide me. I also worry that Papa is not being taken deep enough into the causes of all his aberrations. The first time at Mayo's, I think the doctors did disabuse Papa of his immediate hallucinations, but aren't there deeper things that have to be touched? I don't even know what electric shock is supposed to achieve."

"Are they giving shock again?"

"The last time I spoke to the doctors they said they were going to start a series of them. But I don't even know how many that would be. What alarms me, though, is his talk about returning home. One thing I am sure of is that a repetition of the last three months would destroy me in one way or another. That isn't a threat; it's just a fact. So I just wondered if you could go to see Dr. Renown and ask his advice. For me to do it on the phone, he not knowing me, seems an awkward way of getting at this problem. Maybe we should make a new attempt at transferring Papa to Menninger's. Perhaps you could ask Dr. Renown about that, too."

As a result of my subsequent meeting with Dr. Renown, I learned something about Ernest's condition. Dr. Renown first spoke in a general way about obsessions and delusions and explained that very little was definitely known about the interrelationships of various symptoms—obsession, phobia, depression, delusion, depersonalization, anxiety and others—and the various shifts of emphasis that may make one more prominent today and another, tomorrow; but that the classic symptomatic digression is from obsession to delusion. An obsession is an idea that obtrudes itself on the psyche. The person is aware of its lack of logical basis and regards it as alien to his ego or self, but he succumbs to it in order to avoid the anxiety that he experiences if he challenges or ignores it. A delusion, Dr. Renown went on to explain, is a false belief that is impervious to logical and factual demonstration of its falsity. In some instances, he pointed out, this fine line is crossed in one way and then in the other; thus there may be obsessional behavior in one area and delusional in another.

Applying this general background to Ernest's specific behavior, Dr. Renown said that the previous October in Madrid, Ernest's anxieties over his excess baggage and keeping his name off the manifest and taking a slow, old airplane to avoid detection, were all obsessions. But his later anxieties that his phone was bugged and that the Feds wanted to arrest him for impairing the morals of a minor and for not paying nonexistent taxes, were delusions. His obsessions could be dispelled by insistent logic, as witness our eventual hard-won triumph over the excess luggage anxiety. But these obsessions had hardened into delusions and no amount of persuasive logic or evidence could now have any effect on Ernest. The obsession had surrounded itself with an impregnable shell, and the fact that that delusion-shell was impenetrable necessitated the use of electrical treatment.

As for the electrical treatments themselves, Dr. Renown said that ECT (Electro Convulsive Treatment) was a concept that was now obsolete. He explained that in modern treatment the patient receives an injection that puts him to sleep, thereby eliminating the convulsion that was characteristic of the early use of shock. That once terrifying experience is now no more than an awareness of the injection, then oblivion until the patient wakens a few hours later, when he may or may not have a headache. A patient usually shows some response to three or four treatments, then the series of ten to twelve is completed in order to "fix" the improvement, although it may be necessary to extend the number to as many as twenty. If improvement is sustained a week or two after the completion of the series, the prognosis is good. If there is indication of relapse, a treatment a week may be given for several weeks, often with very good results.

I asked Dr. Renown whether the electrical impulses were directed to a particular part of the brain. He said there are fifty organic and fifty psychodynamic theories to explain how electrical treatments are effectual, which is, of course, a comment on our ignorance. We use many treatments in medicine, he said, that we are unable to explain: digitalis in heart failure; insulin in diabetes. We know only that they work. The electrical treatments are applied by placing the electrodes on each temple and the entire brain is affected. No one knows where memory is stored but it probably is closely related to molecular chemistry of the cells.

I asked him about Ernest's complaints that the shock doctors were ruining his memory. He said that the two most prominent side effects of electrical treatments, loss of memory and confusion, both disappear in a short time. It is true, he said, that details of illness and hospitalization may never be recovered to memory—this could be a function of the treatment or of the illness, but he felt that such details were not important anyway. But he was very definite that all facts and experiences that predate the illness become as available as ever, once the treatments have ended.

Dr. Renown speculated that Ernest's fears of impoverishment and of being in jeopardy physically and legally were probably related to his feelings of impoverishment as a writer, with attendant jeopardy of his identity and stature. His psychopathological symptoms, Dr. Renown thought, were a defense against recognizing this. They were so dominant that he was not accessible to psychotherapy until they could be neutralized by the electrical treatments.

During the month of May, Ernest received a number of electrical treatments. When they were completed toward the end of the month, Mary was permitted to visit him for three days. She reported that Ernest was even more infuriated with these treatments than the previous ones, registering even bitterer complaints about how his memory was wrecked and how he was ruined as a writer and putting the blame for all this on the Mayo doctors, who had finally acceded to his demands that they stop giving him the ECT's. At the heart of this conflict between Ernest and his doctors was the fact that he would not admit that he had a condition that needed such drastic' treatment. Apparently the doctors had not yet been able to make him face up to the magnitude of his problem.

He did not talk to Mary any more about killing himself and, in fact, firmly stated that he was all over thinking about suicide, but the delusions remained the same. By now they had broadened to include hostility against Vernon Lord and against Mary herself. The first night she was there he accused her of having dragged him to Mayo's to get hold of his money. But the following day he was loving and appreciative toward her. His moods oscillated wildly. He had developed a new delusion which had turned him against Ketchum: he could not possibly go back there because they were lying in wait to nab him and throw him into jail for not paying state taxes, and he accused Mary of secretly working with them and maneuvering him into going back there so they could nail him.

"How can we persuade him to have the treatment that he feels isn't necessary?" Mary asked. "How can we make him see the extent of his problem, to admit that he even has one, so the Mayo doctors can work on it? They don't seem to be able to make him realize why shock is necessary. Maybe we could. And seeing him there, all cooped up, never allowed out without an escort, was terrible. Poor darling. Isn't there some place where he could be outdoors? You know how Papa loves the out of doors. He talked about going abroad, even wiring friends in Spain and France, so maybe he'd go to a clinic in Switzerland or somewhere like that. It's so confusing seeing him there needing help, the help all around him, but not getting through to him. There must be a way."

Ernest's mind seemed to have constructed an intolerable prison from which there was no escape; projecting from the reality that he could never return to his house in Havana, delusion had built three other walls: he could not stay in Rochester for they were ruining his memory; he could not go to his apartment in New York for they would nab him for having impaired the morals of a minor who lived in that city; he could not go to Ketchum for they would get him for state taxes.

About the same time that Ernest was permitted to see Mary, he was allowed, by prearranged appointment, a few monitored telephone talks with me. He must have known they were monitored, for there were very few references that involved his delusions and even those were oblique.

What he was mostly concerned about in those talks was a sudden and new compulsion to have a motion picture made of *Across the River and into the Trees*. For ten years he had turned down all picture offers for the book, the most persistent of which came from Jerry Wald, and on one occasion he had returned a fifty-thousand-dollar option check from Columbia Pictures. It's true that he had agreed to let Cooper do it, but that was a gesture of accommodation rather than desire. Now, however, it was a vital matter. He wanted to know who I thought could play the role of fifty-year-old Colonel Cantwell. He asked about an actor, whose name he couldn't recall, who lived in Switzerland and who had been proposed by Jerry Wald for the part. I identified the actor. He said that was exactly who should *not* play the colonel. He then tried to think of two other actors who he thought *could* play the part but could not recall their names either, and he raged out at what they had done to his memory.

In these phone talks Ernest was very businesslike and uncharacteristically crisp. I had the distinct impression he had in front of him a list of items to be discussed and he seemed to hurry from one to the next without paying too much attention to my responses, as if the list were an end in itself. Also, the natural slow rhythm of his speech had changed and his voice was a tape being run through the machine too fast.

As for *Across the River*, I simply put him off by saying I would look into it, but I didn't.

In the beginning of June, on my way back from Hollywood, I rented a car in Minneapolis and drove the ninety miles to Rochester through lovely spring countryside. The town seemed a little less forbidding decorated with green leaf. The nature of Ernest's hospitalization had been well publicized. *Time* magazine had wormed its way into the hospital's confidential records and had smeared its pages with the contents of the file on Ernest, including the number of shock treatments he had received. Where the facts were missing, *Time* filled the gaps with conjecture.

When I approached Ernest's room, he was standing at an elevated hospital table with a newspaper spread before him; I stood at the open door, not able, for the moment, to enter; whereas on my previous visit he had appeared attenuated, now the man he once was had disappeared and the man before me was only a marker to show where he had been.

He was very happy and, in a peculiar and incomprehensible way, proud that I had come. He called in nurses and other floor personnel, and introduced them to me, each introduction followed by an effusive endorsement of my past, present and future. When the doctors came they readily gave their consent to Ernest's request to go for a drive.

In the car I started to tell Ernest about Honor, who had obtained her first job, but he cut me off quickly. To my dismay it was as before: the car bugged, his room bugged, all the same persecutions. He directed me onto a small road that carried us through a wooded section and then climbed steadily up to the summit of a blunt hill. We parked the car and walked a short distance through woods along a trail that emerged upon a clearing. The view was a three-quarters sweep of all the surroundings; the sky was cloudless and busy with birds cavorting in the green-scented air.

Ernest noticed none of it; he immediately took me through a catalogue of his miseries: first, poverty complaints; then accusations against his banker, his lawyer, his doctor, all the fiduciary people in his life; after that, his worries over not having the proper clothes; and then the taxes. There was a great deal of repetition.

My first inclination was to let him talk himself out, hoping that perhaps that would help release the pressures within him, but as I watched him pace about, his eyes on the ground, his face contorted by the miseries he was recounting, there rose in me a kind of anger, and finally not able to hold back, I stepped into his path, causing him to look up, and said: "Papa, it's spring!"

He looked at me blankly, his eyes fuliginous behind his old glasses.

"We missed Auteuil again." Reality. Make him come into my world. Restate the reality. "We missed Auteuil again, Papa."

The eyes stirred. He moved his hands into his pockets. "And we will miss it and miss it and miss it," he said.

"Why?" My words pounced on his. I didn't want to lose the wedge. "Why not next fall? What's wrong with a good fall meet? Who says Bataclan can't run in autumn leaves?" Mention the good associations.

"There won't be another spring, Hotch."

"Of course there will. I can guarantee it . . ."

"Or another fall." His whole body had relaxed. He went over and sat on a busted fragment of stone wall. I stood before him with one foot up on an overturned rock. I felt I should get to it quickly now, and I did, but I said it very gently: "Papa, why do you want to kill yourself?"

He hesitated only a moment; then he spoke in his old, deliberate way. "What do you think happens to a man going on sixty-two when he realizes that he can never write the books and stories he promised himself? Or do any of the other things he promised himself in the good days?"

"But how can you say that? You have written a beautiful book about Paris, as beautiful as anyone can hope to write. How can you overlook that?"

"The best of that I wrote before. And now I can't finish it."

"But perhaps it is finished and it is just reluctance . . ."

"Hotch, if I can't exist on my own terms, then existence is impossible. Do you understand? That is how I've lived, and that is how I *must* live—or not live."

"But why can't you just put writing aside for now? You have always spent a long time between books. Ten years between *To Have and Have Not* and *For Whom the Bell Tolls* and then ten years more until *Across the River*. Take some time off. Don't force yourself. Why should you? You never have."

"I can't."

"But why is it different now? May I mention something? Back in 1938 you wrote a preface for your short stories. At the end of it you said you hoped you could live long enough to write three more novels and twenty-five more stories. That was your ambition. All right—*For Whom the Bell Tolls, Across the River and into the Trees* and *The Old Man and the Sea*, not to mention the unpublished ones. And there're more than twenty-five stories, plus the book of Paris sketches. You've fulfilled your covenant—the one you made with yourself—the only one that counts. So for God's sake why can't you rest on that?"

"Because—look, it doesn't matter that I don't write for a day or a year or ten years as long as the knowledge that I *can* write is solid inside me. But a day without that knowledge, or not being sure of it, is eternity."

"Then why not turn from writing altogether? Why not retire? God knows you have earned it."

"And do what?"

"Any of the things you love and enjoy. You once talked about getting a new boat big enough to take you around the world, fishing in good waters you've never tried. How about that? Or that plan about the game preserve in Kenya? You've talked about the tiger shoot in India—Bhaiya's invitation—there's that. And at one time we talked about your going in with Antonio on the bull ranch. There's so damn many things . . ."

"Retire? How the hell can a writer retire? DiMaggio put his records in the book, and so did Ted Williams, and then on a particular good day, with good days getting rarer, they hung up their shoes. So did Marciano. That's the way a champ should go out. Like Antonio. A champion cannot retire like anyone else."

"You've got some books on the shelf . . ."

"Sure. I've got six books I declare to win with. I can stand on that. But unlike your baseball player and your prize fighter and your matador, how does a writer retire? No one accepts that his legs are shot or the whiplash gone from his reflexes. Everywhere he goes, he hears the same goddamn question— What are you working on?"

"But who cares about the questions? You never cared about

those phony tape measures. Why don't you let us help you?
Mary will go anywhere you want, do anything you like. Don't
shut her out. It hurts her so."

"Mary is wonderful. Always and now. Wonderful. She's been
so damn brave and good. She is all that is left to be glad for.
I love her. I truly love her." A rise of tears made it impossible
for me to talk any more. Ernest was not looking at me; he was
watching a small bird foraging in the scrub. "You remember I
told you once she did not know about other people's hurts.
Well, I was wrong. She knows. She knows how I hurt and she
suffers trying to help me—I wish to Christ I could spare her
that. Listen, Hotch, whatever happens, whatever . . . she's good
and strong, but remember sometimes the strongest of women
need help."

I couldn't manage any more. I walked a short distance away.
He came over and put his hand on my shoulder. "Poor old
Hotch," he said. "I'm so damn sorry. Here, I want you to have
this." He had the horse chestnut from Paris in his hand.

"But, Papa, that's your lucky piece."

"I want you to have it."

"Then I'll give you another."

"Okay."

I stooped down to pick up a bright pebble but Ernest stopped
me. "Nothing from here," he said. "There's no such thing as a
lucky piece from Rochester, Minnesota."

I had a key ring that one of my daughters had given me,
that had a carved wooden figure attached to it, so I removed
the figure and gave him that.

"If I could get out of here and get back to Ketchum . . . why
don't you talk to them?"

"I will, Papa, I will." I felt suddenly elated. "And you should
work hard to think about the things you care about and like to
do, and not about all those negative things. That's the best
thing that can happen."

"Sure. Sure it is. The best things in life and other ballroom
bananas. But what the hell? What does a man care about?
Staying healthy. Working good. Eating and drinking with his
friends. Enjoying himself in bed. I haven't any of them. Do you

understand, goddamn it? None of them. And while I'm planning my good times and worldwide adventures, who will keep
the Feds off my ass and how do the taxes get paid if I don't
turn out the stuff that gets them paid? You've been pumping
me and getting the gen, but you're like Vernon Lord and
all the rest, turning state's evidence, selling out to them . . ."

I lashed into him. "Papa! Papa, damn it! Stop it! Cut it out!"
A heavy quiver shook him, that thin old lovely man, and he
held his hand against his eyes for a moment before he started
to walk slowly back along the path to the car; we didn't say
another word all the way back to the hospital.

I stayed with him for a few hours in his room. He was pleasant
but distant. We talked about books and sports; nothing personal. Late in the day I drove back to Minneapolis. I never
saw him again.

On the flight back to New York I thought about Mary's suggestion about a place that had access to the out of doors where
Ernest could enjoy good air and scenery while receiving treatment. I knew now that he could be reached. On the hilltop he
had been momentarily clear and lucid about his troubles. Sitting there in the plane, I could not help but try to reason out,
from what he had said, what the forces had been that had
crushed him. He was a man of prowess and he did not want
to live without it: writing prowess, physical prowess, sexual
prowess, drinking and eating prowess. Perhaps when these
powers diminished, his mind became programed to set up distorted defenses for himself. But if he could only be made to
adjust to a life where these prowesses were not so all-
important . . .

I found myself thinking about his *dicho:* man can be defeated but not destroyed. Maybe it could work that way, even
though Ernest favored its contrary brother. Ernest Walsh's
words came back to me: "It will take time to wear him out.
And before that he will be dead."

Mary was living in New York now, and we both consulted
Dr. Renown about a new place that would be better suited to
Ernest's needs. He suggested The Institute of Living in Hart-

ford, Connecticut—small cottage residences, open grounds in a scenic setting, fine staff, long-term intensive care a specialty. Mary flew up to inspect it and consult with the director.

She thought that in all aspects the institute would be splendid for Ernest and brought back brochures and literature for me to look at, but again she faced the problem that transfer was not possible without Ernest's consent. Since this was a psychiatric institution and there was no way to disguise that fact, his resistance to it was foreordained. She wrote to the Mayo doctors, asking their assistance in influencing Ernest, but they replied that they would not aid in such a transfer since they did not feel it was to the patient's best interest. On the other hand, the institute was very deferential to Mayo's and insisted on playing a completely passive role.

On the evening of June 14th Mary came to dinner at my apartment. She had arranged a conference call with the Mayo doctors, and when it came through she asked me to listen in on an extension. The Mayo doctors said that Ernest was showing marked improvement and would suffer a lack of confidence in treatment if he were transferred. Mary asked what the marked improvements were. She was told that he was swimming every day, that he had promised to give up worrying about clothes, that he was making more mental effort, as evidenced by the fact that he had started to read a book—the first book he had read in the six weeks he had been there—and he was writing down notes about it. Mary asked the name of the book. She was told it was *Out of My League* by an author named George Plimpton. (The doctors had obviously not noticed Ernest's endorsement of the book on its dust jacket. Mary let it pass.) The doctors said that another good sign was Ernest's heightened interest in getting back to Ketchum and getting to work. Mary asked whether they planned to give any more shock treatments; they answered vaguely and it was my impression that they did not.

Mary then said that she was planning to go to Ketchum for the summer and asked whether, on the way, she could visit Ernest without upsetting him. To the contrary, the doctors said. It would be highly beneficial for Ernest to see her, and perhaps it might not be a bad idea to let him return to Ketchum for

the summer to see whether he really could get to work. Mary
became very disturbed at that suggestion, and said that she
did not want to take on such a responsibility, that Ernest's
letters did not reflect the degree of progress that would make
her feel secure in having him back home. She said she did not
want to come to the clinic on that basis. The doctors acquiesced,
and said they would not promote Ernest's return just yet.

I was getting ready to leave for Europe, but Mary and I
managed one last meeting before I left. She told me that she
had consulted Dr. Renown after the Mayo phone call and told
him how terrified she was that Ernest would be sent back to
Ketchum at that time. He had telephoned the Mayo doctors
and argued strenuously that, in his opinion, the cycle of electrical treatments had not been completed and that Ernest was in
an unstable condition because he had been suspended in the
middle of the series. He urged that the full cycle be adminis-
tered and then followed by extensive psychotherapy, with a
weekly electrical treatment if needed. Because the Mayo doctors had resisted this suggestion, he urged Mary to redouble
her efforts to effect the transfer to The Institute of Living; but
she had told him that she was fearful of the sensational and
notorious publicity this would undoubtedly set off. She said
that Dr. Renown then pointed out to her that there might be
some advantages to inside-page news items about going to the
institute, in contrast to front-page headlines about his suicide.

That was the situation when I left for Europe. Toward the
end of June I received a note from Mary telling me that when
she had arrived in Rochester the Mayo doctors had put pressure on her to let Ernest go along to Ketchum. In fact, they
had already told Ernest that he could go, and he was counting
on it. The doctors said that they felt Ernest was on the threshold
of a new phase and needed to prove to himself what he could
do in Ketchum. Mary said she had again brought up the institute, but the doctors very firmly said that such a transfer would
definitely set Ernest back and couldn't be considered; that, in
fact, it would destroy the new confidence which they had so
painstakingly built up. They said that Ernest was between sixty
to seventy percent of his normal self and that that was plenty

good to sustain him. Mary said she tried to protest but that with such little psychiatric knowledge it was futile. So she was resigned—fearful but resigned. She had rented a car and George Brown was flying out from New York to drive them through the northern states to Ketchum.

On July 2nd I flew from Málaga to Madrid, where I stayed overnight to catch the morning jet for Rome. As I was leaving the hotel elevator to go to the airport the morning of the third, Bill Davis hurriedly entered the lobby. He had driven all through the night, virtually the length of Spain, to tell me that Ernest had shot himself and to be with me at this moment. I was glad he had. But what Ernest had done did not really hit me deeply at that time. It took months for that to happen.

On the flight to Rome I read the details of what had happened. As Dr. Renown had predicted, there were banner headlines on the front pages of newspapers everywhere I went. The Associated Press dispatch said that Ernest had been cheerful during the three-day drive through the northern states and appeared to enjoy himself. That on his first night home he had had a pleasant dinner and had even joined Mary's singing one of their favorite songs, "Tutti Mi Chiamano Bionda." Then, according to Mary, early the following morning a shotgun exploded in the house. Mary ran downstairs. Ernest had been cleaning one of the guns, she said, and it had accidentally discharged, killing him.

I could not fault Mary for covering up. She was not prepared to accept what had happened and that's what came out when she had to explain. What difference does truth make about a thing like that? Does truth bring back anything? Or assuage the torment?

I found myself remembering a question from the interminable interview years before with the German journalist at the Felipe II. He had asked, "Herr Hemingway, can you sum up your feelings about death?" And Ernest had answered, "Yes—just another whore."

I sent Mary a long cable, but I did not go to Ketchum for the funeral. I could not say good-bye to Ernest in a public group. Instead I went to Santa Maria Sopra Minerva—his church, not mine—because I wanted to say good-bye to him in his own place. I found a deserted side altar and sat there for a long while, thinking about all the good times we had, remembering forward from the first tentative meeting at the Floridita in Havana. But when it came time to go, all I could think of to say was, Good luck, Papa. I figured he knew how much I loved him, so there was no point in mentioning that. I lit a candle and put some money in the poor box and spent the rest of the night alone, wandering through Rome's old streets.

Ernest had had it right: Man is not made for defeat. Man can be destroyed but not defeated.